RELATING THROUGH TECHNOLOGY

This book answers one of the most critical questions of our time: Does the vast connectivity afforded by mobile and social media lead to more personal connection with one another? It offers an evidence-based account of the role of technology in close relationships that confronts such pressing questions as where face-to-face communication belongs in this digital age, whether social media is harmful to our well-being, and how online communication spills-over into our offline communication and relationships. Each chapter explores the positive and negative influences of media on relationships, coalescing into a balanced assessment of how technological advancement has altered our connections with each other. By zeroing in on communication with the most important people in our lives and tracing the changes in computer-mediated communication over time, *Relating through Technology* focuses the conversation about media on its use in our everyday lives and relationships.

Jeffrey A. Hall is Professor of Communication Studies at the University of Kansas, USA. He is the founding Editor of the journal, *Human Communication and Technology*, and won the 2015 Early Career Award from the Interpersonal Communication Division of the National Communication Association.

Advances in Personal Relationships

Christopher R. Agnew
Purdue University
John P. Caughlin
University of Illinois at Urbana-Champaign
C. Raymond Knee
University of Houston
Terri L. Orbuch
Oakland University

Although scholars from a variety of disciplines have written and conversed about the importance of personal relationships for decades, the emergence of personal relationships as a field of study is relatively recent. Advances in Personal Relationships represents the culmination of years of multidisciplinary and interdisciplinary work on personal relationships. Sponsored by the International Association for Relationship Research, the series offers readers cutting-edge research and theory in the field. Contributing authors are internationally known scholars from a variety of disciplines, including social psychology, clinical psychology, communication, history, sociology, gerontology, and family studies. Volumes include integrative reviews, conceptual pieces, summaries of research programs, and major theoretical works. Advances in Personal Relationships presents first-rate scholarship that is both provocative and theoretically grounded. The theoretical and empirical work described by authors will stimulate readers and advance the field by offering new ideas and retooling old ones. The series will be of interest to upper-division undergraduate students, graduate students, researchers, and practitioners.

Other Books in the Series

Attribution, Communication Behavior, and Close Relationships
Valerie Manusov and John H. Harvey, editors

Stability and Change in Relationships
Anita L. Vangelisti, Harry T. Reis, and Mary Anne Fitzpatrick, editors

Understanding Marriage: Developments in the Study of Couple Interaction
Patricia Noller and Judith A. Feeney, editors

Growing Together: Personal Relationships Across the Lifespan
Frieder R. Lang and Karen L. Fingerman, editors

Communicating Social Support
Daena J. Goldsmith

Communicating Affection: Interpersonal Behavior and Social Context
Kory Floyd

Changing Relations: Achieving Intimacy in a Time of Social Transition
Robin Goodwin

Feeling Hurt in Close Relationships
Anita L. Vangelisti, editor

Romantic Relationships in Emerging Adulthood
Frank D. Fincham and Ming Cui, editors

Responding to Intimate Violence Against Women: The Role of Informal Networks
Renate Klein

Social Influences on Romantic Relationships: Beyond the Dyad
Christopher R. Agnew, editor

Positive Approaches to Optimal Relationship Development
C. Raymond Knee and Harry T. Reis, editors

Personality and Close Relationship Processes
Stanley O. Gaines, Jr.

The Experience and Expression of Uncertainty in Close Relationships
Jennifer A. Theiss

Contemporary Studies on Relationships, Health, and Wellness
Jennifer A. Theiss and Kathryn Greene, editors

Relating Through Technology

Jeffrey A. Hall

University of Kansas

CAMBRIDGE
UNIVERSITY PRESS

University Printing House, Cambridge CB2 8BS, United Kingdom

One Liberty Plaza, 20th Floor, New York, NY 10006, USA

477 Williamstown Road, Port Melbourne, VIC 3207, Australia

314–321, 3rd Floor, Plot 3, Splendor Forum, Jasola District Centre, New Delhi – 110025, India

79 Anson Road, #06–04/06, Singapore 079906

Cambridge University Press is part of the University of Cambridge.

It furthers the University's mission by disseminating knowledge in the pursuit of education, learning, and research at the highest international levels of excellence.

www.cambridge.org
Information on this title: www.cambridge.org/9781108483308
DOI: 10.1017/9781108629935

First published 2020

A catalogue record for this publication is available from the British Library.

Library of Congress Cataloging-in-Publication Data
NAMES: Hall, Jeffrey A., author.
TITLE: Relating through technology / Jeffrey A. Hall, University of Kansas.
DESCRIPTION: Cambridge, United Kingdom ; New York, NY : Cambridge University Press, 2020. | Series: Advances in personal relationships | Includes bibliographical references and index.
IDENTIFIERS: LCCN 2020009221 (print) | LCCN 2020009222 (ebook) | ISBN 9781108483308 (hardback) | ISBN 9781108704724 (paperback) | ISBN 9781108629935 (epub)
SUBJECTS: LCSH: Interpersonal communication–Technological innovations. | Information technology–Social aspects. | Online social networks. | Interpersonal relations.
CLASSIFICATION: LCC HM1166 .H35 2020 (print) | LCC HM1166 (ebook) | DDC 303.48/33–dc23
LC record available at https://lccn.loc.gov/2020009221
LC ebook record available at https://lccn.loc.gov/2020009222

ISBN 978-1-108-48330-8 Hardback

To all of my friends

CONTENTS

FIGURES

TABLES

Introduction

> When you are playing a DJ set, you are not exactly making anything. You are contending with work that other people have already made, reorganizing it, repurposing it. It's creation, in the sense that I'm bringing a mood into existence, but it's curation in the sense that I'm looking through existing songs to see which ones I'm going to select.
> —Questlove (Thompson, 2018, p. 178)

I considered dozens of ways to start this book and none seemed fitting. A technical introduction that reported billions of mobile connections or trillions of texts was tempting, but would be outdated before the book went to press. A personal anecdote about the ubiquity of social and mobile media in everyday life would be in the spirit of the book, but I figured no one who had not already noticed this on their own would need it described for them. I needed something else.

Questlove – drummer for The Roots, DJ extraordinaire, epicurean, and author – helped me think about this book in another way.

There I was laboring away on this volume you hold in your hands, becoming keenly aware of the enormity of media research. With each chapter I wrote, I realized I was constantly summarizing, borrowing, and reiterating the thoughts of many outstanding thinkers. I kept wondering what my contribution would be in writing this book. Doubt was the devil on my shoulder and I was looking for the angel on the polar. I found it in Questlove's concept of the curator as creator as described in his book *Creative Quest*.

Museum curators, chefs, and DJs share a similar place in the creative spectrum: they select choice bits and arrange them among other selections. Through juxtaposition the tasty bits become tastier, more aesthetically appealing, or even revelatory. When Questlove DJs, he loves to see people who were thinking about ditching the party drawn back in again by his choice of song. This type of creator chooses ingredients from the cupboard, mixes them into new creation, and then presents the new creation to the audience for their consumption. The curator connects with the audience through arrangement and selection.

I am an academic curator and composer. I have scanned the breadth of research on the intersection between personal relationships and technology, and I am presenting my exhibit for you. I dug through the e-crates of academic records and this book is my set list. This book will report new findings from my own research, but it is primarily an act of curation. The order and assembly of this book is a unified exhibit, a spectacle meant to reveal my understanding of the intersection between relationships and technology.

I am humbled by this opportunity to play academic DJ with the ideas of others. I hope that my picks – expressed in ten book chapters – bring together ideas that you may have come across before, but never considered in relation to one another. Or maybe it exposes you to totally new ideas. Like a good playlist, I hope that the chapters fit together in ways that promote repeat visits. I hope this book sets your mental taste buds alight.

I have done my best to be a respectful creator – to warmly and accurately present the work of others, to give credit where it is due, and to provide proper context for any critique. And if any of this research is yours, thank you for giving me the ingredients from which this ten-course meal has been prepared. Thank you for your commitment to your craft.

SECTION ONE: WHAT'S ON THIS PLAYLIST?

Why do we need a book that offers a relationship-focused approach to the study of personal media? After all, there is an abundance of research on the array of media platforms and services. From the ever-growing literature on social media (e.g., Facebook, Instagram, Snapchat, Twitter) to the two-decade tradition of research on texting, the research on media and technology is so deep as to be overwhelming.

One motivation for writing this book is to refocus the conversation. For my taste, there is too much research on technology rather than on the people using it. A recent bibliometric analysis identified the twelve primary themes of 20,330 articles on social media, and *not a single theme* is focused on personal relationships (Foote, Shaw, & Hill, 2018). The most common theme (i.e., media use) has the key words "Facebook" and "people" but not friends or relationships. Of the twelve most common themes, there were *zero* using the words "relationships," "friendship," "romantic," "personal," "conversation," or "social interaction" (Foote et al., 2018).

Another bibliometric analysis of research on online social networks published in the top scholarly journals the past twenty years made this astonishing claim: articles dedicated to the study of the role of social networking sites (SNSs) in interpersonal relationships "did not necessarily examine the social relationships did not necessarily examine the social relationships mediated by those social technologies" (Fu & Lai, 2020). In other words, these articles did not recognize that relationships are the foundation upon which online social networks are built, not the other way around. This same analysis (Fu & Lai, 2020) found very little research on multimodal relationships because research tends to be very platform specific, rarely accounting for uses of various platforms and modalities. Furthermore, social media research is by and large unconcerned with face-to-face (FtF) contact.

In research on personal media, users' preexisting relationships with communication partners are treated as ancillary or, worse, utterly irrelevant to studying the phenomenon (Fu & Lai, 2020). For example, researchers often prioritize measuring technology use in relation to outcomes like well-being, but rarely consider the preexisting relationship between the people on the sending and receiving ends of messages.

When researchers insufficiently attend to the relational context of personal media use, they are adopting a technology-focused approach. I would like to start a larger conversation about what a relationship-focused approach to personal media use could look like. I want to join my voice with Madianou and Miller (2012), who call for a "re-socialization of media" (p. 184) where each modality is understood by the ways that it nourishes or diminishes human relationships.

One of the core observations of this book is that relationships are and have long been multimodal, and, as such, much communication through media is an extension of those preexisting relationships. Although the media choices are vast, people continue to rely on a narrow set of modes of communication with a small number of important others. I will explain how these seemingly incompatible trends are possible. This book will synthesize and critique existing research on the questions of *whom* do we communicate with, using *which* media, for *what* purpose, and to *what* effect?

This book will focus on everyday social interactions both FtF and through media. Everyday talk between relational partners has been an important topic in communication for at least fifty years (Knapp & Daly, 2011). Similarly, research has long explored how people adopt, become accustomed to, and integrate new technologies and platforms into their everyday patterns of communication. As a research community, we need to transcend the boundaries between offline and online communication: "What happens via new technology is completely interwoven with what happens face-to-face and via other media" (Baym, 2009, p. 721). To do so, this book will focus on daily uses of technology to socially interact, highlight how digital technologies are used for maintaining existing relationships and forming new relationships, and examine the ongoing integration of technology into users' social life. In short, this book will explore the intersection between everyday social interaction and personal relationships as experienced in the digital age.

One thing I want to be crystal clear about: this book will not review research on the use of digital media for information seeking, entertainment, and other instrumental purposes (e.g., shopping). My playlist will exclude all nonsocial uses of technology.

The book *will* take into account choices to *not* socially engage through media, choices to *not* be available via media, and choices to be intentionally alone. It is part of my broader perspective on social ecology, wherein seeking solitude and how we feel when we are alone are critical components of a nourished social life (Hall & Merolla, 2020). For the purposes of this book, intentionally making oneself unavailable through media and seeking times of solitude can be understood from the perspective of relating through technology in a way that shopping for shoes cannot.

1.1 Mode + Feature

Communication, both as a concept and as a discipline, is at the core of the study of media. Mass communication researchers study radio, TV, film, newspapers, and the many forms of digital content. These media are often used to broadcast information in a one-way fashion to a large audience of unknown others. In this book, I will use the term *personal media* to refer to media used to send messages back and forth through some technology, platform, or device. These messages are primarily, but not exclusively, sent to a known other or others. There are several classic personal media (e.g., telephone, posted letter) that are addressed to a specific other and facilitate one-to-one communication. Some old-school mass media can be used as personal media or for the purpose of interpersonal communication, such as CB radios used to connect enthusiasts and personal ads in newspapers used to initiate personal relationships or find estranged loved ones. In such cases, each would qualify as personal media. As a rule of thumb, personal media enables interpersonal communication.

Computer-mediated communication (CMC) refers to messages sent and received through a technological platform or mediated device. Thus, CMC occurs through personal media. For much of the early history of CMC research, these messages were primarily textual. For example, the bulletin-board system (BBS), a precursor to the internet and World Wide Web, was primarily a textual medium because audio or visual files were comparably large and could overwhelm the system's capacity (Delwiche, 2018). Although CMC can facilitate mass messages, such as using a BBS to advertise a community event or a modern-day listserv, CMC can also be directed and interpersonal, which is the primary focus of this book. Media refers to the various modalities and platforms used to convey messages to others. Personal media are technologies that offer the possibility of two-way, interactive communication between known others or between individuals who are seeking to connect with strangers (e.g., looking for a dating partner, posting on a social support website).

The *mode* of communication refers to the different forms media can take. Parks (2017) defines mode of communication as "the basic form into which a message has been encoded (e.g., speech, written text, still image, moving image, touch)" (p. 506). Thus, FtF interactions offer several modes of communicating at once – visual, audio, and tactile. In the nonverbal communication tradition, these are called channels of communication. In CMC and mass media research, channel refers to the "physical mechanisms and software of message transmission" (Parks, 2017, p. 506). Thus, a channel is a distinct and separable technology-enabled mechanism to convey a message.

When I suggest that relationships have long been *multimodal*, I am arguing that people have long encoded messages into several modes of communication – letters, phone calls, and FtF conversations. This gives rise to what Parks (2017) calls mixed-media relationships and I will call *multimodal relationships*, both of which refer to any nominally interdependent relationship (e.g., romantic, colleague, friend) maintained through more than one modality. *Modality switching* occurs when people switch among media to manage the stream of communication between them (Ramirez & Wang, 2008). For example, a woman might follow up on the content of a text exchange with her girlfriend later that day when they are at home together.

1.2 Variability between Modalities

Back when the modes of communication were few, there was a pretty clear sense of what any given mode did or did not do. In the age of social media and mobile applications, software developers actively compete to be the hub of users' engagement with the internet, with other platforms, with other people, and with users' geo-located environment. Thus, it has become increasingly difficult to account for what any given technology or platform actually does or can be used to do.

Throughout this book, I will advocate for a mode + feature approach to distinguish between media. A *feature* is a technological option built into a modality, which may or may not be available at a certain time, to certain users, or with certain devices. Back in the era when landline phones were the primary means of making voice calls, a then-new feature was call waiting. This feature allowed a person to know when another call was coming in while already talking to someone. In the smartphone era, it is more common that features can be turned on or off or enabled or disabled (with greater or lesser ease). Within any given mode of communication, the number of features can be many or few. Features are more numerous, more technology-dependent, and more changeable than core modalities. To be clear, I am asserting there is limited variability within a singular mode. While features vary, modes share core aspects across time, devices, and platforms. Traditional modes (e.g., voice calls, email) and newer modes (e.g., video chat) are distinct.

There are several ways to distinguish between modalities and features, and organizing this variability is important theoretically and practically. In 2010, Baym offered seven key concepts to help differentiate between modes of communication. These concepts have been reevaluated and expanded (e.g., Evans, Pearce, Vitak, & Treem, 2017; Nesi, Choukas-Bradley, & Prinstein, 2018), but it is important to note that all exist on continua rather than a binary fashion.

Synchrony (concept number 1) (as opposed to asynchrony) describes the temporal structure of media, wherein totally synchronous communication is like FtF interaction. When modalities require pauses or breaks between messages, either due to the limits of connectivity itself or due to time needed for reception and response, they become asynchronous.

Text-based exchanges do not contain the amount of nonverbal information that FtF communication does. This concept (number 2) is called *social cues*, which varies based on the number of nonverbal channels available on a given modality (Parks, 2017). The idea of anonymity is sometimes folded into the concept of social cues because given sufficiently low social cues, an individual can (nearly) anonymously send and receive messages (Nesi et al., 2018). Another component of social cues is the degree to which a mode promotes certain cues over others. As a concept that describes variability within a mode of communication, it refers to the idea that some modes of communication include visual media or images (e.g., video chat), and others are primarily textual communication (e.g., texting). This issue is also salient when comparing types of social media (e.g., Twitter versus Snapchat) and what type of social cues they offer and promote.

The next three concepts speak to the size of the audience and permanence of the message, both in the moment and over time. *Reach* (concept number 3) refers to the number of individuals to whom a message is sent. Voice calls used for interpersonal rather than broadcast purposes (such as a webinar) have very limited reach, but tweets on Twitter can be very broad in reach. Reach also speaks not just to the intended audience but also to the potential or final audience size. *Replicability* (concept number 4) is the degree to which a message is permanent (versus ephemeral) or has a left digital trace (Nesi et al., 2018). Combining reach and replicability, some modes of communication have a much bigger reach than may have been intended because their digital trace can be dug up and shared. Concept number 5 is *searchability*, which is closely aligned with digital storage. Voice calls are searchable in the sense that call records indicate the length of a call and that the two numbers that were connected, but are not totally searchable as the contents of voice calls are not stored and thus are not searchable. By contrast, text messages and emails are much more searchable because the message content itself is stored. Searchability includes the related concept that certain platforms make it easier to search an archive.

The *mobility* (concept number 6) of a mode is the degree to which the mode is tied to a particular place, platform, or technology. This refers both to the idea that voice calls on mobile phones are much more mobile than they are on landlines and to the idea that instant messaging (IM) used to be confined to a desktop or laptop computer. This variability of mobility has become nearly zero for all modes of communication enabled on a smartphone. Indeed, we have gotten to the point where nearly all modes of communication, except FtF conversations, are highly mobile. As one important caveat to this presumption of constant connectivity, the lack of consistent access to wireless technology reduces mobility. There are many areas throughout the world that cannot rely on the degree of connectivity the global north has come to demand.

Modes vary by their degree of *interactivity* (concept number 7), which refers to their ability to enable social interaction. This is not to be confused with the idea that some media are more interactive in that they let users manipulate what they see on the computer/internet, like interactive games (Baym, 2010). The opposite of interactivity is that the mode does not allow for or facilitate social interaction. For the most part, the entirety of this book will be dedicated to focusing on modes of communication that are high in interactivity, with the notable exception of Chapter 6, which is devoted to social media, which varies in interactivity.

One final concept that Baym (2010) did not address, but I believe merits inclusion, is *quantifiability* (concept number 8), which refers to the degree to which a mode encourages or makes obvious things that can be enumerated, such as likes, shares, or number of friends. This concept includes both how clearly such counts are presented and whether mode usage itself is quantifiable. Nesi et al. (2018) suggest that some modes of communication are more quantifiable than others. Voice calls have very low quantifiability, although you can check your call records, but social media are highly quantifiable. For example, a "like" on Facebook is a one-click acknowledgment that, by nature, quantifies the audience's actions.

1.3 What about Affordances?

Another popular approach to understanding variability between modes of personal media is the affordance. Bucher and Helmond (2018) offer a thorough history of this hotly contested concept, pointing out that different theorists have used it in very different ways at different points of time. One of the challenges of the concept is that an affordance is defined by how people use media (e.g., technology affords user the possibility of doing X), *and* an affordance entails the impact of technology on users' practices of use. An affordance is concerned with both how the technology alters people's communication habits and practices and how users shape technology (Bucher &

Helmond, 2018). Thus, affordances are ultimately a network of relations between users' behavioral patterns and a technology's capabilities. Affordances are *not* objects you can point to.

Bucher and Helmond (2018) note that since there has been such a multitude of ways to approach affordances conceptually, there are many ways to fruitfully use the term. The eight sources of variability between media listed above could be thought of as *high-level* affordances (Bucher & Helmond, 2018). Indeed, in their theoretical review, Evans et al. (2017) identify high-level affordances: anonymity (i.e., social cues), persistence (i.e., searchable and replicable), and visibility, whether a feature is promoted within the platform and the degree to which information can be easily found (i.e., quantifiable and replicable). By contrast, *low-level* affordances could be thought of as the features of a modality: at that level "affordance becomes a way of talking about the technical features of the platform" (Bucher & Helmond, 2018, p. 240).

Given the great deal of complexity and confusion around the concept affordance, I will avoid it. Yet this is not to dismiss its value out of hand. The mode + feature approach is compatible with the affordance perspective in several ways. In addition to idea that the eight concepts I discussed above could be seen as high-level affordances, the affordance perspective is consistent with the idea that a particular mode of communication (e.g., mediated person-to-person chat) can be used on various platforms (e.g., iMessage, GroupMe, Facebook Messenger). Both perspectives are consistent with the idea that the various modes of communication are shaped by features of the modality and the practice of using it within the context of a relationship.

Chapter 2 will offer a more thorough discussion of the fact that just because a feature exists on a platform or because a mode of communication was developed to perform a particular function does not mean that people will enable the feature or will use a mode for that purpose. Although much of this book will focus on more traditional and enduring modes of communication (e.g., voice calls, texting, FtF), Chapter 6 will explore social media and their constantly evolving features, wherein much of the affordance debate is centered.

SECTION TWO: SCOPE OF THE BOOK

2.1 Fundamental Theories: Chapters 1–3

My relationship-centered approach to understanding media starts with laying out assumptions about why relationships matter to people and how media is in the service of those relationships. The first stopping point on this curated tour of ideas (aka Chapter 1) is to introduce the idea of social ecology. This chapter introduces the idea that relationships are a fundamental component of human existence, but there is a limit on the number of relationship partners we have and maintain. This chapter introduces the idea of the *core network* (or the two to five most important people in your life) and the *first fifteen* (i.e., the primary members of your personal network). Chapter 1 explains why the social context of relationships is important for the study of personal media.

Chapter 2 examines the social construction of technology (SCOT) perspective. This addresses why people shape technology use for their own ends, and why deterministic models fail to account for media use. This chapter contrasts a relational approach with competing perspectives, especially technology-centered ones. This social constructivist perspective is brought into dialogue with constructivist theories of personal relationships (e.g., Duck, 1994a) and with dialectical and ironic (Arnold, 2003) perspectives on media's influence on relationships.

Chapter 3 reviews classic theories of CMC that are relevant to understanding personal media use, including media richness theory, social presence theory, social information processing theory, and media multiplexity theory. The chapter also explores models and perspectives of personal media use that are emergent and important, such as relationship interdependence and mundane mediated relationship maintenance.

This chapter also introduces my theory, the communicate bond belong (CBB) theory (Hall & Davis, 2017), which examines how the content of communication, particularly the episode of communication, influences the satisfaction of the fundamental need to belong. One advantage of CBB is its focus on human energy management, which stipulates that humans seek to conserve energy expenditure and invest their time and energy toward future belongingness need satisfaction. From the perspective of CBB theory, personal media use is understood as result of three forces: need satisfaction, energy conservation and investment, and homeostatic balance of social interaction and time alone.

2.2 Modality Comparisons and Contrasts: Chapters 4–6

The three central chapters of the book trace the emergence of today's mobile moment, which is the perpetual state of potential connection created by the widespread adoption of smartphones. Constant access to social media, smartphone applications, and mobile communication (i.e., text, voice call) in the global north means that the typical boundaries of social interaction have all but vanished. Connection is more than ever elective rather than constrained by access to and availability of others.

Chapter 4 introduces the niche and media displacement theories to address the idea that although there is an ever-expanding array of options, the displacement of one media for another has been slow and gradual. This chapter starts by exploring text-based communication in the context of both interpersonal communication and classic CMC literature. The emergence of email and then-new phenomena such as chat rooms, message boards, and the listserv are examined, followed by the emergence of SMS. This chapter also examines the frequency of social interactions on various modes of communication, and concludes by focusing on the coexistence, rather than total displacement, of these forms of communication.

Chapter 5 explores the nature of modern multimodal relationships from a both/and rather than either/or perspective. It explores modality switching, which tracks the flow of communication through multiple media by relational partners. This chapter systematically reviews research that compares modalities to test the idea that FtF communication has greater primacy as a mode of interaction. The chapter discusses the degree to which the privileging of FtF in contemporary and classic CMC research is appropriate and consistent with empirical evidence.

Chapter 6 is about SNSs and social media. Bracketing direct and private communication through traditional modalities (e.g., email, IM), the remaining modes of communication and features of social media are examined. This chapter offers three ways to understand social media use: social media as the *social news*, social media as the *archive of self*, and social media as *bridging social capital*. The social news is the idea that we use social media to advertise the events of our lives and read about the lives of others. The archive of self refers to both the searchability and permanence of our digital connections as facilitated through social media. Theories of social capital were among the first perspectives to develop during the rise of social media, and continue to serve an important function today.

2.3 The Enduring Tensions of Relationships and Technology (Chapters 7–10)

The book concludes with an examination of four important issues at the intersection of relationships and technology – all of which highlight the spillover, overlap, and influence of offline sociability on online behavior and vice versa.

Chapter 7 argues that there are five inherent tensions in the use of media in relationships:

- Hyper-coordination versus micro-coordination
- Personalized and purposeful messages versus generalized messages
- Contributing to the conversation versus virtual people watching
- Intentional attention versus incidental awareness
- Routine access offline versus limited access offline

Chapter 8 addresses the role of media in contributing to digital stress. After reviewing the evidence of whether social media is bad for you,

I introduce five types of digital stress in this chapter. I examine explanations for why individuals experience digital stress and why they continue to use media in ways that contribute to digital stress.

Chapter 9 addresses the long-standing concern that new media technologies are displacing FtF conversations with close relational partners. Starting with the adoption of the telephone, social displacement has been a guiding perspective to understand new technology adoption. This chapter examines evidence of displacement in research on the internet and social media. The other topic tackled by this chapter is where co-present media use competes with partner attention and affects conversational quality.

Chapter 10 grapples with one of the most important questions of our time: Has greater access to others through media (connectivity) contributed to our sense of connection or furthered our isolation from one another? The current nearly constant state of connectivity is contrasted with the importance of connection through social interaction with close others. Bringing back theories and perspectives introduced throughout this book, this chapter examines why connectivity does not necessarily make us feel more connected.

SECTION THREE: CONCLUSION

This book is a strategic argument about how to understand both the use of media in relationships *and* the role of relationships in media use. The content and organization of this book offer a template for how future research can theoretically and conceptually adopt and develop this argument. Thus, this book is no simple playlist.

As Questlove notes (Thompson, 2018), curation requires mindful tending and pruning. Herein, the research of many scholars is framed and juxtaposed in unorthodox ways to make a case for the importance and viability of a new and coherent understanding of the intersection between technology and relationships. I do not summarize for the sake of summary. I selected and pruned extant research, including my own work, to make a novel contribution.

I made countless creative choices to bring you this work. I have composed new songs and remixed prior tracks of my own. Like a DJ, I sampled the work of hundreds of scholars to make something new. Each choice, each selection has been creatively interpreted through my own understanding of how to think about media as used in personal relationships. The ten chapters of this book form a single argument.

This book will offer an alternative approach to studying contemporary uses of personal media that differs from platform-specific or media-centric constraints. This will push back against research that focuses on zero-acquaintance and ecologically artificial conditions. It will privilege the daily, mundane, and relationship-oriented use of personal media. In other words, this book is about how regular people use personal media in day-to-day life to relate to one another.

With this argument, I hope to speak beyond the boundaries of the scholarly community. The act of curation is always personal. This book speaks to what I believe to be one of the crucial challenges of our time: maintaining the vital connection we have to one another as the degree of digital connectivity ever rises. To do so, we must understand how, when, and why we relate through technology.

1

Social Ecology and Personal Media

1.1 What Is Social Ecology?

Who did you see today? Who did you interact with? And who do you truly care about?

In a typical day, you might have seen and been seen by scores or perhaps hundreds of people. Just as when you saw people and they blurred into the margins of your consciousness – neither notable nor memorable – you too were part of the "other people" to everyone else (a fact that never ceases inspire awe when I dwell on it). Perhaps you increased the reach of who saw you today because you posted a selfie on Instagram or shared family photos on Facebook. Thanks to the algorithms embedded in social media, we do not know who among our networks of connections actually saw these photos. As such, our audience is unlikely to be the same people we thought would look at it (Bernstein, Bakshy, Burke, & Karrer, 2013). Even when seen, our photo likely receded into the background of viewers' consciousness – neither notable nor memorable – even if it received a "like."

You undoubtedly socially interacted with far fewer people than you saw. Applying inclusive standards, a head nod, a smile, or a verbal acknowledgment might constitute an interaction. You likely shared a short back-and-forth conversation with a small portion of those you acknowledged. Maybe you texted with a few friends as well. Nonetheless, by any metric, the number of interactions you had was far fewer than the number of people you saw and acknowledged.

And only some of those people you talked with really mattered to you. Only about 40% of our social interactions are with close relationship partners (Hall, 2018a; Sandstrom & Dunn, 2014). You likely saw, greeted, and interacted with your romantic partner or your roommate after you awoke. Maybe you had lunch with a friend or maybe you called your mom today, which is generally a good idea (Seltzer, Ziegler, & Pollak, 2010). Unfortunately, there are many people you truly care about but you did not see and did not talk to today or even recently.

These three questions (i.e., who did you see, who did you interact with, and who is important to you) frame this book's approach to understanding interpersonal mediated communication. I call this approach social ecology. I define social ecology as the study of the number and nature of human relationships and the pattern and content of the social interactions that create and sustain them. This perspective has origins in evolutionary theory and social network analysis, embraces a constitutive approach to interpersonal communication, and sees everyday social interactions as the key unit of analysis.

1.2 Relationships Are Part of What It Means to Be Human

For the vast majority of human history, people lived in small groups comprised of people they knew most of their lives. For most of human history, the questions of who did you see, who did you interact with, and who do you truly care about were responded to by pointing to the people living right next to you. The routineness and familiarity of this life created extraordinary *stickiness* to human relationships; they were durable, long-lasting, and highly interdependent.

People had to rely on one another to survive. Pre-industrial cultures in today's world, without access to technologies that permeate developed nation-states, continue to function in this manner. The conditions of human life made it necessary to have family and friends who could help, protect, and take care of each other every day.

Perspectives on human relationships and social behavior that developed from evolutionary theory focus on the necessity of relationships for survival and reproduction. These perspectives have concluded that being favorably regarded and included by others was necessary for survival, procreation, and parenting – the three primary forces of evolution (Brown & Brown, 2006; Seyfarth & Cheney, 2012; Tooby & Cosmides, 2008). Investing resources in other people – sharing food, tending and caring for others, protecting others' welfare and reputation, and coming to others' aid in times of need – was essential for our genes to be passed on to future generations.

Evolutionary theorists have argued that humans adapted mechanisms – motivational, affective, and cognitive – that direct our feelings and actions toward the goal of being included by others. In evolutionary terms, heritable traits enabling and encouraging the formation and maintenance of enduring social bonds were selected for, while traits maladaptive for the individual's inclusion within the social group were selected against (Brown & Brown, 2006; Tooby & Cosmides, 2008). From an evolutionary point of view, we have adapted to form and maintain multiple durable relationships because it was advantageous for passing along our genetic code.

Compared with other intelligent and social mammals (e.g., dolphins, elephants, primates), human relationships are distinct in nature and number. Some animals form a long-term pair bond with a mate. Far fewer have long-term bonds with non-mates. Even fewer bond with others that are neither mates nor genetically related. Tackling the question, do animals have "friends" (or whatever the animal equivalent of one would be), Seyfarth and Cheney (2012) found the most prominent examples of such relationships were between primate kin – often mother–daughter pairs. Other intelligent animals are able to remember and prefer particular others in the group; for example, dolphins can maintain an alliance with dolphin friends for twenty years!

By contrast, human beings are a class apart in the duration, the number, and in the non-kin nature of our social networks. This uniqueness convinced anthropologist Terrell (2015) to suggest humans have the *trait* of friendship. Before carrying on about what is a friend, perhaps we need to start one step below: What constitutes a relationship?

1.3 What Are Relationships?

Although a *relationship* is one of the most important concepts in social scientific research, it is also one of the least theorized. Brown and Brown's (2006) definition of a social bond is "a tie between two or more individuals that is stable over time and across contexts" (p. 4). In addition to stability, a relationship requires individuation from a group and some degree of mutual influence or interdependence (Reis, 2001). To be said to be *in* a relationship or to *have* one, both partners must identify, differentiate, and recall the characteristics of one another beyond sociological or cultural categorical distinctions.

These three defining characteristics of a relationship (i.e., stability, individuation, interdependence) help people figure out who they know and how they know them, and who they can count on in times of need or when seeking intimacy and assurance. Our ability to even conceive of a relationship facilitates social decision-making, rendering relational decisions easy and consistent without being memory-taxing or requiring an utterly inefficient review of a tit-for-tat balance sheet.

As opposed to those who maintain technology-based theories and perspectives, I reject the concept that the weak-tie versus strong-tie distinction is enough to understand how relationships influence media use. In such perspectives, weak ties are often defined as acquaintances and strangers. Given the above criteria, I would argue that we do not have a relationship with many of our acquaintances (Morgan, 2009), and certainly do not have a relationship with strangers. If this book were heavily focused on ties yet to be made (i.e., latent ties) or on bridging social capital, a process by which we access resources from weak ties, then this weak/strong distinction might be sufficient. But, for the purposes of this book, it very much matters what kind of relationship we have with people we communicate with using technology.

Finally, my definition of relationships excludes one-sided associations (e.g., parasocial relationships). No doubt many people feel they have a relationship with celebrities, but this does not count as a relationship from my social ecology perspective.

1.4 As a Trait, What Does Friendship Do for Us?

Consider that if we had no ability to distinguish who is our friend, we might wander about conversing with whomever was around, unable to discern who they are in relation to us, and how they regard us in return. This would seriously complicate decisions about with whom to share information and ask for help, and in whom to invest our care and concern. The mutual recognition of a relationship streamlines these decisions; knowing someone is a friend or loved one is a powerful heuristic for social decision-making. It also makes reciprocity possible.

In other words, the material and emotional resources invested in others would not benefit us if relationships did not exist or were not able to endure over time and context (Hall & Davis, 2017; Terrell, 2015). The tendencies toward bonding with others, seeking their aid in times of exclusion or danger, and repairing impressions in times of embarrassment would have no effect if we lacked a relationship with that person. More than any other characteristic, willingness to offer aid in times of need is the most consistent characteristic of friendship across pre-industrial cultures throughout the world and through-out history (Hruschka, 2010; Terrell, 2015).

From an evolutionary point of view, a relationship between two individuals is adaptive to *both* partners because it implies future reciprocity. Both parties gain from a mutual tie because of the reciprocity implicated in the existence of a relationship. Relationships (as an evolved trait) exist to vastly increase the availability and ordering of reciprocal resources, which makes help or resources offered in the past available in the future, often in a situationally suitable form.

1.5 Relationships Are Good for Us

Another less clinical way to consider what relationships are good for is to ask the question, What is the evidence that people are better off if they have relationships? Study after study has shown that having more close friends and family is a consistent predictor of life satisfaction (Helliwell & Wang, 2011; Lucas & Dyrenforth, 2006), well-being and health (Helliwell & Putnam, 2004; van der Horst & Coffe, 2012), and less loneliness (Pinquart & Sorensen, 2003). Famous studies of human longevity (e.g., the Terman study, the Harvard

Grant study) show a long and healthy life is fundamentally a social life with meaningful human relationships (Friedman & Martin, 2011; Vaillant, 2012). All of this evidence can be interpreted as a sign that relationships are a precious human resource; without relationships we are unlikely to survive, much less thrive (Hall & Merolla, 2020).

SECTION TWO: SOCIAL NETWORKS

2.1 There Is a Limit to How Many Relationships a Person Can Sustain

Given the definition of a relationship, we are in a relationship with far fewer people than we recognize. If an individual's social network is only composed of others with whom the individual shares a relationship, then social network size is constrained in three important ways for modern and ancestral humans alike. The first is simply a limitation of time, both within a day and over a lifetime. We do not have the time in our lives to make and maintain a very large number of relationships. My own research suggests that it takes forty to sixty hours just to make a casual friend, and more than 200 hours to make a close friend (Hall, 2019). And this does not take into account the countless hours maintaining a friendship after making it.

Second, each relationship is accompanied by an obligation of support, regard, and fair treatment. The closest relationship partners entail the greatest obligations, and emotionally distant others have the fewest obligations. A failure to meet those obligations at either level is associated with disappointment and less satisfaction in friendships (Hall, Larson, & Watts, 2011). But, whether emotionally close or distant, each additional relationship accompanies a minimal obligation to the other person. Thus, larger social networks increase total obligations, and the addition of any network member, but particularly emotionally close others, can increase the net obligation significantly. Anyone who has felt frustrated that a friend is not as available to hang out as they used to be once they have a new romantic partner knows that new relationships take time and attention away from the rest of the network.

Robin Dunbar has done more than any other thinker and theorist to promote the idea that there is an upper limit on the number of "friends" you can have. In 1996, he presented an evolutionary model of human relationships that explained the size of social groups in relation to the volume of the neocortex relative to the entire volume of the brain. This *social brain hypothesis* suggests that there is a limit to the number of individuals with whom a person can maintain a "coherent face-to-face relationship" (Dunbar, 2010, p. 24). This limits the number of friends a person can have.

The limit (~150) emerged from three constraints: temporal, obligatory, and cognitive (Dunbar, 1996; 2012; 2016). The volume of the neocortex constrains the cognitive ability to recognize another person as a unique individual, to recall information about and prior interactions with that person, and to comprehend their associations with others (Dunbar, 1996; 2012). Obligations of concern and support constrain people's ability to create new relationships. The time constraint affects the initiation of new relationships (Hall, 2019; Miritello et al., 2013) as well as the maintenance of old ones (Roberts & Dunbar, 2011).

2.2 Your Relational Network: A Deep Dive into the Ones That Matter

For decades, sociologists and social network analysts have been quantifying the number of relationships a person is said to have. There are many different types of social networks that shape the whole. A discussion network is comprised of the people with whom you discuss with important matters (Small, 2017). A network of intimates is comprised of people who are personally important to you, whether you discuss important matters with them or not (Hampton, Sessions, & Her, 2011; Small, 2017). There is also a network of people you might seek out to help you out – an instrumental support network of people nearby and willing to lend a hand (Mollenhorst, Volker, & Flap, 2014). Depending on the way the question is asked, people will often identify different people in response to each question. Across these various ways of asking, there is strong evidence that the number of vitally important others is quite small.

There are two to six people in the core network. The core network is comprised of the closest relationships we have in our lives. These are our parents, our romantic partners, our children, and our best friends. A recent probability sample of Americans reports that respondents had only two people in the discussion network, and one additional person in the intimate network who was not in the discussion network (Hampton et al., 2011). For example, you might deeply care about your children, but not discuss important matters with them. A nationally representative and longitudinal study from the Netherlands reports an average of two people in the discussion network and two more who can be called on to help out in times of need (Mollenhorst et al., 2014). This network of two to six people is very stable throughout life (Milardo, Helms, Widmer, & Marks, 2014; Morgan, Neal, & Carder, 1996). When emergency hits and we need material help or someone to talk to, the core network is there for us. In times of real crisis, such as life-threatening medical treatment, these close partners become increasingly important, while others fade into the background (Hruschka, 2010).

The fifteen in the personal network matter the most. We have about fifteen important people in our lives at any given time (or about ten additional people beyond the core network). The first fifteen are variously called "near intimates" (Milardo et al., 2014), the "sympathy group" (Dunbar, 2012), or the "personal network" (Wrzus, Hänel, Wagner, & Neyer, 2013), the latter of which is the nomenclature that I prefer. People have an equal number of friends and family in a personal network. In the core network there are likely more family than friends, but friends are more plentiful in the second circle of closeness (Boase, Horrigan, Wellman, & Rainie, 2006).

These people are critically important throughout life. We depend on them and they depend on us. We go to them in times of need (Mollenhorst et al., 2014) and share the tribulations and celebrations of life with them. They provide "close emotional support that allows us to fine-tune emotional well-being and stress reduction" (Sutcliffe, Dunbar, Binder, & Arrow, 2012, p. 156). They celebrate our successes and share our sorrow. These are our true friends. They are our family.

Although these relationships are very durable, they still change more than the core network over life. About 50% of members of discussion and help networks are still in those networks seven years later (Mollenhorst et al., 2014). Although people keep in touch with the other half who are no longer among the first fifteen, the composition of one's personal network changes considerably in less than a decade (Mollenhorst et al., 2014). This change often happens during times of transition, such as when moving or starting school (Small, Pamphile, & McMahan, 2015). Unfortunate or tragic events like divorce or loss of a loved one alter one's personal network composition, and not just due to the loss of a core network member but also because the event itself tends to rearrange our personal network (Mollenhorst et al., 2014; Wrzus et al., 2013).

One of the other critical facts about the first fifteen is they occupy a lion's share of our total social time and relationship maintenance effort, particularly our core ties (Binder, Roberts, & Sutcliffe, 2012). Friendships are particularly in need of care and communication to maintain closeness (Roberts & Dunbar, 2011). This centralization of maintenance times is reflected in our use of personal media. Nearly half of all mobile calls are distributed among only three other people (Saramaki, Leicht, Lopez, Roberts, Reed-Tsochas & Dunbar, 2014), and most texts are shared with five to seven relational partners (Ling, Bertel, & Sundsøy, 2012). We relate to others through media in a fashion that reflects the priority we put on them.

The bottom line is that the unequal allocation of relational concern and effort among our entire social network heavily shapes how we use media, whom we talk to through media, and whether we use certain types of media at all.

2.3 More Distant Circles

Although there is a robust history of research on core and personal networks, research on the size and characteristics of peripheral relationships is less developed. Dunbar (1996; 2010; 2012; 2016) suggests that after the first 15, there is a "rule of three," wherein you have 40–50 in the next group of intimates, and then 120–150 in the outer group. Notice though that these are neither weak ties (e.g., acquaintances) nor strong ties (i.e., the first fifteen). So, who are the people in these layers of intimacy?

These two groups include less emotionally close friends and family, which represent a huge storehouse of past care, concern, and time. These are people who helped shape our identities in the recent and distant past and still support our sense of self today. They are people with whom we were once close or people who we once invested a lot of time and energy into, especially those in the 40–50 group (Mollenhorst et al., 2014). Old friendships tend to fade away, particularly because of less routine interaction, but they do not necessarily disappear from our circle of care. They often take up residence in our mental community of friends even if not part of our daily interaction routines.

The 150 "friends" include those whom you have a relationship with, have contact details for, wish to keep in touch with, and simply prefer compared with other people you may know (Dunbar, 1996; 2010; 2012).They are not people whom we feel particularly close to – less than friends and close friends – and we expect a lot less from them (Binder et al., 2012; Hall et al., 2011). This group is more likely composed of casual friends, neighbors, or distant relatives, such as aunts and cousins, and preferred others we see every day in our workplace or school. In this layer of intimacy, new people are likely coming and going all of the time. New environments, new social opportunities, and increased motivation to develop a relationship likely all encourage people to refashion their broader social network. This group has individuals we might forge a closer relationship with when time or opportunity presents (e.g., if you were to move to where old friends and distant family live). In some ways, these people are in the relationship minor leagues, available to be called up if opportunity or need arises.

2.4 Interaction Networks and Core Networks

Sadly, the people who you care about may not actually be the people whom you talk to. The people you talk to on any given day comprise your interaction network. This network draws on "a broad array of network sectors, including intimates, more distant kin, friends, and acquaintances" (Milardo et al., 2014, p. 41). Only 40% of our social interactions are with close relationship partners (Hall, 2018a; Sandstrom & Dunn, 2014). Daily contact with the ten most important friends and family who do not live in the same residence is exceedingly rare: for 50–70% of people, monthly contact or less is typical (Tillema, Dijst, & Schwanen, 2010). Communication with people whom you actually interact with daily (e.g., work colleagues, neighbors, classmates) is much more instrumental and constrained in nature (Hall, 2018a). That is, you *have to* talk with people in your interaction network, but such talk is unlikely to be relationally oriented or engaged in for its own sake.

On entering the work world, those who you interact with frequently are often not those who you are the closest to (Tillema et al., 2010; Wellman, Carrington, & Hall, 1988). For example, friends are key members of one's personal network (aka the first fifteen) but are rarely part of one's active interaction network. People forget to stay in touch and do not prioritize maintaining communication habits with friends, even with close friends (Milardo et al., 2014).

This observation – that whom we care about and whom we talk to may or may not be the same group of people – is central to the social ecology approach (Hall & Merolla, 2020). This approach is critical to understanding patterns of media use and the role of social media in relationship mainten-ance, and this approach puts into context why the *who* on the other side of a text, call, or video chat matters when explaining its effects.

SECTION THREE: SOCIAL INTERACTION

3.1 Why Are Social Interactions Important?

Social interactions are the means by which relationships come into being. The inimitable interpersonal theorist Steve Duck (1994a) convincingly argues that relationships exist because of talk. All three definitional characteristics of a relationship – its mutuality, its endurance, and its interdependence – are brought into existence through everyday mundane conversation. Thus, a "relationship" merely stands in for the aggregation of talk between people over time. There are two implications of this approach.

First, the constitutive approach suggests that thinking that we "have" a relationship or thinking that we really "know" someone is an illusion. We can know someone only inasmuch as our shared talk permits a partial understand-ing of how they interpret their own experiences and ours. The development of a shared perspective is the means by which our relationships are established and grow (Duck, 1994a). Our understanding of another person is known only in part and changes while we are out of touch, living separate lives. The level of mutual regard of a relationship cannot be assumed, nor can it be directly known or measured. Rather, human beings act in ways that are reflective of where they perceive relationships to be or where they wish them to be (Duck & Pittman, 1994). This perceptual rendition of relational state is the best indicator of the health and strength of a bond. In other words, how we act toward and talk about our relationship, both with our partner and away from them, makes that relationship real and is the best indicator of its status.

If this philosophical approach does not convince you of the importance of talk, consider how important it is for global well-being. Study after study has demonstrated that socializing with others, particularly close friends and family, uniquely contributes to life satisfaction (Helliwell & Putman, 2004; Helliwell & Wang, 2011; Okun et al., 1984; van der Horst & Coffe, 2012) and is associated with less loneliness (Pinquart & Sorensen, 2003). These benefits are *in addition to* the number of relationships we have. We are healthier, happier people when we make time to talk to others, particularly those in our personal network (Hall & Merolla, 2020).

3.2 So Then, What Constitutes a Social Interaction?

People *know* what a social interaction is, but academics hold a variety of perspectives on the matter. Some have offered overly restrictive and others have offered overly encompassing definitions of social interaction (see Figure 1.1). On one side of the continuum is social attention, defined as the awareness of the presence of others, and subsequent adjustments in behavior in response to that awareness (Schlenker, 1980). On the other side is interpersonal communication, as conceptualized by Miller and Steinberg (1975), who were so restrictive in their definition that they believed "some people may never communicate interpersonally with anyone" (p. 27).

Two important points of distinction lie upon this continuum. The first point lies between mutual acknowledgment and intentional engagement with

Concept	Social Attention	Unfocused Interaction	Routine Impersonal Interaction	Focused Social Interaction	Deep Communication
Research Focus	The Public Self	Civil Inattention	Scripted Interactions	Pure Social Interaction	Intimacy
With Whom?	Everyone: Receiver-based definition of communication	Everyone: Sender-based definition of communication	Others in role positions	Acquaintances	Close relational partners
Characteristics and Examples	Presence of others necessary; Mutual acknowledgment not necessary	Greetings (both verbal and nonverbal)	Memory organization packets; Scripts	Less scripted conversation; Conversations	Intimate conversation; Deep self-disclosure
Social Media Examples	Social surveillance (e.g., browsing, lurking)	"Like" and "Favorite"	Happy birthday; Re-tweet and re-post (share)	Chatting; Commenting; Tagging photos	

↑	↑	↑
1. Other-directed behavior 2. Mutual acknowledgment 3. Reception of behavior	Conversation	1. Discussion 2. Interactants recognized as individual 3. Interactants treated uniquely

FIGURE 1.1 Face-to-face and mediated social interaction

others, and the second is between scripted, impersonal, or role-based social interactions and social interactions with acquaintances. Social attention occurs at the moment of awareness that other humans are present and can observe the self (Schlenker, 1980). A colloquial term for social attention is *people watching*. Moving conceptually from social attention toward social interaction, Goffman (1963) defined an *unfocused interaction* as mutual acknowledgment between two or more strangers or familiar others, such as an exchanged nod, smile, or greeting.

The second point of distinction lies between impersonal, role-based interaction and social interactions with acquaintances. Goffman (1963) privileged *focused social interaction*, wherein relational partners share a mutual focus of attention and engage in conversation. Focused social interaction requires that conversation partners recognize one another as unique individuals. When individuals communicate solely based on roles they occupy, as with a cashier, they are not engaging in focused interaction (Goffman, 1963). In fact, many research studies on social interaction do not require participants to recall or report on interactions such as these (see Hall, 2018b).

3.3 Mediated Social Interaction

There are many types of mediated social interactions that are clearly examples of focused social interaction, such as voice calls and video chats. Texting and one-on-one chats (e.g., Instagram chat) can also be social interactions, but only when there is back-and-forth exchange between people who are both jointly attentive to the exchange. The majority of this book focuses on mediated social interactions: phone calls, video chats, texting, and instant-messenger type chats.

By contrast, very little of social media use is social interaction (Hall, 2018b). The unique forms of relating made possible by social media will be examined in Chapter 6. In the meantime, social interaction through social media includes only private, direct messaging (e.g., chat programs) and back-and-forth text exchanges that are publicly visible (e.g., directed comments on Facebook posts).

SECTION FOUR: CONTEXT MATTERS

The final component of my social ecology perspective is a concern for context. There are three issues I wish to draw attention to throughout this book: life course, forming versus maintaining relationships, and what you see is not what you get. All of these issues profoundly shape and are shaped by who you see, how many people you interact with, and the nature and number of relationship partners you have.

4.1 A Life Course Perspective on Relationship Goals

There are many surveys that describe generational divides in personal and mobile media use, including studies with nationally representative samples (e.g., Nielsenwire, 2013). This work points to disparate adoption of and preference for media based on age. In Chapter 5, I explore closely how the choice of media is associated with relationship stage. In Chapter 2, I explore the ideas that relationship partners influence how media are used and that media send different messages about the closeness of the relationship. However, here I want to point out how stage of life influences the size and nature of people's social network. With the notable exceptions of Bhattacharya, Ghosh, Monsivais, Dunbar, and Kaski (2016), Chan (2015), and Ling et al. (2012), very little research has explored the intersection between personal media use and relationship development and maintenance that is sensitive to people's life course and offers useful comparisons between age groups.

The stage of life or change in life circumstances influences media use *because* the stage of life influences relationship-related motivations and choices. Underlying social and relational reasons explain why different age groups use media in different ways. These patterns of use are reflective of what is going on with people at different times of life, not only a matter of preference for one type of media over another.

I would argue that life stage plays a critical and yet poorly understood role in the type of media a person prefers as well as how it is used. For example, the size of one's personal network (i.e., the first fifteen) is an average number that obscures meaningful numerical differences over the lifetime. As mobile records (Bhattacharya et al., 2016) and an analysis of social network size (Wrzus et al., 2013) demonstrate, the decade between fifteen and twenty-five years of age is where the number of relationships people are trying to maintain is higher than at any other point of life. This size peaks at twenty-five years old. Then, a period of decline in number of relationships follows until the early forties where it stabilizes for a while before falling again (Wrzus et al., 2013).

This means that one particular period of life (i.e., fifteen to twenty-five years old) is a time of rapid growth in the number of relationship partners. The three central tasks of that stage of life are making new friends, finding potential romantic partners, and separating oneself from the identity of one's family of origin (Carmichael, Reis, & Duberstein, 2015). New relationships play an important role in the process of forming an identity, and having that identity confirmed by others is crucial. From the period of adolescence to young adulthood, people are transitioning and becoming more fully realized in who they are and what they want to do with their life. In the present era, media are an important means of accomplishing these goals (Chayko, 2018; Nesi et al., 2018).

This is also a period of rapid context shifting. In the United States, nearly 70% of students who graduated high school in 2016 were enrolled in college or university by the following fall (Bureau of Labor Statistics, 2016). Although the portion of young adults living at home has increased in the last decade, more than half of adults under twenty-five have found accommodations elsewhere (St. Clair, 2016). These are critical times in new relationship formation. From the beginning to end of the fifteen- to twenty-five-year-old decade, young people must navigate changing relationships from high school to university or college, wherein the embedded, stable, and familiar relationships of high school that offer more closeness and commitment are replaced by emerging adult relationships that are comparably nascent, unstable, and driven by choice, not by routine (Parks, 2007). Consider that new friendship development coincides very strongly with these sorts of shifts of context (Hall, 2019; Small et al., 2015). Moving for school or for a new job offers new opportunities to make friends and try on different identities. Lifelong friends and confidants are made and built during that key decade (Carmichael et al., 2015) in part because of the poignant need to create new relationships in new contexts, particularly in the case of finding romantic partners.

All of this coincides with the fact that a high percentage of research on digital media, particularly social media and texting, is done on this exact age group (Huang, 2010; Liu & Yang, 2016). This means that what is collectively known about the importance of media is based on findings for people who are going through a period of life that is fundamentally different from that of the remaining adult population, and different from what the young people themselves will experience later in life (Ling et al., 2012).

The unique relationship challenges of this demographic – new romantic partners, new friends, new contexts, and new people to meet – undoubtedly affect research findings, but, sadly, it is hard to know the degree to which research-based conclusions are distorted by this overreliance on young people. Acknowledgment of the unique relational motivations, conditions, and stressors based on time of life that indubitably affect media use is a blind spot in research on personal media. Researchers must be more sensitive to the fact that research findings themselves (e.g., about stress, loneliness, well-being) reflect the challenges at that time of life and are applicable to the participants in the study, but are relatively insensitive to and unrepresentative of the population as a whole.

To illustrate, I would like to offer three quick examples of how taking into account stage of life in conjunction with social network characteristics provides unique insights about digital media use.

My recent project on mobile entrapment (i.e., Hall, 2017a) is illustrative of how network size influences the experience of using digital media. Entrapment is the experience of guilt and anxiety to be available to and responsive to others via one's mobile device, particularly through SMS or texting. In my first study, I found that when people report having more friends, they are more likely to experience mobile entrapment. By closely documenting *whom* people were interacting with through their mobile devices using experience sampling, I found that entrapment is related to using the mobile phone to communicate with less close relationship partners. In combination, the experience of texting is much less pleasant and connected, in part, because of these practices of using technology in the context of one's social network. Although a larger social network appeared to contribute to entrapment across all age groups, it was also the case that the youngest participants were trying to maintain largest social networks.

Reinecke and colleagues' (2017) analysis of digital stress in a representative sample of Germans demonstrates how sensitivity to age enhances our understanding of media use. Across all age groups, those who experienced a greater information load (i.e., sending, receiving, checking messages) were more stressed. Trying to manage this amount of information indirectly contributed to burnout and anxiety. However, older adults navigated these demands more productively. Younger participants experienced greater social pressure to be available via media compared with older users, so they turned to multitasking to manage this demand. Unfortunately, multitasking was associated with even more stress, anxiety, and depression. Therefore, compared with older adults, young adults turn to a strategy to manage digital stress that likely exacerbates digital stress (see Chapter 8).

Finally, dana boyd's *It's Complicated: The Social Lives of Networked Teens* (2014) points out that adolescents are often desperate to spend time with their friends but are constrained by a lack of autonomy to leave their home and a lack of public spaces to congregate, and are upset by the feeling of being overprogrammed. Adolescents turn to social media and texting to converse, share their experiences, and plan to get together or reflect on the events of the day with their friends. Although parents contribute to the constraints that adolescents face, parents tend to blame the media and perceive their children as addicted to social and mobile media. As boyd notes, this fixation on the media is a product of social anxieties that are particularly salient at one critical time of life – adolescence.

4.2 New Relationships Are Different from Ongoing Ones

Another relationship factor that helps to add context to the use of personal media is the difference between new relationship formation and the maintenance of ongoing ones. There are two pertinent ways this matters: the use of media to find new people and the use of media in interdependent relationships.

Nowhere is this issue more important than in the realm of online dating. Since 1997 there has been a sea change in both attitudes toward and adoption of technologies facilitating romantic relationship development (Finkel, Eastwick, Karney, Reis, & Sprecher, 2012). A weighted national sample of Americans married from 2005 to 2012 found that more Americans met online than any single offline location (e.g., work, through friends, school), and 35% of all Americans who married in that time interval met online (Cacioppo, Cacioppo, Gonzaga, Ogburn, & VanderWeele, 2013). The role of media in forming romantic relationships has recently expanded as geo-located smartphone applications for dating and matchmaking have multiplied and become commonplace (Manley, 2017).

By contrast, the vast majority of personal media (not including applications and services for online dating) is used to relate to existing partners, not to form new ones (Bhattacharya et al., 2016; Bryant, Marmo, & Ramirez, 2011; Ling et al., 2012). Despite the fact that social media actively steers people to gain new "friends" or "followers," two-thirds of social media users have *zero* friends or followers they have *not* met in person (Duggan, Ellison, Lampe, Lenhart, & Madden, 2014; Quinn & Papacharissi, 2018). In the 1990s, new technologies such as chat rooms enabled strangers to meet online (see Chapter 4), but these functions did not have a strong sway after the emergence of Web 2.0 and social media. This may be because a broad demographic of people went online for the first time at the turn of the last century to connect with existing friends and family (Rainie & Wellman, 2012), not to meet new people.

This is important because different types of relationships result in different kinds of outcomes. In a classic study by Valkenburg and Peter (2009), adolescents using IM to maintain existing close friendships experienced the positive benefits to social connectedness and well-being, but using IM to make new friends and meet strangers did not have such effects. Granted, there are important places for new relationship development online, such as online dating, online support groups, and online gaming. But new relationship development is not a central use of personal media, and when personal media are used for relationship development, they do not have clear advantages for well-being.

It is also important to recognize that the self-presentational and communicative goals involved with meeting new people are distinct from the communicative practices within established relationships. The results from studies designed to focus on first meetings and studies drawn from populations that are at a life stage of finding new relationship partners are likely quite distinct from studies of established and known relationships. Digital media use is shaped by distinct relationship goals, particularly for those at the most relationship-focused stages of life.

On the other end of the spectrum, interdependence between relationship partners strongly influences media use (Baym, 2009; Caughlin & Sharabi, 2013; Parks, 2017; Ruppel, Burke, & Cherney, 2018). Interdependence is a concept derived from social exchange theory (Kelley & Thibaut, 1978), and is described as the degree to which two people are mutually dependent on each other's actions to achieve relational and non-relational goals. It includes to the degree to which resources are pooled between relationship partners and partners have a shared fate. Highly interdependent partners, such as a married couple, must coordinate finances, plans, and time, or suffer from the consequences of doing so poorly. By contrast, independent friends have very little influence on one another's lives and outcomes, except when spending time together. The degree of interdependence of the partners affects the establishment, stability, and ease of communication both offline and online, and even between offline and online communication.

4.3 What You See on Social Media Is Not What You Get

The final contextual issue that deserves greater research focus is the recognition that what you see on social media is not what you get in terms of the relationships between people. There is a tendency in research on social media to equate the existence of ties or connections with the existence of a relationship (Fu & Liu, 2020). As a direct challenge to this approach, there is evidence that using social media to connect may be inversely associated with relationship closeness.

By design, many social media operate to increase the size of people's network. This will allow the corporation behind the platform to swallow any other competing social media and will further embed users in the platform, making it harder to for them to leave. Thus, social media promotes connection to other users through social matching algorithms and searchable identities – making the network much larger than it might be otherwise (Dunbar, 2016; Quinn & Papacharissi, 2018). Thus, individuals' social networks, as represented in their social media profiles, are highly distorted: both people who are important but not in the network are not counted, and those counted as being in one's social network are often of negligible closeness (Quinn & Papacharissi, 2018).

Several studies have found that closer partners are poorly reflected in social media. A minority of Facebook friends are actual friends: Ellison, Vitak, Gray, and Lampe (2014) report that 37% are actual friends; Manago and Vaugh (2015) report that 21% are close friends and family; Dunbar (2016) reports that only 28% of Facebook friends were genuine friends; and Burke and Kraut (2016) report that 12–18% of friends are those with close ties. What this means is that researchers who look at social network membership uncritically or unreflectively may falsely conclude that a social media network is a network of meaningful or close social relationships.

The opposite may be true. Bryant and Marmo (2012) recognized early on that social media bring together weak-tie relationships. Indeed, Facebook features are more frequently used between relationship partners who are not close (Ellison et al., 2014). Strong ties not only connect elsewhere (Bryant & Marmo, 2012; Ellison et al., 2014), but weak ties are likely to disappear or stall out in terms of closeness if they are not reinforced in some way offline (Manago & Vaugh, 2015). This means the most visible social media actions are taken by those in weaker relationships.

This ties into functionality of the platforms as well. Friends are much more expected to engage in direct mediated social interaction – both on Facebook through private chat and through various other media – than casual friends or acquaintances (Bryant & Marmo, 2012). These private messages are considered much more intimate than status updates, and people use private messaging to create closeness (Utz, 2015). Even among friends, more public messages on social media are inversely related to closeness (McEwan, 2013). This means that friends often consider themselves less close the more they rely on public social media affordances to communicate.

By making a user's networks easily visible and searchable, social media give the false impression that those who communicate through it are close. Evidence suggests the opposite is more likely true.

SECTION FIVE: CONCLUSION

The current mobile moment is historically different from how technology was used in the past, but let us not come to the false conclusion that it has utterly transformed the centrality of our close relationships or easily enabled interdependence with them. Rather, the constant potential for access, greater ease of connection, and sheer volume of asynchronous communication has removed or greatly weakened the traditional boundaries of time, place, and routine. We now live in a time where people have to reestablish this order, and this book is about how people do just that.

Although much of their analysis is spot-on and extremely valuable, I believe that Rainie and Wellman (2012) often argue from what people *could* do using media rather than what they *actually* do. For example, they claim that "many [people] meet their social, emotional, and economic needs by tapping into sparsely knit networks of diverse associates rather than relying on tight connections to a relatively small number of core associates" (p. 12). I am suspicious of this claim, especially the word "many." The authors recognize that this requires a great deal of time and effort to keep up these weak ties, and even more effort and more time to "conduct deeply satisfying electronic communications" as might be found in geographically close or FtF encounters (p. 12). They nonetheless conclude: "Quantity *does* equal quality ... larger networks provide more overall sociability, support, information, and connections to the rest of the world" (p. 266). However, not only is there a limit to the number of relationships a person can have, but there also appears to be diminishing rewards in terms of well-being as social networks get bigger and bigger (Helliwell & Wang, 2011; Pinquart & Sorensen, 2003). Undoubtedly, if the goal is more information and more social media ties for their own sake, this conclusion is warranted, but I think this goes too far in its assumptions about the benefit of large, loose-knit networks.

Approaching this from the perspective of social ecology, I argue throughout this book that humans' personal and relational internal system is fundamentally unchanged from what it was during the time in which we evolved. The affective, cognitive, and motivational mechanisms that evolved to keep us safe and reproductively fit have and will continue to push us toward intimate social interaction with a small number of core partners. Arguing from an interdependence and personal relationship–centered approach, I argue that modality switching and coordination, between FtF interactions and multiple media, are the primary mechanisms of integrating media into our everyday lives. With some important exceptions, we have not (and likely will not) become autonomous actors at the center of our vast array of weak ties and specialized relationships. This is unlikely to happen, in part because it is entirely too effortful and intentional, but also because interdependence in relationships is the way we build reciprocity of resources and enduring relationships, and ultimately satifsy our fundamental need to belong (Hall & Davis, 2017).

Instead, this book embraces the idea that the possibilities of the age of mobility have created enduring tensions that are echoed in past times of new technology adoption and that are ultimately unresolvable. They are simply part of what it means to relate through technology.

2

The Social Construction of Technology

One of the more endearing qualities of Mr. Weasley in J. K. Rowling's (2000) *Harry Potter and the Chamber of Secrets* is his fascination with muggle (human) technology. Rather than reprimand his son Ron for stealing a flying car to liberate Harry, Mr. Weasley is thrilled to know that the machine was up for the task. Later, we find Harry explaining to Mr. Weasley how to use a telephone, as he is unfamiliar with its purpose when an owl or floo powder is readily available. We laugh at these moments because, of course, everyone knows what cars and telephones are for. But that was not always the case. The contemporary uses of those transformative technologies of the twentieth century were unknown and treated with suspicion when first introduced.

As Fischer (1992) recounts, Americans of the late nineteenth and early twentieth century were deeply concerned about the effects of the telephone on sociality. Social critics had utopian visions of the telephone "enriching social ties with gaiety, solace, and security," saving marriages and relieving rural loneliness (pp. 24–25). Social critics also had dystopian fears that telephone conversation created a "palatable emptiness" and would steer society to superficiality and ennui (p. 25). Accounts of dread due to encroachment of new technologies are at least as old as Western civilization; Plato worried about the effects of literacy on memory and the oral tradition in *Phaedrus*. Such fears are worth recounting because there is something very human about worrying about the consequences of adopting new technologies.

As Mr. Weasley's actions illustrate, technology does not inherently *do* anything. Humans invent and build technologies, tinker and modify them, and teach others to use the technology in *specific ways*. When they become obsolete or broken, most technologies have little use than their material value, such as repurposing a flip-phone for a paperweight or old computer monitor as a flowerpot.

Admittedly, there is intuitive appeal to giving agency to technologies. This is certainly reflected in our discourse about technology. Publicly and privately, people are deeply worried about what smartphones or video games or social media are *doing* to us or to our children. Language of the irrecoverable harm *caused* by technology is deeply entrenched in popular discourse. The original mission statement of the Center for the Humane Technology (founded in 2018) plainly stated: "Technology is hijacking our minds and society." Stanford communication professor Jeffrey Hancock, a respondent to a panel on the future of social media research at the 2018 International Communication Association Conference, cautioned the audience of seasoned researchers to stop saying that "social media causes anything." Rather, people use all media to their own ends and in their own ways. It is admittedly difficult to guard oneself, as a parent or scholar or a wizard or muggle, against the temptation to believe that technology is doing things to us. But there is another way to think about technology.

SECTION ONE: THE SOCIAL CONSTRUCTION OF TECHNOLOGY

1.1 Technological Determinism

Scholars who have adopted a social construction of technology (SCOT) perspective have pushed back vigorously against claims of technological determinism for generations. Technological determinism is best identified by its rhetoric. Its language situates agency *in* the technology, the device, or its content. Technological determinism views any way of using technology as being either in accord or in discord with a known and predetermined purpose. The object's designers and its marketing team decide the purpose of technology; it is said to be "built in" and humans are "hardwired" to use it in that way. Technological determinism tends to see users as hapless, clueless, and unsophisticated saps or as mindless consumers who are led to ruin by technology.

Those who fear technology and those who champion technology both speak the language of determinism. I was a speaker on a local panel at a private school on resilient kids in the age of social media. I felt like the only panelist who was not promoting a state of panic about what technology *was doing* to our teens. Everyone was quite comfortable with the idea that technology makes teens do and feel certain things. I shared a story of how as a teenager I exploited the cutting-edge technology of call waiting to talk to my girlfriend late at night without the phone ringing at either of our homes. At a pre-arranged time, I would call a number that reported the current time and temperature and then wait for call waiting to alert me that she was on the other line. The call waiting feature was my accomplice, but the technology did not make me want to talk to my girlfriend.

1.2 The Roots of SCOT

For more than three decades, SCOT advocates have argued forcefully that technology cannot be divorced from the way it is used by people (Fischer,

1992; Fulk, 1993). People give meaning to technology from the initial stage of conceiving of it to the way users make it part of their daily life. The end uses of technologies are rarely fully imaged by their creators: "Mechanical properties do not predestine the development and employment of an innovation" (Fischer, 1992, p. 16). A common theme in the origin stories of personal computers and the internet as well as the phonograph and telephone is that people use new devices for purposes that the producers of technology could hardly have foreseen or desired. Examples of this can be seen in using the phonograph to play music or sharing files of live recordings of the Grateful Dead on the proto-internet (Baym, 2018).

This does not mean that technologies do not have functional elements that point toward particular patterns of use. The SCOT perspective does not require users to be computer programmers or to hack into their mobile devices to play a role in reshaping the use of media. Rather, users bring about subtle and impermanent changes in the technology itself. When studying media, Baym (2010) recommends keeping a tight focus on specific capabilities and consequences of using media in a particular way. The primary questions should include *how* users employ the technology, to what ends, under what circumstances, and, most importantly in this book, with *whom*.

1.3 The Changing Meaning of Media

Another critical lesson of the SCOT perspective is that media use evolves over time. In Fulk's (1993) classic article, she links the origins of social constructivist theories about technology to the challenges inherent to making sense of new technologies: "Technologies provide unusual problems in sensemaking because their processes are often poorly understood and because they are continuously redesigned and reinterpreted in the process of implementation and accommodation to specific social and organization contexts" (p. 922). In the early stages of the internet, academics used message boards in different ways and for different purposes than music fans (Baym, 2018). Make no mistake, both groups contributed to imagining how the internet *could* be used; both foresaw its present-day functions.

There is an additional challenge to understanding technology use: technology has internal contradictions both within and between users (Fischer, 1992; Fulk, 1993). Said simply, people can use the same technology in positive and negative ways, and one individual's way of using technology can be in itself contradictory.

Considering the adoption of mobile devices, Arnold (2003) describes such tensions as Janus-faced. Janus was the Roman god who looked both into the future and into the past. For Arnold (2003), this duality underscores the paradox of the mobile phone. His predictions have borne out in nearly two decades of research on the tensions of mobile use. For example, mobile phones enhance autonomy *and* enhance family cohesion (Donner, Rangas-wamy, Steenson, & Wei, 2008). Dependence on mobile phones in adolescents' lives is a source of confusion, neither fully embraced nor fully rejected (Mihailidis, 2014), both cheered and jeered (Weinstein & Selman, 2014). In romantic relationships, the negotiation of availability *itself* is a source of conflict and stress, and is associated with feeling controlled by one's partner (Duran, Kelly, & Rotaru, 2011; Miller-Ott & Kelly, 2016). It is deliciously ironic and predictable that romantic partners fight about how much they should be available: a desire for connection through media brings about disconnection and discord.

The SCOT perspective reinforces some key lessons from decades of research on new media adoption. Technologies are used in a variety of ways. These uses can be contradictory both within people (e.g., to feel free and to feel tethered) and between people (e.g., to be available and to be independent) (Fischer, 1992; Hall & Baym, 2012). Media effects are *ironic*.

As one added layer of complexity, as technology is used, the patterns of use are reflected back to developers who modify it based on those same patterns of use (Fulk, 1993). Technology and its usage are in a nearly constant state of flux and redefinition. To assume a singular or "right" purpose for any given technology or a single or constant outcome arising from its use is unfounded.

SECTION TWO: THE DOMESTICATION OF MEDIA

2.1 What Is Media Domestication?

The SCOT perspective allows for a move toward domestication, which is the mundane and trivial day-to-day use of technology. To domesticate a pet, one must make it familiar with the conditions of its new environment, decrease or eliminate its unwanted behaviors, and train it to engage in new patterns of behavior, conforming to the wishes and commands of its new owner. In the process of domesticating a technology, people similarly integrate technology into everyday life through becoming more familiar with its functions and capabilities (Chayko, 2018) and eliminating or reducing unwanted programs, functions, or capabilities of the technology (Barkhuus & Polichar, 2011).

All of us can recall the experience of learning and relearning how a new computer or mobile device works. Each time, you had to go through the process of learning its functions and capabilities, turn off unwanted programs, and prioritize wanted ones. You sought to make it work to your own ends. The domestication approach typically focuses on the period of time that follows the adoption of a new medium by a large set of users. The focus of this approach is integration and habit formation.

The best sign that a new(-ish) medium is domesticated is when it is no longer considered new and is now just a given. Many theorists have argued that the ultimate outcome of domestication is being able to ignore the device (e.g., Barkhuus & Polichar, 2011; Humphreys, 2018). It becomes folded into everyday life and is merely part of the daily routine. Once people are unfamiliar with the idea that their life was impacted or augmented by the technology at all, then its domestication is complete. In other words, when people respond to the question, "How is your life affected by technology X?" with a "Huh?" or "What do you mean?" or "I haven't really thought about it, it just always seemed like it was there," then media domestication is finished.

As a quick precursor to Chapter 3, I might point out that domestication steers individuals toward a low energy-expenditure state. As stated by communicate bond belong (CBB) theory (Hall & Davis, 2017), technology use inherently steers us to lower energy use. While initial patterns of use – those involved with learning, becoming accustomed to, and habituating the functions – may require large initial investments of energy, CBB theory would suggest this is all toward the purpose of conserving energy in the future. Furthermore, using technology in less energy-intensive ways in the context of relationships is consistent with CBB theory. Known, socially sanctioned norms are comfortable, and uncertain norms are anxiety-producing, especially when the relational partner at the other end of the medium is either unknown or highly desirable or both. This provides some insight into why many online daters report feeling deeply taxed by the process, especially newcomers to the service.

2.2 Is SCOT the Same as Domestication?

Humphreys, Von Pape, and Karnowski (2013) integrate SCOT with domestication under the broader lens of media ecology. They suggest a singular perspective called the appropriation of technology (AT) model. The AT model suggests that patterns of usage emerge and stabilize over time, as do "the symbolic value," such as the technology's "appropriateness or style" (p. 493). This model focuses on the routine use of technology, and what we think about using them in terms of both value (e.g., is it good?) and purpose (e.g., what does it mean when you call rather than text?). The AT model advances the idea that social life influences media adoption and use, which directly follows from the SCOT perspective. This influence can be cultural, normative, or relational (e.g., a romantic couple).

In his account of the widespread adoption of the landline telephone, Fischer (1992) points out that there are many systems that allow any given technology function – economic, service-sector, advertising/consumption, cultural, social, and relational. Thus, we should never forget that there are social forces that *enable* use of technology in general and *encourage* the use of technology in particular ways. The AT model (Humphreys et al., 2013) reinforces the idea that we should attend to the local and societal economic and social circumstances of technology adoption and use.

Sometimes these social circumstances are organizational. Fulk's (1993) seminal article recognized that norms of technology use within a workplace influence its utility and adoption. That is, *other people* play a critical role in how we use technology. We can think about these other people as more distant or closer to us in the same manner addressed in Chapter 1: the billions of "other" people; people in our sociological groups; people we see but do not know; people we recognize; our social network; our personal network; and finally our core network. It is on these three final groups that this book is focused, not on the broad cultural or economic trends. And rightly so. As Ling and colleagues (2012) point out, our close relationship partners exert the strongest influence on mobile patterns and normative conventions.

The end purpose of bringing the SCOT perspective into dialogue with domestication is that both offer important insights on how people envelope their various devices and programs into everyday life. The *polymedia* perspective of Madianou (2014; Madianou & Miller, 2012) offers another example of blending SCOT with domestication. This work explores the social and emotional consequences of using media to communicate among migrant families. Drawing from these exemplars, I will explore three ways that media are integrated with relationships: social influence, media matching, and making do.

SECTION THREE: SCOT AND RELATING THROUGH TECHNOLOGY

3.1 Social Influence

Fulk's (1993) original work on SCOT was focused on the role of social modeling in the adoption of new technologies. She argued that technology use within organizations was a function of characteristics of the group, characteristics of the technology (e.g., channel richness), and the broader social structure in which both the group and the technology were embedded. The ways we use technology reflect the rules and relationships in which they are used. Thus, when interacting through technology, the rules and resources of the interaction structure are not only reified, but they are normatively translated into the medium's functionality through often implicit norms.

Consider that early telephone users had to figure out how to answer it. Famously, there was a debate about whether "Hoy, hoy" was a legitimate or desirable way to do so. Even now, social conventions about using the telephone often require a greeting of some sort and an expectation that people will identify themselves – sometimes even if the caller is known – as well as a goodbye at the end. Just hanging up without offering a goodbye of some sort is still considered rude when making a voice call a mobile device. Contemporary users of mobile phones confirm that this formal call structure is still normative and that it requires quite a bit of effort and attention, compared with a text message, for example (Eden & Veksler, 2016; Rettie, 2007). However, there is good reason to believe that these conventions are holdovers from the landline and may yet disappear in the future. In the meantime, past conventions of use still influence how people make phone calls.

This is neither new nor particularly problematic; new technologies always challenge social norms (Fischer, 1992). Social norms are "a framework through which people determine what behaviors are acceptable or unacceptable" (McLaughlin & Vitak, 2012, p. 300). Norms are a necessary part of social order. They can be thought of as social order itself. Rather than existing as absolute standards, norms are continuously in flux. They differ among social groups, genders, generations, relationships, and cultures. Norms help to make things predictable and understandable, and when norms change, people tend to respond with anxiety and confusion, and even vitriolic condemnation.

Technologies, particularly when they are new, require norms to change rapidly. Social norms must change or be developed from scratch with anything that is new. People have to decide whether this thing is like *this* or *that* familiar thing, which makes conflicting norms particularly likely with new technologies (e.g. Ling, 2008; Ling & McEwen, 2010; McLaughlin & Vitak, 2012).

3.2 Case Study: The Norms of Mobile Phone Use

Rainie and Wellman (2012) document the remarkable rise of mobile device adoption, in terms of both voice calls and texting, in the United States and around the world from 2000 to 2010. With all of these new mobile phone users making voice calls, norms of taking calls in public had to be navigated rapidly.

At that time, there was a great deal of public debate and some academic study about when to take calls in public and how one should behave while taking that call (Arminen, 2005; Axelsson, 2010; Baron & Hård af Segerstad, 2010; Humphreys, 2005). This was a period of norm redefinition and, not coincidentally, a great deal of normative debate. Frankly, it was a quite stressful time and it inspired strong statements of moral value and decrepitude, especially as hangers-on to past norms (i.e., older adults) looked in condemnation at younger users' behavior. Much of this upset was about when and how to take a mobile call in public. In shared spaces, onlookers judged norm violators negatively, expressing irritation and moral outrage (Arminen, 2005; Humphreys, 2005; Ling, 2008). Echoes of this tension can be seen in discussions about Google Glass, and likely will be heard again for any public technology use, especially ones that require a reformulation of when, where, and how technology can and should be used in public spaces. The degree to which a new technology is perceived to challenge the norm of "acceptable" public behavior will be directly proportional to the degree of moral outrage felt and expressed.

Consider the rise of texting. The debate about appropriate use shifted as people became accustomed to public mobile use and as trends of mobile use shifted toward texting instead of voice calls (Lenhart, 2012; Rainie & Wellman, 2012). At this juncture, people began to question the degree to which texting or using their mobile phone for other online functions was problematic. News media frequently offered dire warnings that mobile phones were ruining relationships, and gave tips for avoiding unfavorable outcomes. "Whether it's your cell phone or your Twitter account," warned *Cosmopolitan for Latinas*, "technology can quickly propel your relationship down the drain" (Nagi, 2012). In many ways, these fears have persisted and even become more piqued as the mobile app use becomes widespread (see Chapter 9 for co-present device use).

Yet in my own work on mobile phone etiquette with Nancy Baym and Kate Miltner (2014a), we found a remarkable degree of consensus about the "rules" of public mobile phone use, and participants agreed that it was important to adhere to these norms. In retrospect, it is remarkable how quickly these norms became the new standard.

Furthermore, we found that when having dinner or drinks in public or at home with a partner, the norms of use were built into the company one keeps. The more that people saw their partners adhering to their own norms of mobile use, the more they enjoyed and felt close to their partners (Hall et al., 2014a). They also adhered to their own sense of what was normative when they were in satisfying relationships. When both partners recognized the mutually agreed-upon norm and acted in accord with that norm, they were expressing and reflecting care for one another. Thus, the construction of social norms of technology use is a relational as well as a public, social act.

3.3 We Keep Using Media Because of Who Is There, Not Because of What the Media Do

When the commercial boundaries of the internet were opened for business in 1994, text-based chat rooms hosted by America Online were places to meet new people. Less than a decade later, Swedish high school students reported feeling that chat rooms were on their way out of style (Thulin & Vilhelmson, 2005). These highly wired teens had moved to using mobile phones to communicate with friends – primarily through voice calls. By 2011, a Pew Internet survey concluded that texting had taken over voice calls for young adults in the United States (Lenhart, 2012). And in 2017, after a second year of declining use of Facebook among young people, and Instagram and Snapchat receiving more teen and young adult users, some commentators were ready to crow over the inevitable death of Facebook (e.g., Lomas, 2017). Only a year later in 2018, a friend from London told me, "as we all know, Snapchat is dead." She insisted that people had moved on to apps like WhatsApp, which is (comically) owned by Facebook.

Being social is one of the primary purposes of personal media across time and across countries throughout the world. Thus, in times of transition, personal media displace other media (a topic given full attention in Chapters 4 and 8). What does this mean for the SCOT perspective? People adopt a new medium and keep using it because of who is available on that medium. A social network analysis approach called the diffusion of innovations (Valente, 1995) would predict that one's personal network shapes the choice to adopt new technologies, partly through network exposure and partly through social norms. I would argue that this process is sped up considerably when the use of an innovation or technology is dyadic and relational in nature.

Adopting most technologies does not expressly require other people to do it too. A new media player that I buy will work for me whether anyone close to me buys one or not. My friends might be influenced to buy the same product based on my experience with it (Valente, 1995), but my friends do not really *need* to have it because I do.

Social media and mobile media are quite different in that the use of them is socially interdependent. Additionally, with some exceptions (e.g., email, voice calls), many personal media platforms are not able to communicate with each other. This, by the way, is quite intentional on the part of developers. They would prefer something like this to happen: "Oh, I downloaded this new video app, you should download it too so we can share videos." This influence is vastly more direct compared with influence borne through observation or recommendation. Sometimes it even requires active persuasion or a willingness to set up or buy the technology for a loved one of another generation or of limited means (Madianou & Miller, 2012). As discussed in Chapter 1, the primary benefit of personal media is the access they offer to important relationship partners.

This means researchers ought to pay close attention to *who* is on the other side of mediated messages because it is a crucial factor in the use of a medium. It is hard to fathom people using personal media composed of users that the person has no need to talk to and is unlikely to develop a future relationship with. This may seem like an obvious observation, but few people who study media ask the question, To what degree is media choice (in adoption and amount of use) predictable by mapping it onto the core network, the first fifteen, the social network, and to the 150? I believe that the reachability and responsiveness of desired communication partners is the ultimate driver of the adoption and continuing use of personal media (see also Barkhuus & Polichar, 2011; Fulk, 1993; Rettberg, 2018).

Consider the finding that when young adults choose to use social media to directly communicate with one another, they do so due to known patterns of use (e.g., "My friend is on Snapchat all the time, so I know they at least saw that message") (Eden & Veksler, 2016; Rettberg, 2018). This motivation for use is presumptive of access to a specific person. A medium and its features are irrelevant if the person you would like to talk to does not use it now or stops using it in a predictable fashion.

This point has several important implications for understanding media use at different periods of one's lifespan. As discussed in Chapter 1, between the ages of fifteen and twenty-five, people are acquiring new friends and new romantic partners while they are experimenting with new identities and new trajectories in life. Social activity is particularly acute for teens in that they are at a point in life where constructing an identity and having that identity confirmed by others is a crucial task of development (Chayko, 2014; Nesi et al., 2018). To be able to "claim" a new identity, teens and young adults must be able to experiment with their self-presentation and receive feedback from important others on that identity construction (Humphreys, 2018). Teens are driven to use media by these motives (boyd, 2014; Nesi et al., 2018).

At later stages of life, when the core network has stabilized and personal development goals are expressed through one's professional identity, media use morphs to suit new goals. As a person who has counseled recent college graduates on their social media presence, professional identities must be carefully tended, but for different audiences than young adults are accustomed to. The reputational and career risks of a careless tweet, email, or shared photo are considerably different from the side-eyed disapproval of peers in moments of Snapchat foolishness.

SCOT embraces the idea that the use of media is influenced by how others use media (Baym, Zhang, & Lin, 2004; Fulk, 1993), but this perspective can be taken a step further. I would argue that people adopt and continue to use media most crucially because of *who* is there, and to a lesser extent because of the specific, functional nature of the media. If the narrative at the beginning of this section accurately reflects the constantly shifting choice in platform, then the nature of any given platform or app is less important than who is on it. A small network of new adopters of mobile texting in 2003 begins to look a lot like a small network of WhatsApp users exchanging private texts with one another in 2020. We tend keep our networks small across media, so the modalities and motivations for media use in general are remarkably stable.

3.4 Making Do

The dual revolution of mobile devices and social media documented by Rainie and Wellman (2012) has been joined by two other dramatic changes that have unfolded recently: the rise of wireless internet and use of mobile applications. In 2017 alone, 180 billion apps were downloaded from the Apple app store alone. Although many of these apps are not social in nature, the magnitude and variety of online dating apps, messenger apps, gaming apps, and others that allow people to communicate with one another is astonishing from a media choice perspective. SCOT is fundamentally concerned with the interplay between media companies' attempts to capture our attention and time, and users' choice, adoption, and routine (Humphreys et al., 2013).

The combination of these four mini-revolutions (i.e., mobile devices, social media adoption, wireless internet, smartphone apps) has effectively removed nearly all of the traditional boundaries of time, space, and access in our social routines. Now we have to reestablish this order for ourselves. How do we do that? This will be explained further in Chapter 10, but for now, the answer lies in part with the last domain that I would like to bring into focus from the perspective of SCOT: what I call "making do."

People have long struggled with and engaged in back-and-forth negotiations during periods of new media adoption. In his review of domestication of the landline telephone, Fischer (1992) states, "As much as people adapt their lives to the changed circumstances created by a new technology, they also adapt that technology to their lives" (p. 5). In adapting technology, it changes. It has become clearer in recent years that technology is chosen from an ever-expanding list of options, then it is enabled to some degree, leaving users to *make do* with a combination of programs and functions they already know and are familiar with and new ones they experiment with and fuss over. Making do is a process of domestication through personalization.

People make the best of their media options, but also are careful to take into account the media to which their loved ones have access (Madianou & Miller, 2012). When young adults deliberate about which modality to use to contact their parents, they embody a make-do attitude (Platt, Bourdeax, & DiTunnariello, 2014). To keep in touch with their parents, young adults both conform to media comfortable to their parents and show a preference for media they grew up with, rather than adding modalities or programs for their own sake. Both American college students and international migrants exploit the capabilities (and limitations) of the modalities to achieve their relational goals when trying to keep in touch with loved ones (Madianou, 2014; Madianou & Miller, 2012; Platt et al., 2014).

Barkhuus and Polichar (2011) were among the first researchers to recognize that the era of mobile option personalization was only just beginning. They called this process of personal crafting of phone devices toward personal use *empowerment through seamfulness*. This is a process of making do rather than a process of optimization. As features are negotiated, people create workarounds and compromises. Barkhuus and Polichar (2011) point out that much of this is because the toll of learning or relearning or unlearning new technology can feel interminable and deeply irritating. Their analysis was prescient in that these days users are increasingly asked to switch between mobile devices or apps or operating systems. Users have to adapt to unbidden and unwanted updates by the platform itself. Users' loyalty is taxed as they are expected to endure yet another change in program functionality.

To be clear: I believe the most pertinent aspect of SCOT in the present era, particularly in the case of mobile device use in relationships, is this make do aspect.

Barkhuus and Polichar (2011) offers three ways this happens. First, we can select it – I'll download or try this app, but not that one – and the growth curve of apps suggest we are doing this more and more. Second, we can blend it or circumscribe it: I'll use this device with that program, or I'll use this program, but only for this purpose on this device. Certainly, relationship partners make blending decisions constantly. For example, I'll send a text to alert my friend to a change of plans, but I'll call to try to figure out what we are doing before it turns into a mess. As Arnold (2003) and others predicted, selecting then blending technology creates a leash to that technology (Barkhuus & Polichar, 2011). In choosing to download, learn, and become familiar with some device, app, or platform, users feel they are now leashed by those choices. This commitment may exist for no other reason than the frustrating start-up costs of learning something new and convincing others to use it too. Finally, Barkhuus and Polichar point out that *making do* means that all of these adjustments are a given part of modern life with technology. Thus, such decisions are not typically consciously acted toward or against. In other words, people do not usually think about it that much; they have adjusted to having to make do with the technology that is there.

Since Barkuus and Polichar's work on seamfulness, there has grown a larger discourse around the need to push back against technology. The idea that users fashion technology to their own ends is illustrated when they have to figure out how to uninstall an app or silence their device to push back against its buzzes, vibrations, beeps, and notifications (Humphreys et al., 2013). In testing a new app that helped romantic partners keep track of which text conversation fits into which category (Andalibi, Bently, & Quehl, 2017), couples reported that keeping track of life as negotiated through texting is very difficult, but trying to learn how to use an app to organize those texts was just more work piled on existing work. We find ourselves forced to manage the constant encroachment of personal technology into our lives, and to manage this, people would rather make do than optimize.

This issue of making do can also be understood in terms of an externality, or undesired or unexpected effect of use. Fischer (1992) points out that the consequences of use often illustrate that "technology can be a both a *tool* for an individual user and, aggregated, become a *structure* that constrains the individual" (p. 19). This means each choice of using a technology then also becomes a constraint to stopping using it. Any Facebook user who wishes they could quit, but realizes there are few means of sharing kid photos with grandma or hearing what old friends are up to that are as convenient. One person cannot reconstitute their online network alone.

The issue of externality also applies to electing not to use it. For example, if you choose not to use a particular app or texting program your friends prefer to organizing getting together or coworkers use to make plans, it feels as if you are forcing others to go to extra trouble for you. This means there are consequences, practical and relational, of electing not to use any given program, platform, or app.

SECTION FOUR: THE SOCIAL CONSTRUCTION OF RELATIONSHIPS

Interpersonal communication's social constructivist tradition shares similar assumptions as SCOT, but as far as I can tell these two perspectives have not yet been formally brought into dialogue with one another. The final goal of this chapter is to introduce the social constructivist perspective of interpersonal communication, referred to in Chapter 1 and expressed in the work of Steve Duck. I will show how bridging these perspectives can strengthen and expand the scope and vision of SCOT.

4.1 Relationships as a Social Construction

Well before the four mini-revolutions of personal media, interpersonal communication had developed a social constructivist position. Aspects of this theoretical orientation can be found in Goffman's (1959) belief that the public performance is the self-in-action, in Rawlins's (1992) book on the conversational dialectics of friendship, and in Baxter's relational dialectic theory (Baxter & Simon, 1993). However, this perspective was given its fullest development by Steve Duck in a series of key works (e.g., Duck, 1994a; 1994b; Duck & Pittman, 1994).

This approach sees everyday talk as serving a core relationship constituting function. Although talk obviously has other functions, such as to convey information, the constructivist position articulates how the content of communication reflects the nature of a relationship. Duck (1994a) even went so far as to argue that everyday talk *is* the relationship; no relationship exists that is not initiated, sustained, and ratified by talk. One of the implications of a constitutive approach is that relationships are not fully knowable, thus how people interact is a projection of what they believe the relationship is or wish it to be (Duck & Pittman, 1994). This renders everyday talk a fundamentally relational act.

The constructivist approach celebrates the idea that much of talk is practical, mundane, and routine. Conversational routines are relational routines. Thus, relational change is a communication achievement, not a state willed into being by a single partner's wishes or perceptions. Duck (1994b) offered the metaphor of the difference between an official report of attending an academic conference and the reality of being there. Little moments of acknowledgment and the content of conversation are totally lost in the official report, which focuses on papers presented or sessions attended. Mundane talk is the vast majority of what people do and is deeply constitutive of the relationship, but many approaches to human relationships instead prefer a neat "official report."

Duck was a trailblazer in methods too, using his Iowa Interaction Record (Leatham & Duck, 1990) to document these mundane moments of communication. I suspect that because his work focused on FtF communication, issues germane to relating through technology have yet to be integrated with a social constructivist perspective.

4.2 Relational Force

Applied to mediated social interaction, the constitutive approach would suggest that the content of the texts we send, the photos we share, and the choices we make about which medium to use to communicate should be given greater attention as a method of *relationship-making*. Essentially, these choices indicate *this* is the type of relationship we are going to have – one sustained through these media practices but not those, one that privileged *this* modality of interaction but not *that* one. Duck's perspective would certainly agree that we reflect something about the relationship in each of those choices. Perhaps he would suggest we are creating the relationship itself through these choices. One can only say they are *in* a relationship with someone because of the way they interact with that person (Duck, 1994a; Duck & Pittman, 1994). There is no other relationship than the one enacted through media and in FtF talk. We communicate relationships into being.

An example of the relationship-constitutive function of media can be found in an innovative paper on the WhatsApp program (O'Hara, Massimi, Harper, Rubens, & Morris, 2014). O'Hara and colleagues suggest that technologies are a means of relational meaning production. In the case of WhatsApp, the relational function is not for learning, catching up, or getting to know one another (participants even resisted calling WhatsApp communication "conversation"). Rather, talking to each other through the app is constitutive of *being in* relationship with each other. O'Hara and colleagues call this *dwelling* within mediated communication. Commitment and faithfulness toward one another – shown by patterns of WhatsApp use – stand in for the ongoingness of the relationship itself.

From this perspective, how might we think about mediated social interaction? One concept I have found useful in explaining the importance of particular ways of communicating is *relational force* (Hall, 2018a). Duck (1994a) defined this concept as the commonality of experience brought into awareness through talk. For example, spending time catching up brings the conversational partners up to date with one another in the present moment. This talk contributes to a sense of commonality and mutuality both in the past and in the present (Rawlins, 1992). Empirical evidence supports the value of such talk: it is associated with some of the highest levels of in-the-moment relatedness and affective well-being compared with all of the other ways people could converse (Hall, 2018a). Talk that has greater relational force brings a bond into being in the present. Different media used in different ways may also have distinct relational force.

A quick phone call to tell grandma about something cute the grandkids did, a text to a friend going through a hard time, or a scheduled video chat with a long-distance romantic partner can all have relational force. The continuing task of *talking the relationship into the present* is the central function of everyday social interaction, both mediated and otherwise. I believe such communication constitutes a relationship as one worth bringing into being over time and over space. Duck (1994b) intriguingly suggests such routine actions are similar to hygienic care; conversation keeps the relationships healthy – and without a commitment to social hygiene, relationships deteriorate, just like your teeth.

4.3 The Social Construction of Relationships Through Media

The roots of a relational approach to SCOT can be found in Fischer (1992), who noted that using the telephone to keep in touch implied the existence of a meaningful friendship. Ling and McEwen (2010) argued that the way people use texting is an expression of partners' shared communication norms, developed both online and offline. Barkhuus and Polichar (2011) point out that texting does not exist in isolation of relationships, but, rather, allows for a continuance of shared events in the process of being understood. A message that mentions shared events implies and likely requires a shared understanding of those events. Whatever modality partners use to communicate also has a symbolic value. IM was once reserved for hanging out with friends (Mesch, Talmud, & Quan-Haase, 2012) and Facebook was once reserved for college classmates. The first phone call between potential romantic partners is interpreted as a sign of relationship development (Yang, Brown & Braun, 2014), and has been seen that way for a long time. And, of course, making a relationship "Facebook official" is a public sign of its development (Duran & Kelly, 2017; Lane & Piercy, 2017). All of these perspectives acknowledge the ways that technology is integrated into relational development.

Acknowledging the contributions of these researchers, Brown, O'Hara, McGregor, and McMillan (2018) wrote a valuable article in what I hope will be an ongoing articulation of the social construction of relationships through personal media. This is a remarkable paper both in method and in exposition. They analyze audio recordings of people talking about the content of their personal media exchanges with others who are co-present. This is people talking FtF about their texts and chats with others who are not physically there. Through a series of fascinating examples, they illustrate "how these technologies and encounters are experienced as a part of the ongoing production of our relationships and sociality over time" (Brown et al., 2018, p. 19).

When two friends talk about a text exchange with another friend, they are talking the relationship into existence "in that it produces relationships as stable, objectively visible parts of the participants' lives" (Brown et al., 2018, p. 12). Just as Duck (1994b) claims that mundane exchanges bring a relationship into existence, Brown et al. (2018) argue that talking about the content of mediated social interactions makes the online conversation meaningful to FtF communicators. Brown et al. (2018) suggest that channel blending does not provide a sufficient conceptualization for what is going on. Like Barkuus and Polichar's (2011) note about the *ongoingness* of relationships as illustrated through texting and O'Hara et al.'s (2014) analysis of relating through WhatsApp, Brown et al. (2018) firmly situate the relationship as constituted by coherent social acts that take place over time and across channels:

This ongoing sociability is made up of the various interactions, exchanges, and encounters with others experienced across a wide range of media and contexts, both face-to-face and remote. These interpersonal encounters are not experienced as discrete entities in and of themselves, but rather as interrelated encounters, with meaning and significance woven together in the production of social relationships over time. This means that not only do encounters having a bearing on past and subsequent interactions, but that this network of encounters produces our sociality with others.

(p. 2)

Duck (1994b), too, suggests that everyday talk embodies the relationship, and through talk, people come to share a social reality. As Madianou and Miller (2012) recognized: "Social life is lived in (rather than with) different forms of media practices and mediated interactions" (p. 174). Through everyday talk we are a witness to each other's sense of reality, and when sufficiently motivated and attentive to apprehend this reality, we produce the relationship itself.

SECTION FIVE: CONCLUSION

A fully articulated perspective that would integrate the assumptions of SCOT and interpersonal communication's theoretical approach would acknowledge the following six tenets:

1. Everyday talk can occur on various modes as well as FtF. Thus, mediated social interaction serves a relationship-constitutive function.

2. Personal media use is influenced by the capabilities of the media *and* by the types of relationships users are creating and maintaining with those media.
3. The choice of personal media has relational significance; each has a different relational force that is socially constructed and negotiated.
4. The norms of talk on media and the norms of talk in relationships mutually influence each other. People attend to both norms when relating through technology.
5. People make do with the media they have and are familiar with. That any given medium or app is available does not imply that people will use it to maintain relationships. In conditions of less choice, people will make do with what they have to keep relationships maintained and in good repair.
6. All social interactions – mediated and FtF – can talk a relationship into being.

Taken together, these tenets extend Duck's concepts into digital communication practices. They allow for the idea that all modes of communication have the potential to bring relationships into being. Each mode of communication has social significance attached to it, and this significance is not the individual's alone to navigate but is a product of social practices of technology use as well as social practices of *doing* relationships. The nature of mediated talk – whether rich or lean in terms of social cues or more or less synchronous – is reflective of the status of the relationship, and reflect past patterns of relating. It is an expression of where the interactants would like the relationship to be by picking up where it has been. Communication flows through various channels picking up and dropping topics, which reinforce or diminish situated and relational meanings of both topics and partners. Importantly, this means that the meaning of the messages is not fully visible in any given channel, and is often intrinsically dependent on shared knowledge rendered invisible by its implicitness. This should give researchers pause when attempting to infer these implicit meanings of the mediated content of communication unmoored from relational context.

Each interpersonal speech act has a rhetorical vision (Duck, 1994a), which is a projection of the past, present, and future of the relationship. This vision is located, in part, in the style and content of the talk, and, in part, in the shared meaning system of the relationship partners. Thus, each medium will vary in relational force and significance, but communication partners can remake the meaning of both the medium and the message within their co-constructed shared system.

The consequences of a technology on the user and the relationship are, then, quite likely the exact ends the users seek. Thus, the relational force of any given mode of communication is not determined by the type of relationship wherein it is used or in the inherent features of the technology. Rather, the relationship force is to be found in the mundane content of ongoing mediated and nonmediated social interactions that assert a rhetorical vision of ongoing connectedness.

3

Theoretical Perspectives on Personal Media and Relationships

When we study how technology is used in the context of personal relationships, particularly if that perspective is housed in the communication discipline, there is a set of assumptions about what it means to *be in* a relationship. Coming from that perspective myself, I would like to take a moment to clarify what I think those assumptions are. As I discussed in Chapter 1, human relationships are necessary for human survival both now and during our evolutionary past, but our ability to form and maintain those relationships is limited practically by time and cognitively by our relational carrying capacity. Thus, at any given moment, we are accompanied by only a few important others as we venture on this caravan through life.

At the end of Chapter 2, I stated that relational maintenance is necessary for relationships to form and continue to exist, and that social interactions, both mediated and FtF, are the place to study how we relate to others. As Parks (2007) eloquently put it: "Relationships live in communication" (p. 24). Interpersonal communication research is grounded in social interactions and the talk within them, and less so in internal or psychological factors. It is through social interaction that we come to understand, make meaning, and feel connected to one another. Although this perspective asserts that talk makes relationships manifest, the evolved mechanisms that steer us toward others, such as needs and motivations, require attention as well. Although there are other assumptions that accompany the study of interpersonal communication and the study of media (and these are not necessarily the same assumptions), from my perspective they can be summarized as: relationships are fundamental to survival and thriving, are constituted by talk, and need maintenance to exist.

Although I may imply a great deal of clarity about the shared assumptions of how we could study relationships and technology in unison, there is no such continuity inside the discipline or across disciplines. Researchers will strongly disagree (as they should) with what should be the appropriate unit of analysis (e.g., perceptions, platforms, words, episodes). In this chapter,

I review a set of theories with which one *might* initiate inquiry or offer an explanation for how personal media and relationships interact. I will also offer my own theoretical perspective (e.g., Hall & Davis, 2017) toward that end.

But, why oh why, you ask, do we need theory? As Scott (2009) persuasively argued, we simply cannot keep up with the speed of technological change, "so we need theory and models that can" (p. 754). Seminal CMC theorist Joseph Walther (2011) notes that theory gives us a basis for initiating inquiry, reasons and rationale for why certain constructs merit attention, and, when the research is programmatic and thorough, a set of empirically grounded answers to questions. However, any given theory is one explanation among many. Thus, by engaging and contrasting several theories, we are more likely to form a complete account of the phenomena at hand.

SECTION ONE: COMPUTER-MEDIATED COMMUNICATION THEORIES

1.1 Social Presence Theory and Media Richness Theory

No discussion of theories of CMC can begin without acknowledging the importance of social presence theory (Short, Williams, & Christie, 1976) and media richness theory (MRT) (Daft & Lengel, 1984). Drawing from a conceptualization of communication that saw co-present nonverbal immediacy as a causal agent in producing feelings of connection and that focused on modes of communication that were exclusively textual, these two theories established many of the guiding assumptions in CMC research. This text-only, low social cue environment was expected to have all kinds of effects, including less warmth, less normative behavior, less civility, less empathy, and less friendliness (Baym, 2015; Walther, 2010; 2011). Remarkably, these theoretical predictions have failed to generate strong empirical support, but the "concept of social presence as an inherent consequence of multiple cues remains alive and well" (Walther, 2011, p. 446). How can it be that theories that have performed so poorly empirically have such an enduring pull over how we understand relating through technology?

From MRT's perspective, the richness of media is its carrying capacity, which includes the amount of nonverbal cues, the use of natural language (i.e., spoken language), and synchrony (Daft & Lengel, 1984). Richer media are assumed to be more efficient when resolving uncertain situations (i.e., high equivocality), such as conflict. Predictions derived from MRT have often held up in the domain of task accomplishment, but not as well in relational contexts (Baym, 2015; Walther, 2011). This may be because the primary outcomes of the theory (e.g., efficiency) are more pertinent to organizational settings than interpersonal ones. Additionally, effectiveness and efficiency are more relevant outcomes for tit-for-tat rather than communal relationships

(Clark, Mills, & Powell, 1986). Efficiency is not a good reason or motivation for keeping in touch with close friends.

These theories also have other limitations, such as that situational uncertainty and equivocality are poor predictors of a mode's suitability to the task (i.e., whether the task is performed efficiently and effectively) (Walther, 2011). Experimental work has also demonstrated that nonverbal communication is not necessary to convey emotion, to shape sociality online, and to influence and be influenced by partners' behavior – text-only communication is more than sufficient (Grebe & Hall, 2013; Tong & Walther, 2015).

This should come as no surprise for anyone who has ever written or received a letter or lengthy personal email. For millennia, written correspondence was the primary means of keeping in touch over distance with colleagues and intimates alike (Farman, 2018). The ability for written text to be personal or professional, simple or complex, demonstrates that reduced channel environments are not necessarily deficient of meaning. For ongoing relationships, the richness of media alone is a poor predictor of its use; who it is used with and why it is being used are much better predictors (Park, Chung, & Lee, 2012; Scissors & Gergle, 2013).

Another challenge for richness approaches is that the number of cues enabled by a modality, its synchrony, and users' ability to employ natural language are three distinct aspects by which media vary (see the Introduction). That is, these three aspects are not uniform in richness. Some of these features strongly co-occur or enable one another (e.g., video chat by nature is high synchrony and has high social cues), which makes it challenging if not impossible to know what characteristic is the driving force in forming impressions, influencing one another, and conveying meaning (Walther, 2010).

Given that the richness of the media provides, at best, a weak understanding of how it will influence communicative outcomes, does it at least tell us something about generating social presence? *Social presence* is defined as "the degree of salience of the other person in the interaction and the consequent salience (and perceived intimacy and immediacy) of interpersonal relationships" (Short et al., 1976, p. 65). Other definitions of social presence have focused on "states of awareness of the self and other" (Walther, 2011, p. 446), or feelings of intimacy experienced during mediated interactions. These definitions suggest that social presence should be the highest when people interact FtF, and lower in reduced social cue contexts. But this link has not held up under scrutiny (Walther, 2011). Inasmuch as behavior or perceptions change when people communicate online versus offline, the lack of nonverbal cues does not seem to be a major factor in explaining those differences. Although it is quite conceivable that different modes of communication convey different levels of social presence, it does not appear to be strictly a function of fewer nonverbal channels with which to communicate.

Instead, people reintroduce cues through textual features to convey meaning (Grebe & Hall, 2013; Tong & Walther, 2015). People artfully and intentionally use written language and emoji to convey whatever meaning they wish – aggression or support, humor or formality (Walther, 2017).

In a remarkable conclusion, Walther (2011) suggests that while the lay public and researchers seem to agree that social presence varies in important and salient ways by modality, there is no clear theoretical reason why and how that happens. Exceptions to the rule prove the point. Gaming research suggests that abstract representations, such as avatars, stimulate the greatest experience of social presence (Walther, 2011). That is, people *feel* that avatars enhance social presence. From the perspective of the theory, a digitized avatar cannot possibly convey the nonverbal immediacy of FtF conversation, as it disguises the user and masks their nonverbal expression, so this should not be possible, theoretically speaking.

As a final point, the vast majority of research guided by MRT and social presence theory is conducted in zero-acquaintance environments where participants are strangers to one another, and is often conducted in organizational or professional settings (Walther, 2010). It is quite likely that many of the findings have little bearing in understanding when and why people choose one medium over another in ongoing relationships, especially in interdependent relationships that frequently channel-switch between online and offline communication. In that vein, Walther (2011) concludes: "It remains to be seen whether social presence or some other construct and framework will emerge to account for why individuals use various media for various relational activities" (p. 446).

1.2 Channel Expansion Theory

If a reduced cue environment does not create the deficiencies of connection that are implied by the above two theories, then what theories might help understand the empirical evidence? One perspective that is limited in scope but interesting in implication is channel expansion theory (CET) (Carlson & Zmud, 1999). While CET builds on a theory I will review shortly (i.e., social information processing theory), it is a suitable rebuttal to the reduced social presence presumptions. The primary idea of CET is that users' past experiences with the mode of communication, the topic of communication, the context, and the preexisting relationship of communication partners all contribute to the perception of media richness. Prior experiences with the technology help people accomplish their communication goals, no matter their equivocality or complexity (Walther, 2011). Harkening back to MRT, CET suggests that a modality can be perceived as richer as a function of past experiences. This means that media richness is not a property of the modality alone. In the case where communication partners are emotionally close and have a lot of familiarity with the modality, the theory would predict that the perception of the medium's richness will be similar between partners as well as higher in general (Carlson & Zmud, 1999). In a study of social interactions across relationship partners, Vlahovic et al. (2012) found that interactions that were more humorous fostered happiness no matter the medium, which the authors interpret as being supportive of CET. "Channel expansion theory offers an antidote to the inconsistencies of media richness research" in the sense that experience with the medium and sharing that medium with a particular partner likely enhances social presence (Walther, 2011, p. 457). CET clearly explores some important factors to study relating through technology, including the preexisting relationship between communicators and their past experiences with the modality; thus, it is well suited to explain perceptions of media richness across modalities.

1.3 The Hyperpersonal Model

Another perspective that has had an important role in shaping how we theorize about CMC is Walther's (1996) hyperpersonal perspective. Rather than assuming that the reduced social cue environment of CMC (again, think primarily of text exchanges) creates an impoverished relationship, the hyperpersonal perspective asserts that intense, high self-disclosure, and very positive relationships can be initiated through CMC. There are two concepts inherent to this perspective that are particularly pertinent to explaining how such effects are possible: the role of the actor and that of the audience. Although actors and audiences are interchangeable during initial mediated social interactions (i.e., people take turns sending/receiving messages), the media environment affects each role in a slightly different fashion. Due to the delay in composing and sending a text-based message, actors have more time to craft messages that are positive and appealing. Because the receiver has no other information to call on to confirm that perspective (again assuming an initial interaction with a stranger), impressions formed are often exaggerated when made in text-based modalities, such as in online dating (Ramirez & Wang, 2008; Sharabi & Caughlin 2017a). This means idealization (i.e., inferring that the actor has extremely positive characteristics) occurs.

This process is assumed to be cyclical and reinforcing. When positive impressions are constructed, increasingly positive impressions are made. When both communication partners participate, the relationship can escalate quickly, becoming not just personal, but hyperpersonal. Many of us have experienced rapid, personal disclosures online that are characteristic of the hyperpersonal perspective, and can attest to its intuitive appeal.

The hyperpersonal perspective represents an important shift in theoretical thinking. Specifically, it marks a move away from technological determinism and a move toward recognizing that people exploit the features of the modality to achieve communication goals. MRT and social presence theory trend toward determinism, in part, because of the implicit disparagement of online modalities (Baym, 2015; Walther, 2010). They show linear thinking regarding the effects of characteristics of the media. The hyperpersonal perspective represents a step forward because it recognizes that people augment and modify technology by making mindful decisions during message construction.

One of the core outcomes predicted by the hyperpersonal perspective is self-disclosure. Specifically, mediated interactions should become deeper and more personal than FtF interactions. This application is influenced by the media on which the theory was based; written communication is where evidence of both self-presentation modification and emerging intimacy would be found in CMC modalities of the time.

Yet a recent meta-analysis has cast doubt on this conclusion. Ruppel, Gross, Stoll, Peck, Allen, and Kim (2017) identified twenty-five studies (thirty-one effect sizes) with more than 6,200 participants measuring self-disclosure in CMC and FtF environments. They concluded that across studies there was greater self-disclosure FtF than in CMC environments ($r = 0.276$). There was more self-disclosure FtF than in text-based conversations, and self-disclosure was greater FtF than in video-chat conversations ($r = 0.132$). The authors conclude that there is strong evidence in support of MRT, which assumes that a lean cue environment would decrease self-disclosure, than there was support for social information processing theory and the hyperpersonal model.

Sprecher (2014) found similar results when experimentally manipulating modality. Initial interactions that were FtF resulted in higher liking, closeness, responsiveness, and enjoyment than either Skype or voice calls, which, in turn, were significantly higher than text-only exchanges. Ruppel et al. (2017) and Sprecher (2014) point out a significant limitation of past studies: they focus on social interactions in zero-acquaintance experiments rather than interactions in developed relationships. This, again, calls into question the degree to which the hyperpersonal model explains how we relate through technology in ongoing relationships rather than in initial interactions with strangers.

As a final note, much of the excitement associated with the early days of online communication may have contributed to some of the enthusiasm for CMC as relationship-promoting in general (Chayko, 2018). The idea that CMC inspires a cascade of positive impressions and self-disclosure that promote intimacy (i.e., the core assumptions of the hyperpersonal perspective) may have resulted from recognizing an already-existing phenomena in a new environment – namely, the stranger on the plane. As a person who is often a stranger on the plane having a deep conversation with a person I just met, I can attest to the fact that it does not require a lean cue environment to confide in a stranger. I am not alone in this. People often find themselves confiding in strangers and people they just met, especially in environments suitable to such types of disclosures (Small, 2017). Disclosures about your child's health and well-being may be considered very private, yet the fellow parent in the waiting room in the doctor's office becomes a quick confidant. As such, it is quite possible that deep disclosures in online support groups or Facebook groups around a personal illness or experience may be more due to the feeling of a shared experience or a sympathetic audience than because it is online. This explanation may require a rethinking of this perspective (see Ruppel et al., 2017), and greater attention to the context and/or the people in that context who are comfortable self-disclosing (Small, 2017).

1.4 Social Information Processing Theory

The one of only two CMC theories to have its own chapter in the second edition of *Engaging Theories in Interpersonal Communication* (Braithwaite & Schrodt, 2015), social information processing theory (SIPT) is an important theory in explaining how people use technology to relate. The original model (Walther, 1992) began with a set of assumptions about the ways in which uncertainty motivates people to act in initial conversations. In FtF interactions, a great deal of information is (accurately) conveyed through a person's appearance, clothing, and nonverbal behavior prior to speaking (Amady & Skowronski, 2008). Assuming that individuals are at least somewhat motivated to learn about their conversational partners in CMC environments, this enhanced uncertainty motivates them to use text to showcase their personality and signal relational intent. Thus, textual cues substitute for nonverbal information. During first interactions between strangers using IM, textual exchanges can be used to seek and show affinity (Grebe & Hall, 2013). When getting to know one another through IM, individuals who more accurately interpret text messages' level of affinity were more likely to feel closer and connected to their partners. In online communities, simple cues, such as a shared discussion board membership or a person's online handle, can be used to infer information about their personality. A recent meta-analysis (Tskhay & Rule, 2014) suggests that simple online information, such as a creative email address (e.g., DJdadrock@), can be used to infer personality significantly above chance rates. SIPT stipulates that language is a primary source of forming first impressions online, and empirical evidence suggests this is a reasonable assumption.

Another assumption of SIPT (Walther, 1992; Walther, 2015) has to do with the nature of temporality in the development of relationships. Because textual information substitutes for lost nonverbal information, and because nonverbal information in initial FtF interactions is abundant, SIPT suggests that the lower bandwidth of CMC environments requires more time for relationships to develop. This conclusion is supported by a meta-analysis that found CMC interactions require more time to develop than FtF interactions (Walther, Anderson, & Park, 1994). Time also figures prominently in the theory because information conveyed by text messages builds up over time, so in cases of less synchrony or slower response rates, the theory would predict that people form impressions less fully and relationships develop more slowly. Thus, once accounting for time, there is much more similarity between CMC and FtF environments than would be predicted by MRT or social presence theory (see Mesch & Talmud, 2006). Similarly, Sprecher (2014) found that in zero-acquaintance interactions, more time fostered more relationship development (i.e., closeness, responsiveness, enjoyment) in general, and particularly so for newly acquainted strangers using the text-only medium. As an important caveat though, Sprecher also found that after accounting for the effects of time, FtF was still superior to all other modalities in terms of relationship development (see also Walther, 2011).

Walther (2015) suggests that SIPT does not have to be limited to understanding impressions formed in initial interactions between strangers. In a test of SIPT, Chan and Cheng (2004) compared online friends – both made and maintained online –to offline friends. Initial results suggest that offline friends scored higher across the board (with large effect sizes) for friendship characteristics (e.g., interdependence, understanding, commitment). However, these differences decreased over time, as SIPT would predict. Although offline friendships were stronger and deeper when they had been maintained for less than a year, online friendships that lasted a full year or greater started to look like offline friendships that lasted a similar amount of time (Chan & Cheng, 2004). Although there were still differences favoring offline friendships, online friendships showed a notable ability to grow and strengthen when given time.

Walther (2015) concludes that SIPT has been supported in many contexts and is adaptable to the changing media landscape. No doubt, it is an important theory in understanding how people adapt media to their social ends and why time is a crucial element in understanding how lean cue environments allow for relationships to develop. Pertinent to this book, Walther (2015) concedes that modern relationships will nearly always multimodal, so the theory needs to be changed or adapted to account for the choice and preference of modality.

1.5 Media Multiplexity Theory

Media multiplexity theory (MMT) is the other CMC theory to have a chapter in the second edition of *Engaging Theories* (Braithwaite & Schrodt, 2015). The theory is pertinent to understanding how media influence relationship closeness (Haythornthwaite, 2005), and has become increasingly relevant for how closeness influences media use (Taylor & Bazarova, 2018). The two primary components of the theory are number of media and tie strength. Drawing from the social network analysis tradition, where a multiplex tie is one that contains more than one type of relationship (e.g., advisor *and* friend; wife *and* coworker), media multiplexity is the number of distinct channels of communication. Tie strength, which is also derived from social network analysis, is an amalgam of the length of the relationship, the emotional intensity, reciprocity, intimacy, and reciprocal services exchanged in a relationship. Although the association between these two concepts is thought to be mutually influential (Haythornthwaite, 2005), the theory posits that tie strength is the driving force in the use of media (Ledbetter, 2015). I feel compelled to point out, however, that the theory is frequently *not* empirically tested in that way. Finally, MMT presumes that each additional channel is associated with developing tie strength because multiple media are needed to sustain strong ties in an ever more connected world. For weaker ties, new channels of communication are assumed to play a bigger role in promoting tie strength than for stronger ties (Ledbetter, 2015).

One of the central theoretical challenges in MMT regards the directionality of the association between tie strength and number of channels. There are a host of studies that have found support for this basic association (e.g., Baym & Ledbetter, 2009; Caughlin & Sharabi, 2013; Hall & Baym, 2012; Ledbetter, 2010; Ledbetter, Taylor, & Mazer, 2016; Ruppel, Burke, & Cherney, 2018). Because the association is assumed to be bidirectional, the rationale for why this association occurs is somewhat unsatisfying. Haythornthwaite (2005) suggests that the addition of new channels creates new opportunities to communicate, which can make the tie stronger. But common sense would tell us that just because a person has communicated with a relationship partner using a new medium, it does not follow that this new dab of content will bring them closer together (see McEwan, 2013; Utz, 2015). On this point, Rains, Brunner, and Oman (2016) found that heightened volume of online self-disclosure was inversely associated with relationship satisfaction and liking. More talk is not necessarily better for the relationship – offline or online.

The theory also presumes that there should be an effect brought about by changes in channels; that is, the subtraction of a channel is presumed to alter the tie (Ledbetter, 2015). But this conclusion has not stood up to scrutiny either. In a longitudinal study of romantic partners' personal media use over the course of six weeks, Taylor and Bazarova (2018) found that initial relationship closeness predicted the number, the frequency of use of, and the amount of self-disclosure on personal media in the future. However, adding media did not predict changes in closeness over time, nor did it predict increasing frequency of use of or amount of disclosure through media. These results call into question the bidirectional effect. Adding or subtracting channels alone does not seem to *cause* a change in tie strength.

MMT could be understood from an interdependence perspective (Caughlin & Sharabi, 2013). In finding an association between online relationship maintenance and interdependence, Ledbetter (2010) notes that while Haythornthwaite (2005) did not use the term "interdependence," it is conceptually synonymous with "influence strength," which is one of the original (many) components of tie strength in MMT. Conceiving of interdependence as the driving force of adding media is consistent with the organizational origins of MMT (Haythornthwaite, 2005), but it also squares with recent findings that fail to support the assumption that each channel contributes to tie strength (e.g., Ruppel et al., 2018; Taylor & Bazarova, 2018).

Furthermore, romantic relationship partners (Caughlin & Sharabi, 2013) and parents and children (Madianou & Miller 2012; Platt et al., 2014) engage in channel segmentation, wherein particular types of communication are saved for particular channels. Similarly, Taylor and Bazarova (2018) found that "romantic partners tended to use some media more often and other media less often," which "extended to their self-disclosure patterns" (p. 16). That is, partners limit certain types of interactions to their preferred channels of communication (Scissors & Gergle, 2013). In friendships, the use of any given modality seems to be dependent on the relationship – more channels alone will not produce a better friendship (Ruppel et al., 2018). Supporting the theory of the niche (see Chapter 4), this suggests that not all channels are equivalent. Ledbetter and colleagues (2016) offer this revealing conclusion in their investigation of MMT: people may just prefer the "taste" of certain media: "effective media choice does not match medium to message so much as medium to person" (p. 155). These research findings square with Parks's (2017) strong critique of MMT where he notes that the theory offers little insight into how media are used or when they are chosen.

Although certainly a relevant theory for exploring the widespread and consistent association between number of modes of communication and tie strength, there appears to be growing evidence that the relationship and its interdependence drives the addition of and amount of use of media, not the other way around. Indeed, Yang et al. (2014) suggest that adding personal media in an unfamiliar or counternormative order (e.g., placing a voice call after looking up a romantic partner on Instagram) could be seen as a break of protocol and could damage the relationship's development. Consistent with SCOT and the theory of niche, personal media have different meanings that are defined by the relationship as well as by broader social forces.

1.6 Channel Complementarity Theory

The theory of channel complementarity (TCC; Dutta-Bergman, 2004) pushes back against many prior theoretical assumptions of CMC. In a multimodal world, Dutta-Bergman (2004) argues against media displacement theory's assumption of a zero-sum game. Instead, she suggests that the motivation to interpersonally communicate drives mode use. Coexisting modalities do not exist in a zero-sum fashion. Rather, TCC presents inter-personal modality choice as additive; those who communicate on one medium likely communicate on others as well. Dutta-Bergman (2004) illus-trates this idea in the context of communicating about the 9/11 terrorist attacks; voice calls with friends and family were more common among those who also emailed or instant messaged about the attacks than among those who did not. Those who are motivated to interpersonally communicate do so using several media.

TCC has similar challenges of MMT in that the raw number of media used is a weak approximation of how many media are used and for what communicative purpose. The original theory was proposed in the context of a national tragedy, but has been expanded to explore long-distance friendship maintenance (e.g., Ruppel & Burke, 2015; Ruppel et al., 2018). Although types of media use were associated with both weak and strong tie relationships, the patterns of associations (media X and Y with this relationship, and Y and Z in that relationship) are neither intuitive nor neatly aligned with TCC. Although not using TCC as a basis for interpretation, Kim, Kim, Park, and Rice (2007) found that media pairings were highly dependent on the relationship between conversation partners. Email and mobile phone use are paired for salaried workers and professionals at work, but such pairings are absent in students' relationships with other students. Another study found that as relationships become closer, texting and phone call use are highly tied together, but other forms of communication (i.e., social media, email) drop off (Park et al., 2012). This suggests that as intimacy grows, media preference changes (Liu & Yang, 2016; Ruppel & Burke, 2015).

Particular patterns of media use are specific to particular relationship types. There is considerable variation of media use across relationships but also within specific relationship types (e.g., coworker *or* friend) that is obscured when focused on the global trends of strong associations between using two or more types of media.

TCC has also received criticism for a lack of specificity about the needs or motivations that are being satisfied by any given modality (Parks, 2017). As the SCOT perspective would argue (see Chapter 2), the ways in which media are used within relationships shape the patterns of use as well as the goals pursued on each modality or platform. Ruppel et al. (2018) recommend that future development of TCC should develop greater differentiation of inter-personal functions (e.g., everyday talk versus intimate conversation) by better integrating it with the theory of the niche.

At a more fundamental level, the core idea of channel complementarity is in need of further development. Although it may be true that if I want to interpersonally communicate with someone important to me, I may use more than one modality to do so (thus creating a correlation between the use of those two modes), it does not follow that those correlations would continue ad infinitum. There is no reason to believe that people keep adding more and more and more media to communicate in their close relationships or that more media connectivity better serves relational needs.

SECTION TWO: EMERGENT PERSPECTIVES

Formal theorizing from a post-positivist epistemology requires (1) at least two variables, (2) an association between them, and (3) a clear articulation of why that association is the way it is. There are, however, several important perspectives, models, or approaches that offer important insight on the study of technology in relationships, but do not meet the formal requirements of a post-positivistic theory. I offer three below.

2.1 Mediated Maintenance Expectations

When Nancy Baym and I (Hall & Baym, 2012) introduced the concept of mobile maintenance expectations, we combined two well-known concepts in interpersonal communication: relationship maintenance and relationship expectations. We argued that mobile maintenance expectations are standards of relational maintenance made possible by mobile phone technology at the time, which included communication through text messages and voice calls. The concept combined solidarity from the friendship expectations literature (Hall, 2011) and mundane maintenance from CMC research (Tong & Walther, 2011). Friendship solidarity, or relational maintenance through inclusion and social interaction, is one of the most important expectations in friendships (Hall, 2011; 2012): we expect our friends to include us in activities and want to socialize with us. Baym and I argued that this sense of inclusion can be fostered through mobile communication. Many different modalities, including SNSs and IM, can be used for mundane maintenance over the course of a day (Tong & Walther, 2011).

We characterized the content of mundane mobile maintenance as updates on everyday behavior (e.g., "What are you doing?" "How is your day going?"). Thus, mobile maintenance expectations represented a unification of both concepts: updates, narratives, and short messages that bring together individuals who are not co-present. Furthermore, these expectations are relationally constructed. Reliance on mobile phones to coordinate, share, inform, and pass time with friends establishes strong obligations to be responsive (Baron, 2008; O'Hara et al., 2014; Quan-Haase & Collins, 2008). This obligation can be understood as a relationship maintenance expectation, which is relationship specific and refers to the frequency of the use of a modality as well as the routineness of the content. If it were to be developed and expanded, I believe this perspective could help to sensitize research to the specific relationship and to the couples' modality preferences for maintaining solidarity.

Although we explored this idea in the context of a single friendship (Hall & Baym, 2012), the concept of mediated maintenance expectations could be used to conceptualize and operationalize mediated communication "practices within particular relationships or larger interpersonal networks" (Parks, 2017, p. 3). Reconstituting the collective experience online, groups of friends relive and reflect on their offline conversations and happenings by "dwelling" on WhatsApp (O'Hara et al., 2014), as they once did through IM (Quan-Haase & Collins, 2008). This relationship-specific pattern of use points to a limitation inherent to thinking of the use of any given modality or platform as simply additive.

The idea of relational maintenance has long embraced the idea of routine maintenance (Duck, 1994a), which describes communicative acts folded into everyday talk. Routine interactions are simply a matter of course in one's day, rather than intentional or strategic communication. Similarly, WhatsApp users eschew the idea that they are even having a conversation at all (O'Hara et al., 2014). Within any given relationship, there are expectations of maintenance that are sensitive to channel and idiosyncratic to the couple's modality preference (Barkhuus & Polichar, 2011; Kim et al., 2007; Ruppel et al., 2018). Conceptually, mediated maintenance expectations include the concept that couples or groups vary by the degree to which any given modality is useful for keeping in touch in a routine, daily fashion. Fulfilling these expectations is associated with greater interdependence in the relationship (Hall & Baym, 2012); they are acts of commitment and faithfulness to one another (O'Hara et al., 2014).

The assumptions of the original article (i.e., Hall & Baym, 2012) were built around the two modalities (i.e., voice calls, texting) that were widely available at the time, and the instrument for measurement was geared toward mundane maintenance. Thus, its utility or applicability to other modes (e.g., video chat, group text) or types of maintenance (e.g., a weekly or monthly check-in) is unknown. However, the idea of checking in on someone through a modality (e.g., email, voice call) because time has passed and you would like to know how they are doing is consistent with past research on modality preferences for keeping in touch (Tillema et al., 2010). Furthermore, certain relationships have clear expectations to not rely solely on one mode of communication (Manago & Vaugh, 2015), which suggests this perspective needs to take into account the idea that maintenance expectations may depend on one another. For example, "real" friends are expected to contact one another in ways outside social media (Bryant & Marmo, 2012). Although the conceptualization is flexible enough to account for less close and interdependent relationships, empirical evidence to that effect is wanting. Thus, the concept of mundane mobile expectations is likely most applicable to interdependent and/or close relationships, particularly for the purpose of maintaining routine mediate contact or facilitating an ongoing connected presence.

2.2 Communication Interdependence Perspective

In Chapter 1, I introduced the communication interdependence perspective on technology (Caughlin & Sharabi, 2013) to contrast ongoing relationships with new or nascent ones. Interdependence, derived from social exchange theory (Kelley & Thibaut, 1978), can be defined as the degree to which two people are dependent on the actions of one another for meeting each other's needs.

There are several implications of the interdependence perspective for issues around channel switching and mode segmentation of conversation. For example, as interdependence in romantic relationships rises, people tend to channel-switch with greater ease as they coordinate daily affairs (Caughlin & Sharabi, 2013). Research on texting by romantic couples suggests that texts are extensions of prior conversations and conflicts (Lasen & Casado, 2012; Scissors & Gergle, 2013). That is, the *flow* of communication blurs offline and online boundaries, taking various and unexpected pathways between modalities. Similarly, interdependence has shown to be associated with FtF *and* online relational maintenance (Ledbetter, 2010). As relationships cope with issues that are more complex and require more cooperation, particularly issues that may cause conflict (Scissors & Gergle, 2013), both online and offline communication are likely required. Future research on interdependence should seek to capture and understand the flow of communication between relational partners within multimodal networks (Caughlin & Wang 2020).

Another aspect of the communication interdependence perspective has to do with whether different modalities are used for different communicative purposes. Caughlin and Sharabi (2013) suggest that the segmentation of media for topics of conversation is a sign of a lack of relationship development (Scissors & Gergle, 2013; Taylor & Barazova, 2018). Integration of media is a sign of interdependence in the relationship, and segmentation of media is a challenge more likely faced in independent or newly formed relationships.

The interdependence perspective has many advantages, including its roots in a well-developed relational theory (i.e., social exchange theory) and its superior empirical performance compared with MMT (Ruppel et al., 2018; Taylor & Bazarova, 2018). Another advantage of the perspective is that it explores issues that lie in the spaces between modalities, such as the flow of communication and the separation or integration of modalities by relational partners, which are not addressed explicitly in other theories. It has less to say about the number of modalities used and frequency of use, which are issues at the center of MMT and TCC. But this is not a limitation; instead, it provides a new way of understanding how multimodal relationships operate.

2.3 Social Construction of Technology

Although this theory receives a full treatment in Chapter 2, some important points might be brought up here for the sake of comparison.

Across the theoretical perspectives that I have reviewed, there is a persistent challenge surrounding accounting for three issues: the idiosyncratic nature of media choice within a couple, the normative understandings about what modes should be or are used at different stages or types of relationship, and the positive association between number of modes and relationship closeness. With long-distance friends, modalities are highly relationship specific (e.g., I text and instant message with this friend, I call and email with that one) (Ruppel et al., 2018). Although there are couple-specific preferences, patterns of media use are constructed at a social level as well. Although smartphone adoption continues to increase across the world (Poushter, 2016), specific modality usage varies across countries because it is highly sensitive to reliable access, cost, and varying privacy concerns (Madianou & Miller, 2012; Velasquez, 2018). International students living in Western countries often bring their media preferences with them when maintaining family connections, and their patterns of media use empirically stand out in comparison to Western norms (e.g., Vlahovic et al., 2012; Yang et al., 2014). At the same time, the general trend of more media use in more intimate relationships is a robust finding. Unfortunately, this trend tells us little about the other two issues: preference and societal-level creation of norms of use.

Although the SCOT perspective certainly can account for these particularities and exceptions better than other theories, this is likely more a product of the advantages of the epistemology than of the precision of the perspective. There are some outstanding examples of how qualitative interpretivist research driven by SCOT can provide insight and understanding beyond what can be achieved by quantitative research (e.g., Barkhuus & Polichar, 2011; Brown et al., 2018; Madianou & Miller, 2012; O'Hara et al., 2014). To explain and predict how relationship constructs (e.g., closeness, interdependence, relationship type) influence media choice and use and how media choice and use affects relationships, a linear-variable approach is needed. Although SCOT can certainly be used to support linear-variable models of analysis (i.e., Fulk, 1993), it is also certainly not constrained to such analyses. One solution to many of the problems and limitations of other theories is to recognize that different approaches offer unique advantages and limitations. The goals of interpretivist epistemologies and some lines of qualitative data analysis are to enhance understanding, not to understand trends in the data across studies or to create a predictive model.

SECTION THREE: COMMUNICATE BOND BELONG THEORY

Strictly speaking, CBB theory (Hall & Davis, 2017) is not a CMC theory. Rather, it focuses on the fundamental need to belong, the expression of that need in human relationships, the centrality of social interactions for relational maintenance, and the homeostatic management of social interaction throughout a person's day. Researchers have long noted that relationships are multimodal and that to better understand personal media use, media and FtF communication must be considered simultaneously and in the context of ongoing relationships (e.g., Baym, 2009; Caughlin & Sharabi, 2013; van Kruistum, Leseman & de Haan, 2014). CBB theory offers one possible approach to do just that.

One of the other advantages of CBB theory is its focus on human energy management, which stipulates that humans seek to conserve energy expenditure and invest their time and energy in others for the sake of future belongingness need satisfaction. This offers a new variable that puts in perspective the draw of energy-efficient digital technologies.

Because CBB theory takes into account users' entire social ecology, it offers a theoretical account of how media use with one partner might affect the likelihood of social interaction with other members of a person's social network. While one couple's interdependence strongly influences the amount of social interaction and the choice of media, CBB theory offers a means to understand how the amount of and modality of interaction for that couple influences the modality and type or amount of interaction within a person's social network. CBB theory can take into account modality, type of communication episode (i.e., the content of the conversation), and relationship partner in predicting need satisfaction and social interaction frequency (see Figure 3.1). As such, it has several implications for understanding how, when, and why people relate through technology.

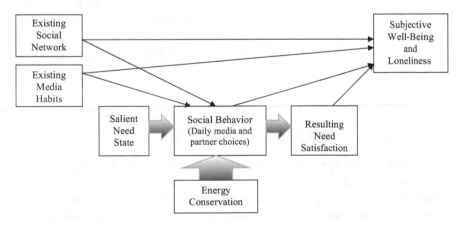

FIGURE 3.1 Communicate bond belong theoretical model

3.1 Social Interactions and Relationships

Consistent with the perspective advanced in Chapter 1, CBB theory suggests that human beings have always needed close and enduring relationships for the sake of survival and reproduction. Thus, the need to belong, or a persistent desire for social acceptance and inclusion, likely evolved to orient our attention and resources toward those goals (Baumeister & Leary, 1995). To satisfy the need to belong, individuals will "seek and maintain some minimum number of strong and abiding relationships with both individuals and groups" (Leary & Kelly, 2008, p. 400). Therefore, humans are instinctually motivated to put forth energy to establish, maintain, and repair existing social relationships (Leary, 2001).

Human motivations are psychological forces that direct mental resources and behavior toward the elimination of unsatisfying need states (Tinbergen, 1951/1970). When a need precedes the action of the organism, it is said to motivate or drive the associated behavior (Hull, 1943/1970). Sheldon and colleagues' work (Prentice, Halusic, & Sheldon, 2014; Sheldon & Gunz, 2009; Sheldon, Abad, & Hinsch, 2011) proposes a two-process model that I later adopted in a formal test of CBB theory (e.g., Hall, 2018a). In the first part of Sheldon's model, individuals experience a dissatisfying need state (e.g., I feel lonely) and then they take action to resolve that dissatisfaction (e.g., I will call mom) (Sheldon & Gunz, 2009). In the second part of the model, if the action taken to resolve the undesired need state results in need satisfaction, then it should increase well-being both in the moment (Sheldon et al., 2011) and over the long term through greater thriving in relationships (Hall & Morella, 2020).

Social interactions of all kinds and types, mediated and unmediated, can be thought of as actions taken to resolve an in-the-moment need to belong and to maintain valued relationships over time. However, actions taken to satisfy needs may not always succeed in doing so – they can miss the mark. When behaviors fail to fulfill needs, it will improve neither momentary nor global well-being (Prentice et al., 2014). Because the action was taken to resolve a fundamental need (i.e., belongingness), that same need state will arise again shortly after engaging in an unsatisfying behavior.

In other words, if the snack doesn't cut it, we'll feel hungry again soon.

3.2 Example of CBB in Social Media

The primary motivation for personal media use in general (i.e., texting, voice calls) (Bryant et al., 2011; Fischer, 1992; Tong & Walther, 2011) and social media in particular (Smock, Ellison, Lampe, & Wohn, 2011) is maintaining relationships and keeping in touch with friends. Personal media can be used both to ameliorate feelings of loneliness and to maintain existing relationships (e.g., Krasnova, Spiekermann, Koroleva, & Hildebrand, 2010; Rae & Lonborg, 2015). According to CBB theory, these two things are part of the same core process. People seek out mediated and FtF social interactions in response to feelings of disconnection, and through social interactions needs are satisfied (or not) and relationships are maintained (or not).

When using social media in ways other than socially interacting, the first component of the two-process model has strong empirical support. Users who feel disconnected use social media more (Wang, Tchernev, & Solloway, 2012), even to excess (Masur, Reinecke, Ziegele, & Quiring, 2014). On the need-satisfaction component of the process, however, evidence is weak. Facebook can sometimes satisfy a need for support (Manago, Taylor, & Greenfield, 2012), but this is dependent on the degree to which Facebook friends' actions are supportive and positive (Blease, 2015; Greitemeyer, Mugge, & Bollerman, 2014; Oh, Ozkaya, & LaRose, 2014). For users most reliant on social media to resolve feelings of disconnection, it fails to alleviate negative emotions (Oh et al., 2014) and may actually increase negative mood (Sagioglou & Greitemeyer, 2014). Although motivated by feelings of disconnection, social media use does not result in a more satisfying bond (Pollet, Roberts, & Dunbar, 2011; Weidman, Fernandez, Levison, Augustine, Larsen, & Rodebaugh, 2012) or satisfy relatedness needs (Reinecke, Vorderer, & Knop, 2014).

This is consistent with one of the assertions of the two-process models: individuals can miss the mark when attempting to satisfy belongingness needs. Wang et al. (2012) suggests that ungratified social needs "drive [social media] use, but are not gratified by [social media] use, and grow larger to stimulate heavier [social media] use in the future" (p. 1837). Chapter 6 will provide a more complete account of how we can understand social media from the perspective of relating through technology, but for the purposes of introducing CBB theory it is a good illustration of how our relatedness needs drive personal media use, and depending on how we use the medium, this choice may or may not satisfy the need to belong.

3.3 Social Energy Conservation and Investment

CBB theory (Hall & Davis, 2017) has implications for multimodal relationships and media choice. Like TCC (Dutta-Bergman, 2004), CBB theory suggests that media choice in relationships is multimodal and driven by interpersonal needs. Like MRT, CBB theory assumes that modalities differ from one another in important ways. Unlike MRT and social presence perspectives, CBB theory directs attention to the concept of energy conservation and investment when trying to explain media use.

The theory offers two formal principles about social energy. First, people will seek to conserve energy or use the least amount of energy possible to meet their needs. Second, people will seek to invest energy where they perceive greater returns on their investment. Given these principles, the theory predicts that people should engage in relationship maintenance actions that engender bonding, but are constrained by the obligations implied with each new relationship and the tendency toward energy conversation. Thus, all social interactions can be interpreted through this relational need to social energy trade-off.

This general tendency toward energy conservation is offset by two important factors: (1) the need to belong and (2) occasions when the use of a low energy medium might increase rather than decrease future energy expenditure. In the first case, when people feel compelled to feel close and connected to others, they will seek out interactions that are most likely to meet those needs, such as with close relationship partners or through social interactions that bring about stronger feelings of relatedness (Hall, 2018a). People feel better when their social interactions have a high connectedness and low energy expenditure ratio in the moment (Hall, 2018a) and globally (Hall & Merolla, 2020). Thus, people may use modes of interaction that are energy intensive when they are motivated to do so and because certain types of communication episodes (i.e., the ones I call striving communication episodes) make people feel more connected. Chapter 5 will explore the idea that different modes of interaction have differing consequences for closeness, loneliness, and connection, but suffice it to say that different modes differ in important ways.

In the second case, CBB theory would predict that people would use a mode of communication that requires more attention and energy expenditure when they experience or anticipate a greater cost in terms of energy or inadequate closeness if they choose a lower energy medium. For example, people can experience frustrations or complications when trying to use texting to communicate (Scissors & Gergle, 2013). CBB theory would interpret the growing frustration or confusion as an energy-intensive state (Hall, 2018a). Thus, a quick voice call might require more in-the-moment energy, but this may be offset by avoiding further energy expenditure in the form of misunderstanding, upset, or conflict.

3.4 Energy Use by Modality

To explore this issue of energy and mode of communication, I will share the results of two experience sampling studies, where people are contacted at random times in a day for five to seven days. At these random moments, the first question they were asked was: Did you have a social interaction in the last ten minutes? If they answered yes, they reported whom they were interacting with, what mode they were using to interact (including FtF), what they were talking about (i.e., communication episode), and how much energy the interaction took. The combined sample of these two studies included

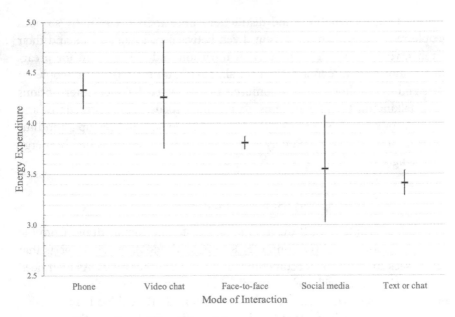

FIGURE 3.2 Energy expenditure by modality

334 people and 4,435 social interactions. Figure 3.2 shows the estimated marginal means for social energy expenditure (with 95% confidence intervals), controlling for participants' age and gender, and the closeness of the interaction partner and content of communication.

The results suggest that voice calls and video chats are quite energy-intensive modalities. Indeed, voice calls are more energy intensive than any other modality. FtF interaction is squarely in the middle of the spectrum, with interactions through social media and text/chat programs significantly below the scale midpoint. These results confirm the idea that texting and social media are relatively low-energy modalities and demonstrate an important distinction between energy and social presence. In contrast with what might be expected from MRT, two modalities are significantly more energy intensive than FtF interactions, which is the usually gold standard for social presence in MRT.

The principle of energy investment may also explain both people's long-standing reticence to talk on the phone (Fischer, 1992) and the unique considerations of voice calls and video chat. Well before the rise of Web 2.0, voice calls had a set of unique characteristics. They often require a high degree of focus and a lack of distractions to successfully complete. As such, they are considered to be more work (Baron & Campbell, 2012; Duran & Kelly, 2017; Rettie, 2007). This is partly because of the challenges of turn taking without prosodic and nonverbal cues (e.g., does silence mean they aren't listening or are they waiting for me to keep talking?). In FtF conversation, interruptions and distractions are experienced jointly so both people respond to them in unison. Even between college students and their parents, voice calls can be seen as an intrusion and are reserved for prearranged moments to connect (Platt et al., 2014; Quinn 2013). Both people on each end of the line can feel confused or distracted by such interruptions when talking on the phone. Thus, to maintain focus, limit distractions, and avoid uncomfortable silences on the phone, people have to keep up a continuous level of attention, which may explain why it is perceived as highly energy expending.

3.5 Homeostatic Principle

As a final principle of CBB theory, the homeostatic principle draws from the social affiliation model (O'Connor & Rosenblood, 1996), which suggests that people seek to be in contact sometimes and alone at other times. As their need to relate rises, they will seek out social interaction and as their desire to be alone rises they will seek solitude (O'Connor & Rosenblood, 1996; Hall, 2017b). This idea is important for three reasons. First, it rejects the "more is better" model of connectivity – both mediated and nonmediated. Thus, CBB theory stands in contrast to any linear model of connectivity that makes such an assertion (or implies it). Second, because the amount of contact seems to be regulated within the day, not between days (Hall, 2017b), the homeostatic state can be meaningfully explored within each person's day. This may give researchers a window for analysis that can look at trends of connectivity and meaningful talk, and may explain a desire to connect late in the day by both phone (Aledavood et al., 2015) and FtF (Hall, 2017b). Third, the homeostatic principle is guided by an underlying need state: relatedness. Thus, to understand how people use media to relate, it would help to understand whether or not media successfully meet their social needs.

3.6 CBB Theory Compared with CMC Theories

Due to its focus on social interactions and personal relationships, modality use is not a central focus of CBB theory. Unlike both MMT and TCC, CBB theory is not concerned with the number of unique modalities people use. Because it draws from an evolutionary model of human behavior, FtF communication is presumptively primary. That is, our motivational and social systems were built for the conditions where and when they developed, not for the present-day media landscape. The theory also focuses on a set of concepts that are quite distinct from CMC theory: belongingness needs and satisfaction, social interactions and episodes, relational closeness, homeostatic regulation, and social energy expenditure and investment. Technologies are seen as a means by which people achieve (or not) these relational goals and alleviate their social needs. CBB theory presumes multimodality and presumes media choices are going to be responsive to relationship-related pressures. Thus, it is consistent with conclusions from Chapter 2, that people use media to relate because of *who* is available on those media first and foremost.

CBB theory assumes a social network of others: it locates the individual within their social network of ties, which vary in emotional closeness. Although media have offered people an incredible range of potential relationship partners to meet or engage with, and social media have strongly embedded individuals within a large network of acquaintance relationships (Brandtzæg, 2012), people still direct a large portion of their total personal media use toward closer relationship partners, whether texting or making phone calls (Miritello et al., 2013; Saramaki et al., 2014) or when engaging through social media (Burke & Kraut, 2014; Utz, 2015). Overall, the theory provides an underlying mechanism for why people relate through technology, why they may choose one modality over another, and why one mode of communication may spill over or affect another relationship partner, mode of communication, or content of communication.

Future questions may directly explore what it is about media that requires more energy expenditure. Perhaps aspects of channel expansion theory should be explored, as CBB theory also assumes that familiarity with a modality and partner choice are important constructs in terms of energy conservation and relatedness, respectively. Familiarity with a technology and a preference for using normative modes would be understood as consistent with the tendency toward energy conservation (Davis, 1997). The MRT concept of natural language, perhaps, could be brought in to explain what it is about FtF interaction that is both more able to meet the need to belong (see Chapter 5) and less energy intensive than phone calls and video chats.

The theory is limited in its applications to media compared with self-determination theory (e.g., Reinecke et al., 2014) because it explores only one need instead of three (i.e., it does not address competence and autonomy needs). However, as CBB is a relational theory, it is more specific in its ability to generate predictions about whom people want to interact with, how they want to interact with them, and when people would desire that interaction. As a cautionary note, because it is a new theory that has not been tested by other researchers, it still is primarily a theoretical explanation and not an empirically supported one.

4

Niche, Media Displacement, and Multimodal Relationships

These days, citizens of the global north have an unprecedented degree of choice in personal media options made possible through the smartphone. Recent surveys indicate that approximately 68% of adults in developed nations and 77% of adults in the United States own a smartphone (Pew Research Center, 2018; Poushter, 2016). In addition to social media platforms and basic mobile functionality (i.e., texting, voice calls), there is an always-expanding menu of downloadable smartphone apps. Whether a person has enabled a narrow or wide range of media platforms and apps on their smartphone, the choices of new ways to communicate that a person has yet to enable on their device are perpetually available and growing.

Yet people obviously do not adopt all of the technologies available to them. Although the potential ways to connect are more numerous than ever before, the actual use of any given personal media tool is very narrow, with few exceptions. As the principle of the conservation of energy suggests (Chapter 3), people tend to stick to media they know and are familiar with. As addressed in Chapter 2, people make do with the technology they know.

This chapter will address the question, Which media do people use to socially interact? As this book excludes the use of media for information gathering (e.g., news, geo-location, shopping) and entertainment (e.g., streaming videos and music), this chapter is focused on relational and social media use. To answer this question, we first have to reframe the issue of media choice, not in terms of the contemporary conception of endless adoption of new modalities, but instead in terms of a historical frame of gradual displacement of media and in terms of corporations competing for users' money, time, and attention.

SECTION ONE: MEDIA DISPLACEMENT THEORY AND THE THEORY OF THE NICHE

To know what media people actually use to socially interact, two lines of comparison need to be drawn: between socially interacting or doing something else, and communicating through one mode versus another. The first question is about displacement and the second is about inhabiting a niche.

1.1 Media Displacement Theory

We could not talk or talk forever and still find things to not talk about.
—Best in Show

Communicate bond belong (CBB) theory (Hall & Davis, 2017) asserts that humans are driven by the fundamental need to belong, which motivates them to socially interact with one another. Two other universal processes offset this need: the tendency toward energy conservation and a homeostatic regulation of social interaction within each day. Thus, when considering how people use their time in general and use personal media particularly, we must keep in mind that constant communication is neither a goal nor a meaningful standard for optimal human functioning. That is, people do not really want to be endlessly communicating, and the effects of any given social interaction depend on a person's internal need state as well as the partner and the content of the conversation. Considered in this manner, social interaction is just one of many things people might do with their time. So, how do media fit in with people's time?

The number of minutes per day that people spend socializing is very low, and appears to be in decline among US adolescents (Twenge, Spitzberg, & Campbell, 2019) and adults (see Chapter 10). Based on the American Time Use Survey of 2003–2018 (US Department of Labor, 2019), people spend about forty minutes per day socializing, compared with two to four hours per day spent watching or streaming TV and movies.

As discussed in Chapter 1, people have eighteen to twenty-six interactions per day on average. No doubt, there is substantial variation in this average depending on the jobs people have and their living conditions. That said, it is important to keep in mind that (1) just because people are around or available does not imply or require interacting with them and (2) just because a person *could* be interacting with others via a smartphone, it does not mean they actually do so. Taken together, this means that much of media use is not for socializing and that the vast majority of people's personal time is not spent in social interaction.

The first line of distinction is between time spent on any given medium and time spent on other activities, which is the fundamental question of media displacement theory. This theory has a long research tradition, which became particularly active during the widespread adoption of television (Bryant & Fondren, 2009). Throughout the 1950s, cinema attendance fell in response to increased TV viewing, and for children, increased TV viewing typically displaced similar forms of in-home entertainment, such as reading comic books and listening to the radio (Bryant & Fondren, 2009). In both cases, a new medium (i.e., TV) displaced similar activities (e.g., watching movies) serving a similar function (i.e., entertainment).

Media displacement theory suggests that people go through the process of *transformation* during periods of media domestication (see Chapter 2). Old routines are altered to conform to new technologies; new habits and routines set in. Another principle of the theory, *proximity*, refers to the perception of new media and old media occupying similar positions physically or psychologically. The TV may have taken the place of a radio in the home, just as the web browser took the place of a dial-up program on the desktop of a personal computer, a laptop might have replaced a desktop PC, or one app replaced another on a smartphone. The concept here is media have *materiality*, or thingness. Media or digital objects (both physical objects and specific programs or icons) that occupy a similar physical or psychological space are more likely to displace one another during the process of transformation.

The final two concepts are *functional similarity* and *marginal fringe activities*. Functional similarity suggests that older activities that are most functionally similar to the new medium (i.e., they serve similar purposes or needs) are the activities most likely to be displaced by a new technology. The principle of marginal fringe activities refers to the concept that new media replace free or leisure time. Unstructured time is more likely to be displaced by a new medium compared with time that media users have less control over. When displacement occurs, the new medium likely borrows time from various unstructured activities rather than one single activity (Bryant & Fondren, 2009; Hall, Johnson, & Ross, 2019a; Robinson, 2011).

One of the core questions of media displacement has long been, Does media displace social activity? This will be given full attention in Chapter 9. For the purposes of this chapter, we will consider displacement from two associated perspectives: Does personal media borrow time from other things people might do? How do people decide which personal media to use?

On the first question, media displacement theory would suggest that when two possible activities occupy a similar space, either physically or psychologically, if they serve similar needs (*proximity*), then they are more likely to displace one another. In that sense, the activities most similar and serving similar needs as FtF social interaction are other ways of socially interacting. In Fischer's (1992) account of American adoption of the landline telephone in the twentieth century, he points out that very early on in that process people used local calls to contact people in the neighborhood rather than walking over to their house, especially when the nature of the call was to ask a question. In that instance, one method of communication was replaced by another method. Because watching or streaming TV is more passive entertainment than social interaction in nature, media displacement theory would suggest that such activities would replace (and be replaced by) other forms of entertainment, not socialization.

Just as internet use primarily displaced time watching TV, listening to the radio, and reading papers (Vilhelmson, Thulin, & Ellder, 2017), social media use appears to primarily displace internet use for adults (Hall et al., 2019a) and print media in various forms for adolescents (Twenge, Martin & Spitzberg, 2018b). However, not all displaced activities neatly correspond to the underlying needs that they serve, which is addressed the principle of marginal fringe activities. For example, both internet use in the early 2000s and social media use in 2007–2017 appear to have displaced a variety of activities, including housework and driving, as well as time spent working and watching children (Hall et al., 2019a; Robinson, 2011; Vilhelmson et al., 2017).

When asking questions about which activities are displaced by media use or consumption, it is important to consider that media in general, and any given medium specifically, serve a host of functions and needs, and many of those needs are not directly social or communicative in nature. The theory of the niche is better equipped to answer the question, Why do people use one personal medium, app, or social media platform over another?

1.2 Theory of the Niche

Dimmick and colleagues' theory of the niche (Dimmick, Feaster, & Ramirez, 2011; Dimmick, Kline, & Stafford, 2000; Ramirez, Dimmick, Feaster, & Lin, 2008) offers a complementary perspective to media displacement theory. The theory is versatile in helping to understand why individuals choose one medium over another. Consistent with media displacement theory, the theory of the niche suggests that media compete with one another to serve particular needs or gratifications (Dimmick et al., 2000). Niche research tends to focus on personal media use and related needs, rather than media use in general. The theory is most useful when the particular need served by a technology is carefully defined by its functional use. Long-distance telephone calls displaced posted letters (Fischer, 1992), just as email replaced long-distance calls (Dimmick et al., 2000), because they served the same function (e.g., keeping in touch with loved ones who lived far away). In both cases, the newer technology had the advantage of being cheaper, more convenient, or more need satisfying. As such, any technology that allows for person-to-person communication (e.g., telephone, chat, text, email) is likely to serve similar relational needs (Dimmick et al., 2011).

Similar to the principle of functional similarity in media displacement theory, niche theory suggests that a medium must differentiate itself among competing media to survive. When there is considerable overlap in the gratifications that two distinct media serve, there is a greater potential for displacement. The theory of the niche has two additional advantages: it recognizes that some media are strongly associated with fulfilling very specific (or niche) needs and that those types of media are rarely fully displaced when new media are adopted.

Once a domain of gratification or need is well defined, then the theory of the niche becomes particularly useful. Within the broad concept of interpersonal communication, the primary needs that personal media serve are belongingness and inclusion, relationship maintenance and initiation, hanging out, virtual people watching, and information exchange. When selecting among media, users evaluate each medium by the degree that it can "amplify or attenuate the opportunities for deriving gratification from that medium" (Dimmick et al., 2000, p. 230). This is consistent with the concept that media functions as an amplifier or modulator of communication. What a medium does is dependent on its use, rather than its design. The focus on gratifications suggests that some media are better than others at getting users' needs met. For the purposes of interpersonal communication and relationship maintenance, media vary considerably in what they can offer, especially in terms of social cues and synchrony, as explored in the Introduction and Chapter 3. Some media functions are broader, meaning they can do several things at once, and others are narrower. When there is a lot of overlap between media, they are called functionally substitutable, which suggests they serve the same gratifications (Dimmick et al., 2000).

The theory of the niche accounts for the well-known phenomena that some media niches endure, while others fall away. This is because some patterns of media use are associated with particular types of relational partners in particular places and at particular times (Dimmick et al., 2011). As IM became widely used, users developed patterns of use that were distinct from voice calls and email (Quan-Haase, 2007). IM offered opportunities for gratifying the need of passing the time, or hanging out online when communicators were not co-present, in a way that other media simply did not (Quan-Haase, 2007; Quan-Haase & Collins, 2008; Ramirez et al., 2008; Sheer, 2011) – at least until the rise of social media, which undoubtedly contributed to IM's demise as the modality of choice among young people.

Research on the theory of the niche also documents how niches can become refined and very specific. Dimmick et al. (2011) reported that voice calls occupied the niche of keeping in contact with close others when on the move, primarily late at night, and texting tended to be more used for keeping in touch with friends at any time of the day and in most places a person could inhabit. In short, the theory is quite adaptable to the constantly shifting menu of media options, and can define the niche of a medium as broadly or narrowly as the patterns of use require.

SECTION TWO: A SHORT HISTORY OF PERSONAL MEDIA

Media displacement and the theory of the niche lead us to a set of questions: Where did the contemporary media landscape emerge from? What is gone? What endures now and might endure in the future? Although a complete history of personal media use is well beyond the scope of this book, it is worthwhile to offer the following overview in trends in personal media displacement in the past thirty years.

2.1 Pre-internet Age

It is important to point out that new technologies have changed how humans relate to one another throughout human history (Farman, 2018). For thousands of years, people have sought to keep in touch with one another over great distances. An example from the American past can be found in *My Antonia* by Willa Cather (1918), who writes about letters sent by loved ones far from home. Such letters were meant to be passed around among family and friends. Thus, letters were ostensibly for keeping in touch, but Cather illustrates that they served broader self-presentational purposes for the writer. These letters were like a long, infrequent status update to a clutch of geographically proximal others. Consider that Twitter content has a remarkable similarity to eighteenth- and nineteenth-century personal diaries that were also meant to be passed around (Humphreys, Gill, Krishnamurthy, & Newbury, 2013). In both cases, authors sought to account for the goings-on in their lives and to share with others the content of those accounts with faraway friends and family.

Skipping ahead to the early 1990s, the dominant options for communicating with others near and far were still posted letters, the telephone, and FtF contact. In 1990, for twenty-nine cents and cost of paper and envelope, you could send a letter across the country. Telephone pricing was much more variable as providers competed for long-distance call traffic, but around that time a new price cut in long-distance calls was promoted: a "10-minute AT&T call during the evening calling period to Los Angeles from Chicago would fall to $1.58 from $1.67" (Rudd, 1989). Given that is more than $3 in 2019 (adjusting for inflation), these ten-minute calls sound quite expensive to me. No wonder I remember my parents being cautious about call length.

Even with those cost prohibitions, at this time, families reported that the telephone was a critical tool for keeping in touch with one another, particularly over long distances (Wellman et al., 1988). In the 1980s, Fischer (1992) reports that people called only a small set of friends and family (about five unique individuals); 75% of all telephone calls were to friends and family. This reinforces the concepts introduced in Chapter 1: social interactions in general and mediated interactions specifically are primarily shared with a small group of others.

Three additional notable trends point to the endurance of patterns of communication over time. People have personal preferences for how they kept in touch. From the moment telephones were available in the early 1900s and through the 1990s, some people loved to chat on the phone and some preferred FtF conversation (Fischer, 1992). More recently, between 10% and 15% of people report having a strong dislike for making lengthy, engaged telephone calls (Baron & Campbell, 2012; Eden & Veksler, 2016; Rettie, 2007). Showing preferences among media options is a core feature of the SCOT perspective (Chapter 2), and it has a long history in media adoption.

Second, as alternatives to posted letters emerged with the telegraph and telephone, different media were understood to convey different types of information. Fischer (1992) reports that people often preferred receiving a letter over a telegram, not because letters were longer, cheaper, or more personal, but because telegrams were often sent to report on the death of a loved one! This makes me wonder whether unexpected phone calls from family might have similar connotations in the near future. Thus, each medium in the past had a socially constructed form and purpose that defines interpersonal patterns of use at the time.

Finally, in the last century, the frequencies of telephone and FtF contact with any given person were correlated with one another – even for geographically proximal friends and family (Fischer, 1992; Wellman et al., 1988). This means that more communication through one modality corresponded with more communication in general (see the description of MMT and TCC in Chapter 3).

In sum, human relationships have long been multimodal and disproportionally focused on a few important others, who construct idiosyncratic patterns of use.

2.2 The 1990s: And Now for Something Completely Different

Even at its onset in 1972, email was immediately recognized as a social medium, although most email was used for professional purposes (Chayko, 2018). It began its integration into domestic environments by the early 1990s. It is important not to overstate the use of email: by 2000, less than 40% of American households had access to the internet at home, and only 21% of American adults exchanged emails on an average day (Rainie & Wellman, 2012). Yet email's potential for disrupting the stranglehold of long-distance calls and posted letters was becoming increasingly clear throughout the 1990s. A random sample of email users in Columbus, Ohio, in 1997 suggested that the adoption of email was displacing long-distance calls (Dimmick et al., 2000). It was far superior for communicating when finding times to talk was difficult (e.g., different time zones, discordant schedules) or when the expense of phone calls was prohibitive (which is fascinatingly similar to the rise of video chat programs).

There were four other forms of personal media that emerged in the 1990s that, in my estimation, were distinct and new at the time they were introduced. Each one of these forms of online communication created the possibility of new media niches, as each was distinct in form and function from other CMC options. The novelty of these forms of communication in the 1970s and 1980s generated a strong sense of excitement among adopters. Chayko (2018) writes, "The feeling of being part of a grand social experiment – a pioneer on a brand new frontier – was frequently invoked among those developing this new kind of social interaction in those not-so-distant times" (p. 30). Part of this excitement was a feeling of possibility and experimentation with new ways of communicating: through text, with strangers far away, on computers, in real time. It must have been at least novel and even shocking or transgressive.

From the perspective of theory of the niche, there were distinct forms that this "revolutionary form of sociality" (Chayko, 2018, p. 30) could take: the listserv, the message board, IM, and the chat room. Both message boards and listservs of the 1990s were most often formed around particular interests or hobbies, such as music or TV shows, or around particular geographic communities or spaces, such as within a city or university (Baym, 2000; 2010). Many listservs were most similar in function to modern mass emails sent to subscribers. By contrast, message boards were shared online spaces that could be accessed remotely. One of the important features of message boards in terms of niche creation was access to individuals who shared an interest in a topic and were not geographically near. This feature offered more opportunities for direct communication with strangers than previously possible. Although much of the communication on message boards was dedicated to its ostensible purpose (e.g., a board dedicated to the Grateful Dead's music talked about the Grateful Dead), relational and interpersonal communication often developed there as well (Baym, 2000; 2018).

Message boards also gave rise to blogging by individual users or collectives, which linked their contributions to one another through a series of hyperlinks to other blogs. This was an earlier precursor to "tagging" people in social media. Thus, much of the technological affordances we tend to associate with SNSs and other social media had clear precursors in the 1990s. Just as with all technologies, these technologies were socially shaped by users through norms and practices of use. Users could identify one another and understand and police the social norms of conduct in their shared online community (Baym, 2000).

The second mediated form of communication emerging in the 1990s was made possible by computer programs that could offer one-on-one chat with someone you already knew. One of the earliest text-based communication programs was called "Talk" (Baym, 2015). This program enabled nearly synchronous and purely textual exchange with someone who was online simultaneously. AOL's Instant Messenger was founded in 1997. One of the innovations of IM was its use of a "buddy list" that informed you who was available for contact, which reinforced the use of IM as a space to hang out with others online (Mesch et al., 2012; Quan-Haase & Collins, 2008; Ramirez et al., 2008). Again, because the internet was typically accessed by a desktop computer and a dial-up modem in the 1990s (Rainie & Wellman, 2012), chats were restricted to people who had a stable internet connection and access to a computer, at the same time of the day.

The chat rooms of the 1990s offered yet another option to meet strangers in online spaces. The exchanges in these chat rooms were open to everyone logged in to the site, but individual users could also elect to privately chat with one another. Again, these online spaces offered a novel way of socially interacting. As a niche, they were distinct from message boards in that private dyadic textual communication was enabled, and the speed of response was generally more synchronous than message boards, contributing to a feeling of social presence. As such, the feelings of relatedness and the possibility of relationship initiation was strong. I recall using online chat rooms as a high school student, and remember feeling excited and curious when messages popped up in the chat window. These chats were not dissimilar to short, superficial conversations with strangers at a party. When a chat partner stopped responding, it could be they were uninterested in continuing the chat, but it was also possible they had lost their internet connection, which was very common at the time. Alas, this face-saving interpretation of being "ghosted" no longer holds much value in today's world of nearly continuous mobile access.

Thulin and Vilhelmson (2005) capture the landscape of these competing media options on a two-wave panel study of high school students in Sweden between 1997 and 2001. For these students, the use of email was at its peak, particularly with long-distance friends and family, but had begun to transition into IM on desktop computers and SMS on mobile phones. Interestingly, respondents reported that chat rooms were considered "childish" and on the way out of fashion. Participants also thought that discussion groups or message boards were for specialized interests, not really for friendship or socializing. Communication within those discussion groups, even one-on-one chats in chat rooms, tended to stay online and not further develop offline (see also Mesch & Talmud, 2006). Of course, this is not to say that relationships were never established online, only that the majority that started online stayed online.

Thus, by the early 2000s, telephone calls and email maintained their central position as a means to maintain existing and long-distance relationships, while the revolutionary promise of communication with strangers (through chat rooms and online communities) was being displaced or segmented for specialized communication purposes – a true niche. This change also signaled the rapid rise of texting, which is one of the most transformational technological developments in relationship maintenance and communication in the past twenty years.

2.3 The Rise of Short-Message Service (SMS) (2000–2007)

The Swedish high school students of the Thulin and Vilhelmson (2005) study were the exact population at the forefront of the change from the technologies of the 1990s to the mobile revolution of the aughts: young, northern European, and wired. In Europe, pricing plans encourage the rapid adoption of texting, in comparison to America where texting was limited by expensive pricing (Baron & Hard af Segerstad, 2010; Ling, 2004). By the late aughts (2006–2011), the rise of mobility and texting grew hand in hand in the United States, nearly doubling (Rainie & Wellman, 2012). In the Netherlands, van den Berg, Arentze, and Timmermans (2012) report that young people were moving away from using the phone to make voice calls and toward the use of IM and texting. These trends came to the United States shortly thereafter. By 2010, the average American adolescent (i.e., thirteen to seventeen years of age) sent and received the most text messages compared with all age groups: 3,339 text messages in a month, or between 50 and 110 per day (Nielsenwire, 2010), and spent around two hours per day texting (Twenge et al., 2019).

The biggest driver of these changes in media practices was the worldwide adoption of mobile phones. A technology once reserved for emergencies was becoming commonplace in countries throughout the world. By 2010, there were five billion mobile connections worldwide, quickly outpacing computers with internet connections by a factor of three (BBC News, 2010). The International Telecommunications Union estimated in 2010 that nearly 80% of the global population used mobile phones, while only 30% used the internet, and less than 20% had fixed phone lines (ITU, 2010). And a good deal of mobile traffic was via text. In 2008, more than two trillion text messages were sent worldwide, and in the United States, SMS topped voice calls on mobile phones (Nielsenwire, 2008). Between 2006 and 2008 the number of text messages sent by Americans increased by 450% (Nielsenwire, 2008).

The rise of mobile connectivity and change in texting pricing was transformative because it merged most of the functions of email, IM, and voice calls into one device. And it had another big advantage: not being tied to a modem or hardline connection on a desktop computer. This was greeted with a powerful feeling of freedom *and* a feeling of being tethered (Arnold, 2003; Baron, 2008). Suffice it to say, the mobile device became the centralized point of entry for prior niches of communication. This change was powerful and transformed the mobility of relationships and communication within them.

The centralization of several niches of communication into one device was also eerily prescient of battles to come among social media companies. Consider the fight about whether a person could take their phone number with them if they changed mobile carriers, which was an issue resolved by the Federal Communications Commission in 2004. The mobile number became more fixed than a street address as people began to "cut the cord," or stop having a landline telephone (Rainie & Wellman, 2012). Now, consider whether a phone number or a social media profile is more fixed. Young adults see each other's social media profiles as a semi-permanent means of keeping track of people, akin to an address book that is constantly being updated by the contact themself (Standlee, 2019). At a broader level, this battle – which company owns the platform that centralizes different modalities (and serves as your permanent address) – rages on as social media platforms become more adept at taking competitor's functions. These are exactly the network effects that Facebook CEO Mark Zuckerberg vigorously fought for in the last decade (Onos, 2018). This debate is also at the core of whether social media should be regarded as a public good, something to be regulated in a manner similar to telephony and the monopoly of Ma Bell.

On a personal media level, these issues speak to two related challenges: the "making do" component of SCOT and researchers needing to become increasingly careful of what they mean when they study mobile communication. The first issue recalls concepts proposed in Chapter 2, namely, the idea that people often do not maximize or take advantage of all possibilities, but instead make do with what they are familiar with. Similarly, as one's mobile device (and mobile phone plan) allowed individuals to do more, they were disinclined to change means of communication wholesale. The added difficulty of integrating contact lists or other ways of keeping an online "address book" (which until recently was stored on the mobile device itself) meant individuals were often happy to make do rather than change swiftly. Additionally, researchers were confronted with a challenge that has only worsened with the rise of social media: What are people actually *doing* on their phone when they say they rely on it or cannot do without it? Reliance on or even "loving" a device tells us little about the interpersonal niche or the actual patterns of use from a niche perspective.

Issues surrounding patterns of use are brought to bear when researchers consider *who* was most influenced by early mobile phone adoption. Mobile habits dramatically varied by age group, with users in their late teens and early twenties leading the way (Ling, 2010; Ling et al., 2012; Park et al., 2012; van den Berg et al., 2012). Ling (2010) makes a compelling argument that texting is a behavior characteristic of a particular life stage. It is a niche that is socially situated in needs and the match with technology for particular types of users. Consider that Ling et al. (2012), analyzing 2007 Norwegian data, found that sixteen- to twenty-two-year-old users send and receive on average almost *60 times more* texts that would be expected if texts were evenly distributed among all users. Nineteen-year-olds, in particular, sent and received *80 times* more texts than one would expect if patterns of use were evenly distributed. Network effects likely further heightened differences in texting between young people and older adults. That is, because teens sent more texts to primarily same-aged others (Ling et al., 2012) and because those who communicate with a wider network of people are more likely to do so through texting (Hall, 2018b; Park et al., 2012), teens most certainly reinforce one another's texting habits. One's most frequent mobile communication partners most strongly influence one's mobile experience (Ling et al., 2012) and media adoption and use generally (Fulk, 1993).

Ling et al. (2012) present strong longitudinal evidence that as people aged, they sent fewer texts. This means that while a new cohort – early adopters of texting – established new texting habits, they do not keep up this pace over time. Among US adolescents, the heyday of texting occurred around 2011 and was displaced by rising internet use in general and social media specifically over the next five years (Twenge et al., 2018b).

As a notable caveat to the incredible number and prevalence of texting, patterns of SMS use still tend to conform to the first fifteen most important people discussed in Chapter 1. It is most prevalent within a core network of three to five others (Ling et al., 2012). Texting was particularly prevalent between close friends, compared with family or romantic partners (Dimmick et al., 2011). Recent data confirms this trend. Bhattacharya et al. (2016) report that phone call time is very unevenly distributed among all contacts. Rather, it is focused strongly on a very few close others. Miritello et al. (2013) report that texting patterns are similarly focused on very few partners (five to eight individuals).

2.4 A Quick Stop at IM

IM and its messenger competitors had its heyday in the early aughts. The relationship between the availability of texting on mobile phones and the use of IM were likely strongly related; countries that offered cheap, available access to SMS were countries most likely to see a drop in IM use (Thulin & Vilhelmson, 2005). In the middle of the decade (~2005), IM appeared to have hits its peak in North America and Israel (Boase, Horrigan, Wellman, & Rainie, 2006; Mesch et al., 2012; Quan-Haase, 2007). Shortly thereafter, the rise of social networking sites in the United States probably further accelerated its displacement. During its peak period, college students reported more interactions with friends on IM than any other mode of communication, including FtF (Quan-Haase, 2007). Its use was confined to the niche of friendship maintenance, particularly those who were geographically close and interested in hanging out online (Mesch et al., 2012; Quan-Haase & Collins, 2008). In terms of media displacement, IM also contributed to the rapid drop in the use of email for friendship maintenance (Quan-Haase, 2007).

As the aughts came to a close, the importance of texting as a relationship maintenance device was undeniable, but a new trend had already emerged: social media. Hampton et al. (2011) reports on a nationally representative US sample collected in 2008: 30% of individuals used social networking sites, 31% used IM, 35% used a photo-sharing application, and 10% were blogging. Data from the Longitudinal Study of American Youth (LSAY) (Miller, 2014) in 2009 suggests even higher rates for members of generation X: 67% had a Facebook account, 23% had a Myspace account, and 18% were still using message boards. For adolescents, between 2010 and 2016 the number of those who report going on social media daily rose dramatically from ~50% to ~80% (Twenge et al., 2018b). The Web 2.0 revolution was well underway.

SECTION THREE: PATTERNS OF SOCIAL INTERACTION

Certainly, we have more choices on the current personal media menu. Yet which media are people actually using to communicate? Below is an assembly of all of the studies that I could find that asked people (1) to identify interactions or social interactions, through (2) several different media (including FtF) in the same study, and (3) using event-contingent (i.e., report every social interaction you have) or experience-sampling (i.e., did you have an interaction when contacted?) methods.

3.1 Daily Social Interactions by Modality

Table 4.1 illustrates the percentage of daily social interactions by modality.

TABLE 4.1 Percentage of daily social interactions by modality

	2004	2008	2009	2012	2014	2015	2018
Face-to-face	64	52	61	60	60	73	73
Voice calls	18	29	16	6	5	9	10
Email	12	11	1	2	2		
IM	4	2	3	10			
SMS/text		6	16	2	24	16	15
Social media			4	2	6	3	
Video chat				19			1
Snapchat					2		
Other		1			1		
Lead author	Baym	Van den Berg	Hall	Vlahovic	Bayer	Hall	Merolla

Note: Details of included studies:
1. Baym, Zhang, & Lin (2004): student sample; event contingent (over three to five days) of each "significant voluntary social interaction"; N = 51; 851 total social interactions.
2. Van den Berg, Arentze, & Timmermans (2012): adult sample; event contingent (over two days) of "all forms of social contact, for instance, visiting, performing a joint activity, having a conversation, face-to-face as well as over the phone or online, sending or

3.2 Social Interactions Are Primarily Face-to-Face

In this multimodal contemporary media environment, at least 50% and as many as 70% of all social interactions are still FtF. Across all of the ways of defining an interaction, across various age groups, and across the methods of collecting interaction frequency, FtF is the primary mode of social interaction.

Why is this so important? It is reasonable (but apparently wrong) for people to assume that FtF communication is being displaced by other ways of communicating. In both academic and popular press writing, one hears of the growing rates of digital media use and its harms. Implicitly, there is an assumption that people writ large are turning their attention away from one another because they are turning toward their mobile phones and other devices. This popular and academic rhetoric may be running into a false dichotomy of social displacement that I will discuss in more detail in Chapters 9 and 10. Despite all of this, the concept that FtF interaction is proportionally in decline just does not seem to hold true among adults. A deeper dive into the specifics of Table 4.1 further supports this conclusion.

First, both the identity of the participants and *whom* they were communicating with merit further attention. The youngest group sampled (i.e., Bayer, Ellison, Schoenebeck, & Falk, 2016, data collected in 2014; Baym et al., 2004; and Hall et al., 2011, data collected in 2009) were first-year college students with mean ages around twenty. Among them, about 62% of their interactions are FtF. This includes both "significant voluntary social interactions" (Baym et al., 2004), social interactions with three friends of varying degrees of closeness (Hall et al., 2011), and "any form of communication between you and other person" (Bayer et al., 2016). This suggests first-year college students

receiving an email, an SMS, a letter or a fax." Definition excluded all social contact at work and people who lived in same home as respondents and excluded incidental contact; $N = 747$; 8,048 total social contact; data collected in 2008.

3. Hall, Larson, & Watts (2011): student sample; event contingent (over five days) of social interactions with one best friend, one friend, and one casual friend, excluding incidental contact; $N = 197$; 2,088 total social interactions; data collected in 2009.

4. Vlahovic, Roberts, & Dunbar (2012): post-graduate student sample; reported number of minutes for event contingent (over fourteen days) of "all social interactions with 5 closest relationship partners"; combined email and SNS; $N = 41$; percentage estimated from mean minutes for each mode.

5. Bayer, Ellison, Schoenebeck, & Falk (2016): student sample; event contingent (over fourteen days) of "any form of communication between you and another person"; $N = 154$; 11,242 interactions; data collected in 2014.

6. Hall (2018b): student and adult sample; experience sample (over five days) of social interactions, not defined; combined all SMS: text, chat programs, and apps, including Snapchat; $N = 116$; 1,909 social interactions; data collected in 2015.

7. Merolla & Hall (2018): adult sample; experience sample (over seven days) of social interactions, not defined; combined all SMS: text, chat programs, and apps, including Snapchat; $N = 128$; 2,525 social interactions; unpublished data set.

are not proportionally decreasing their FtF interactions, significant or incidental, with other people, either emotionally close or distant. Young adults continue to place a great deal of importance on FtF interactions with romantic partners (Caughlin & Sharabi, 2013) and friends (Duran & Kelly, 2017; Eden & Veksler, 2016).

In fact, the lowest percentage of FtF interactions (van den Berg et al., 2012, data collected in 2008) came from a sample that included the largest percentage of older adults, who seemed to favor the telephone to make social contact. However, this study *excluded all social interactions with people who lived in the same house.* Thus, the low FtF percentage and high telephone rate is likely more a consequence of excluding interaction partners who most likely co-present (i.e., the ones who live with you). It may also be due to cultural preference in social interaction, as it is the only non-US (i.e., Dutch) sample.

It is quite possible that the evidence in Table 4.1 is *underestimating* the frequency of FtF interactions. Several studies restricted the count to narrowly defined social interactions (Baym et al., 2004; Hall, 2018b; Morella & Hall, 2018), and classic research on social interaction suggests that incidental contact with service personnel, passing greetings (e.g., Hello, how are you?), and other types of public social behavior are *not* reported as FtF social interaction (Hall, 2018b). Interactions that shorter than ten minutes with people who are not in the study (e.g., strangers, customer service representatives) were likely not counted whatsoever.

By contrast, forms of communication such as quick checks on social media (Bayer et al., 2016) are actually not really social interactions (Hall, 2018b). The point is: there is a whole range of FtF social behaviors that are simply ignored in analyses of the frequency of social interaction, but are undoubtedly communicative and social in nature.

3.3 Mobility Endures

We can also draw other conclusions from Table 4.1. Voice calls appear to be have declined steadily in the fourteen years of the studies. This trend was reported in a study published during that time frame (i.e., Baron & Campbell, 2012), and lines up with data that suggest that voice calls, email, and IM (in that order) were the most dominant mediated modes of communication in the mid-aughts (Boase et al., 2006). It is consistent with the idea of the theory of the niche that other personal media might contribute to that decline, especially as SMS does not require a person to immediately respond or be able to respond through talking. Compared with a voice call, the efficiency of using texting to convey short bits of information, especially information that does not require an immediate response, is one of its core benefits (Eden & Veksler, 2016). Not only can texting be done while doing nearly anything else (and voice calls require much more in-the-moment attention and interruption), voice calls carry a certain degree of formality and politeness (e.g., greetings, goodbyes) that make the exchange temporally longer and more energy intensive (Rettie, 2007). Other differences between modes are explored in Chapter 5.

About 10% of social interactions across all of the samples were conducted via voice calls. Voice calls share many characteristics of FtF communication (Rettie, 2007), particularly in terms of increased nonverbal channels, such as vocalic cues, but also in terms of motivation to have a phone call (Eden & Veksler, 2016). It more fully simulates the feeling of a person being there (i.e., social presence) than text-based media. In fact, some researchers (e.g., Kross et al., 2013) have combined voice calls with FtF communication in their analyses, calling it "direct communication." According to LSAY data from 2009 and 2011, weekly voice calls among members of Generation X actually *increased* over three years (from 4.86 per week to 6.11 per week) during a period of rapid social media adoption (Hall, Xing, & Kearny, 2019b). Although this may be due to the particular time of life of these individuals (e.g., aging into their late thirties and perhaps having children), the phone call niche still has a particular place in American households.

The medium that has experienced the most significant growth in terms of social interaction has been text-based channels of communication. First-year students in 2009 (as studied by Hall et al., 2011) were already using SMS to have social interactions at a rate five times that of IM, further suggesting that IM had hit its peak use only a few years prior.

By the time that mobile integration with social media had begun (i.e., the wireless internet), SMS had to directly compete with chat programs tied to social media (e.g., Facebook chat, Instagram chat), and with stand-alone apps (e.g., GroupMe; WhatsApp). Importantly, all served very similar functions as SMS, although having the characteristic of not being linked to a phone number but to a social media account. This transition can be seen in the growth from 4% to 7% of social interactions early on, to 15–17% by the end of 2018.

3.4 Other Mediated Social Interactions

The remaining options received very little of the total percentage of inter-actions across respondents, studies, and groups. Two to five percent of all social interactions took place through social media. As I reported (Hall, 2018b), this is partly due to the fact that once excluding chat/messenger programs, the vast majority of social media activities are unrecognizable as social interactions to users themselves. As people spend an increasing amount of time on social media, they actually are less likely to socially interact (Hall, 2018b). Furthermore, the highest percentage across studies (in the study by Bayer et al., 2016) had an exceedingly inclusive definition of interaction: any communication on all social media.

Only two studies offered video calls as an option for measuring frequency of social interaction, but reported vastly different results. The more recent sample reported that 1.3% of interactions were on video calls; the other study (Vlahovic et al., 2012) had video calls second only to FtF communication based on number of minutes. I suspect there are two reasons for this. Like voice calls, video chats steer toward conversation, particularly with people who are far away (Eden & Veksler, 2016; Yang et al., 2014). If there is a reason to call, then it is a more intentional, engaged, and time-consuming form of communication.

To clarify these results, I contacted the lead author Dr. Vlahovic via email, and she told me that the sample "had a lot of international students at Oxford who had family, friends, and romantic partners far away," and those who used Skype would "leave it on while they did other activities and interacted occasionally with their partner" (personal communication, July 9, 2018). As indicated by other research (Yang et al., 2014), international students tend to favor Skype and email over other forms of communication, such as voice calls, for pricing concerns among other reasons.

As the options for personal media continue, there is certainly a strong possibility of growth for these media, but according to recent research, they still are distant options compared with FtF, SMS or chat, and voice calls.

SECTION FOUR: ENDURING MODALITIES

[Typologies of media] creating media categories that are exhaustive and mutually exclusive remains a particular challenge.
—Malcolm Parks (2017, p. 513)

As a final component of this chapter, I thought it would be valuable to consider the future of these media niches. As functions and platforms change, especially social media platforms, it is critical be careful of what "counts" for each type of mode of communication. To make such differentiations, I am partial to Baym's (2015) seven dimensions on which personal media can vary (see the Introduction). Among those, the characteristics useful for comparing personal media are the temporal structure, social cues, reach, and mobility. Each of the personal media discussed earlier, with the exception of social media due to the multiplicity of affordances, varies on each of these dimensions.

Focusing on social interaction (not all acts of communication or virtual people watching) and sensitive to the relational purposes of media use, I will try to identify modes of communication that may endure. I am not suggesting they will continue to exist in their present form; rather, they will be folded into existing and new apps and social media platforms that will compete for user attention.

I believe the least mobile form of social interaction, namely, FtF interaction, is not going to disappear. All the other modes discussed below are mediated in some way and all are mobile and likely to remain so. But the perfect synchrony, low reach, zero mobility, and high social cues modality of FtF communication will continue to occupy a central place in the study of human sociality and relationship maintenance. I believe the evidence from Table 4.1 continues to point to its importance during a period of dramatic mobile phone adoption and social media integration.

And as a final point of caution, the more we, as a research community, feel it necessary to document each glance, touch, or acknowledgment at or through one's mobile device as an example of "media use," a true apples-to-apples comparison with FtF communication must take into account each glance, look, and acknowledgment at people who are physically co-present. We must be careful in making comparisons between FtF communication and media use, and must seek to use as similar units of analysis as possible whenever possible.

4.1 High Synchrony, High Social Cues, Low Reach Modes

Two modes of communication are the best fit to these dimensions: voice and video calls. Like FtF communication, both are highly synchronous and convey a great deal of social cues. As reported in Chapter 3, these two modalities stand alone in terms of their high degree of social energy expenditure. Video calls convey more nonverbal cues than voice calls, especially as the strength and quality of the transmission has improved and faces are much clearer. This is also low reach communication. Both voice and video calls have low upper limits to the number of people who can participate before communication becomes unwieldy or takes on a one-to-many form, like a lecture or conference call, which I do not include in this category.

As for the final characteristic, mobility, I expect that the value of being able to place and take calls from one's mobile device will not abate. This does not mean that everyone will choose to hold their conversations while on the go, only that they are unlikely to wish for a return to a time where mobility was restricted to the length of the telephone cord. Rather, I expect that when maintaining personal relationships, people will sometimes favor long conversations, which give ample time for catching up, but at other times people will call to quickly convey and share information (Rettie, 2007), just as they have since the early days of landline phone adoption (Fischer, 1992).

Interestingly, new research (Vlahovic et al., 2012) has suggested that video calls have become a way to increase co-presence by relaxing the standard of needing to communicate while "on" the medium. Other research has reported that young couples in long-distance romantic relationships keep their video lines open throughout the night so they can virtually sleep together (Neustaedter & Greenberg, 2012). Could it be that the formality assumed with telephone calls could break down and the majority of people will become comfortable with leaving video lines open continuously with loved ones?

Would that change people's comfort or energy use when using such media? If video chat becomes a dominant mode of communication, further research will be needed on such questions.

Imagine a tablet hung on a wall in one's home that is a virtual window into the home of grandchildren or long-distance partners. Residents could turn it on or off when available and interested in catching up, similar to IM's available versus busy feature (Quan-Haase, 2007). Families could walk to it, look in and see which family members or friends around the globe are "home" on the tablet. Like walking over to the fence separating neighbors, future media might be comfortable with signaling to loved ones far away that one is interested in virtually hanging out.

4.2 Moderate Synchrony, Low Social Cues, Low Reach Modes

As Rich Ling stated in 2010: "In all likelihood, there will be a strong need for texting or at least mobile, asynchronous, point-to-point, text-based mediation" (p. 289). I restrict this category to text-based communication to few others and kept intentionally low in social cues conveyed. The vast array of conveniences enabled by text-based exchanges, both as shorter SMS and potentially longer emails, is too important for relationship maintenance and convenience to die out. As Ling (2004) documents so well, the value of micro-coordinating schedules, grocery store trips, and family affairs for couples with mobile SMS was big push in the rise of text adoption. SMS exchanges are flexible enough to be personal and conversational, and tend to remain in form and use medium synchrony (as people take time to compose the messages they send back, or get back to the message when they can), yet low in social cues.

Arnold (2003) pointed out that longer forms of communication, in the form of both long conversations on the phone and long form letters, are just the opposite on the dialectic of more engaged and shorter conveyance of personal information (Hall & Baym, 2012; Rettie, 2007). Is it possible that long-form email exchanged for purely for the sake of conversation will die out? To my knowledge, there isn't any research that documents how many people still use email to maintain relationships through long-form, infrequent letters, but I would be surprised if the portion of people doing so has never been very high, especially after long-distance calls were possible and IM use became widespread (Quan-Haase, 2007). While the slow death of the long letter form of communication may continue, I expect it has not been a major component of the majority of people's relationship maintenance for some time.

Will text programs become increasingly supplemented by hypertexts with embedded videos or audio recordings or GIFs? Could text exchanges become a higher social cue medium, perhaps more similar to SNS posts and feed? Sharing pictures through mobile devices has grown dramatically, and the emergence of short videos on platforms such as Snapchat may signal an interest in such forms of communication. Perhaps some version of SMS richly supplemented by nontextual video, audio, and visual cues might augment SMS in the future in a more normative and fully developed manner in the future.

4.3 Moderate to High Synchrony, Low to Moderate Social Cues, Moderate Reach Modes

One of the key features of chat programs since their inception has been the visibility of knowledge about who else is available to chat at any given time (Mesch et al., 2012; Ramirez et al., 2008). Both group texting and chat programs steer users toward a more medium reach mode of communication. Although certainly functional for group correspondence and planning, it also promotes hanging out in a medium (O'Hara et al., 2014). This type of mode of communication steers users toward others who are presently responsive and available, pressing toward more synchrony (see Chapter 3). For the sake of this chapter, it makes sense to me that there may be a continuing niche for modes of social interaction that enable "on ongoing but background aware-ness of the presence or nearness of others" (Chayko, 2018, p. 53). The feeling of others' availability is undoubtedly a key feature of social media, but it is sustained only through steady compliance by users to log in and provide content (Donath, 2007; Orchard, Fullwood, Morris, & Galbraith, 2015). Par-ticularly for tweens and teens whose access to social spaces is scant and becoming increasingly monitored and controlled (boyd, 2014), the desire to maintain access to friends outside the home seems unlikely to come to an end. Online spaces to hang out and feel connected to friends appear to have replaced FtF interaction for adolescents as their opportunities to go to malls and parties or take leisurely car rides all decline (Twenge et al., 2018b).

Early uses of IM steered users toward hanging out online (Quan-Haase, 2007; Quan-Haase & Collins, 2008; Ramirez et al., 2008), and this medium required some text exchange. Through social media, hanging out online often does not include social interaction, "but still sensing others' presence in an ambient way" (Chayko, 2018, p. 54). There is good reason to believe that the niche these types of modes of communication occupy *may not be* one of directly interacting, which means they are underreported in Table 4.1 of social interactions. Instead, the purpose may be to enjoy the sociality without the burden or obligations of reciprocity or response – just to see and be seen.

4.4 Moderate Synchrony, Moderate Social Cues, Medium to High Reach Modes

This form of communication is most notable in online behavior in social media environments with existing networks of others. The value and endur-ance of these modes are given greater attention in Chapter 6.

4.5 Low Synchrony, Low Social Cues, High Reach Modes

The earliest internet enabled the possibility of creating online communities and spaces with others who shared a hobby or interest (Baym, 2000). Formal and informal online support groups are numerous and increasingly studied in terms of their effects on well-being, health, and recovery (Rains & Young, 2009). These modes of communication do not expect individuals to be co-present, and many times one of the benefits of the resources is that they are available at all times. These modes of communication are extremely high reach: one of the interesting characteristics of this mode, compared with all others, is that it invites communication with strangers.

The revolutionary sense of sociality created in such spaces is not a central space for maintaining existing relationships, but perhaps forming new ones and extending beyond one's existing network (Chayko, 2014). They complement FtF relationships and hold the possibility of developing into ones through repeated interaction. There is no question that online-only relationships can proceed and grow without FtF contact, and that this opportunity is unlikely to abate. In some sense, this is still perhaps the most distinct type of mode of relationship maintenance, although also one of the oldest and least used.

SECTION FIVE: CONCLUSION

New options for mediated communication continue unabated, but centrality of FtF communication for social interaction is incredibly stable. This means the potentiality of mediated communication far exceeds individuals' patterns of using media to socially interact. As the voice call to text trade-off suggests, slight adjustments to existing, familiar modes are certainly more likely than wholesale displacement and disruption. No mode is totally displaced, but as niche theory would suggest they coexist. As Chan (2015) points out, after individuals choose to use a new technology, it enables the possibility of forming unexpected or unintended niches. Newer media might yet come to offer means of communicating that are yet unanticipated.

At the same time, the making do and energy-conserving forces discussed in prior chapters suggest that these processes are likely to be slow and gradual rather than disruptive. As Ling (2010) cautions, just because the young people are using a new means of communication does not mean they will continue to do so. This is a particularly important note of caution for researchers or members of the general public who believe that because young people are doing it, it is here to stay and it will disrupt all prior means of communicating. Relationships have long been multimodal, and this fact is unlikely to change. The means of maintaining relationships will shift, but several modes of communication will endure in conjunction with FtF communication rather than in opposition to it.

5

Mode Comparison and Coexistence

In Chapter 4, I argued that the gradual emergence and displacement of personal media can be understood as media competing with one another to occupy users' time and attention. I also asserted that despite dramatic changes in the availability of opportunities to communicate, especially as smartphone apps have multiplied, FtF is still the dominant form of social interaction in the daily lives of most people. Although voice calls have waned and SMS and mobile chat programs waxed, few of the newest forms of communication have dramatically swelled in terms of frequency of use for the purpose of social interaction.

The goal of the present chapter is threefold. This chapter will examine the idea that modern relationships are multimodal and will try to bring the niche perspective into alignment with MMT and CBB theories. Second, this chapter will address a question of comparison: How do these different media line up in terms of psychosocial outcomes and patterns of use? Finally, the concept of layers of electronic intimacy – that some media are more frequently used at particular levels of closeness – will be developed.

SECTION ONE: MULTIMODAL MODERN RELATIONSHIPS

Social life, including important interpersonal relationships, may have become *mediatized*, but it is also the case that the media have become *interpersonalized*. As we have seen, the media individuals use for communication have become increasing aligned with the rhythms and structure of their personal relationships and social networks.

—Malcolm Parks (2017, p. 513)

Daily life is rhythmic. There are well-known patterns of sleeping and waking, eating and drinking, but it is becoming clear that social life also has rhythm. People seek solitude at some times and company at other times (Hall, 2017b; O'Connor & Rosenblood, 1996). In the morning, people seem more content to be alone, while in the evening they prefer to be in the company of or communicating with others (Aledavood et al., 2015; Hall, 2017b; Wiessner, 2014). Most of the time a brief check-in or "hello" will do, but other times deeper conversation is desired. Personal media offer a means of doing both with friends and family near and far.

The idea that media have become *interpersonalized* is consistent with the SCOT perspective addressed in Chapter 2. Media can be tools for relationship building, introduced and folded into the patterns of life. Yes, it is true that the global north is saturated by media, wherein media influence nearly every aspect of citizens' daily lives. At the same time, people across the world, from mothers and grandmothers of Filipino migrant workers (Madianou & Miller, 2012) to Columbian families (Velasquez, 2018), are bending media to their own relational ends.

Chapter 4 documented personal media use from an either/or perspective through the lens of media niche and frequency of social interactions. This chapter argues that once the menu of media options is established in individuals' daily lives, they select media throughout the day to meet their psychological needs and communicative goals (Madianou & Miller, 2012; Parks, 2017; Quan-Haase & Collins, 2008; van Kruistum et al., 2014). I argue in this chapter that modern multimodal relationships must still conform to humans' psychological makeup. In other words, the need to belong will always exist, no matter how many media we have to choose from. The all-too-human struggle to stay present and build nourishing relationships with others underlies the public debates about the influence of media on our lives. One way to understand how people navigate these demands – to select media, to accomplish communicative goals, within the context of relationships – is to explore how and why people engage in channel switching or modality switching (Ramirez & Wang, 2008).

1.1 Both/And, Not Either/Or

I am not the first to suggest that the balance of FtF communication and media use in modern relationships is more characteristic of a both/and than an either/or perspective (e.g., Baym, 2015; Chan, 2015; Parks, 2017; Rainie & Wellman, 2012). Nor am I the first to recognize that research must grapple with the *who*, *when*, and *why* of mediated personal connections (e.g., Arnold, 2003; Baron, 2011). Although the either/or perspective will be given full attention in Chapter 9 where I discuss social displacement, what I hope to establish in this chapter is just how closely media use tracks the nature and interdependence level of the relationship.

There are two ways to think about this association: at the individual level and at the population level. Both are instructive in different ways.

At the individual level, there is a well-known trend that strong ties use more media to communicate – a trend powerful enough to give rise to MMT

(Haythornthwaite, 2005) (see Chapter 3). Among articles that attend to both the closeness of the relationship partner and the type of media, this association has been long known (e.g., Baym et al., 2004) and consistently found in recent work (e.g., Tillema et al., 2010; van den Berg et al., 2012). When relationships are stronger and more interdependent, more modes of communication are used to maintain them. And this is not necessarily a process of replacing FtF interactions. For example, more interdependence in friendships is associated with *both* FtF and online relationship maintenance (Ledbetter, 2010).

At the population level, people who engage in more social interactions are more likely to use more personal media to do so. Although there is good reason to believe this may be due to underlying personality (Requena & Ayuso, 2018; Tillema et al., 2010; Twenge et al., 2019), it may also be due to the practicalities of maintaining a larger social network. If people have a large social network, they tend to engage in more interactions in general (Tillema et al., 2010; van den Berg et al., 2012), specifically, greater use of IM and mobile phones (Hampton et al., 2011) and SMS or texting (Hall, 2017a). This research finding has also been tracked over time. Those who use social media more frequently within a day are more likely to engage in FtF and IM contact six months in the future (Dienlin, Masur, & Trepte, 2017). Those who use more personal media tend to interact more frequently FtF as well (Requena & Ayuso, 2018).

1.2 Media Multiplexity Theory and Communicate Bond Belong Theory

Why is this trend so prevalent? The answer is directly addressed in two of the theories reviewed in Chapter 3. MMT suggests that the association between the number of media used in a relationship and the strength of the tie is bidirectional (Ledbetter, 2015), but there is increasing evidence that tie strength drives media use more than the other way around. A recent test of the theory (Taylor & Barazova, 2018) demonstrates that in romantic relationships the closeness of the relationship appears to drive the addition of new media over time, but adding media did not influence future closeness. In Chapter 3, I suggested that these results offer strong support for the argument that multimodal connectedness between partners is a sign of interdependence (Caughlin & Sharabi, 2013). As the interdependence of a relationship grows, the need for diverse and multiple modalities grows as well.

Chapter 3 also introduced CBB theory (Hall & Davis, 2017), which argued that the need to belong, energy conservation, and homeostatic patterns of sociality should be considered when studying media choice for the purpose of social interaction. While MMT presumes that each channel is equivalent and interchangeable with another (Ledbetter, 2015), CBB theory presumes that channels vary by two important factors: energy expenditure and its ability to satisfy relatedness needs. These two factors should influence which channel people use in relation to their underlying need state. In Chapter 3, I argued that while social media expends very little energy, it is not well suited to satisfy relatedness needs. This complements the interdependence perspective. CBB theory argues that when social interaction is seen from the perspective of relationship building and maintenance, then the purpose of social interaction with close others is for meeting relatedness needs and for ongoing investment in the relationship. Once the assumptions of why we interact with close partners are established, the theory offers additional factors that likely influence media choice in ongoing relationships.

1.3 Channel Switching

There is a developing interest in studying toggling between modalities with a particular relationship partner, which is known as channel switching (Baym, 2009; Caughlin & Sharabi, 2013) or modality switching (Rameriz & Wang, 2008). This perspective assumes that close relationships are multimodal and assumes that streams of discourse between partners flow between various modes of communication (Scissors & Gergle, 2013; Sharabi & Caughlin, 2017a). This perspective suggests that channel switching is unlikely to be motivated by adding modes of communication for their own sake. Rather, the management of communication *across* modes is a crucial and underappreciated factor in understanding media's role in personal relationships. In romantic relationships, channel integration is associated with closeness, and those who struggle to manage communication between channels tend to be less close and satisfied (Caughlin & Sharabi, 2013). More mode segmentation is negatively associated with closeness and satisfaction (Taylor & Barazova, 2018).

Online dating is a great example of channel switching. Although people use online dating services and apps for a variety of reasons, the most common goal of online dating is to eventually meet potential romantic partners in person (Toma & D'Angelo, 2017). Undoubtedly, online romantic and sexual play is titillating and is an oft-promoted feature of some online dating platforms. But when meeting FtF is a goal, online dating is fundamentally an issue of channel switching, and research suggests that timing matters (Ramirez & Wang, 2008; Ramirez, Summer, Fleuriet, & Cole, 2015; Sharabi & Caughlin, 2017b). When people take too long to move from online textual communication to meeting FtF, it tends to predict worse outcomes. When potential dates shared more photos before meeting, it reduces uncertainty and tempers expectations, increasing positive outcomes (Ramirez et al., 2015). Asking questions before meeting also plays a similar role in managing expectations (Sharabi & Caughlin, 2017a). To prevent idealization and dashed expectations, online daters must clarify their expectations and actively learn about one another via the online dating site's features.

I would suspect that coordination between channels may be associated with dating success. Daters inevitably compare online profiles with the person they meet in person (Ellison, Hancock, & Toma, 2012; Toma & D'Angelo, 2017), and may look for other online sources (e.g., Google, social media) to cross-check a potential partner's profile (Toma & D'Angelo, 2017). In initial emails to potential dates, referencing aspects of the partner's profile encourages relationship development (Sharabi & Dykstra-DeVette, 2019). Beyond the link between profile and email, which could be conceived of channel switching, I would guess that daters who effectively recall and integrate online communication content – either from the profile or from the online conversations – into conversation on a FtF date are more effective at moving into the next stage of romantic relationship development. Doing so shows the person has taken the time to learn about a potential partner. Given our multimodal world, this may be a good test of being able to coordinate future streams of communication between channels – an important skill in modern committed romantic relationships.

My enthusiasm for channel switching as a research perspective and research on the timing and process of online to offline switches stems from what I perceive to be a lack of appreciation of differences between channels in research. Too many researchers seem content to add up frequency of communication from a list of modes and platforms and conclude that they have measured communication. This is not to say that the number of channels isn't one part of the puzzle, but doing so collapses the variation between platforms and modes in a way that presumes equivalence between channels. As the next section illustrates, this issue of channel comparison has a long shadow in CMC research and is hotly contested to this day. Differences or equivalences between modes and platforms should not be presumed theoretically, but should be better explored and understood.

SECTION TWO: CHANNEL COMPARISON RESEARCH

Even if we accept that face-to-face communication provides a kind of social connection that simply cannot be attained with mediation, it does not follow that mediated communication, even in lean media, is emotionally or socially impoverished, or that social context cannot be achieved.
—Nancy Baym (2015, p. 64)

Comparing mediated communication with FtF communication was a staple of early CMC research (e.g., Walther, 1995). Both twenty-five years ago and today, technology enthusiasts felt there was an implicit (if not explicit) diminishment of online communication in research that compared various modes of communication with FtF communication. This was likely due to the noted prejudices of MRT and social presence theories (Baym, 2010; Walther, 2011) (see Chapter 3). Due to that long shadow, privileging FtF social interactions is sometimes seen as a prejudice of research itself. What I like about Baym's quote above is that talking about what a medium is like on average is not the same thing as diminishing what it could do or has done for relational partners. (From a statistical perspective, it is important not to conflate variance or range with mean or central tendency, but I digress.)

This section will grapple with the idea of equivalence between channels first from the perspective of usage and then from a perspective of psychological and social outcomes. I hope to clarify the degree to which privileging of FtF in contemporary and classic CMC research is appropriate and consistent with empirical evidence. Then, I share new research evidence from my own unpublished data to explore the overlap between relationship partner type and mode of communication.

2.1 Comparison in Utility or Purpose

To begin, it is important to acknowledge that media are shaped by the way they are used, not by features intrinsic to the technology. That people *choose* to use media in a particular way or for a particular purpose does not mean that the media cannot be used in a different way. Technology may be designed with one purpose in mind, but people may not use it in that way. Instead, people engage with the features of the media, select among them, modify or exploit their features, and test out and develop patterns of use in the context of relationships (Barkuus & Polichar, 2011; Madianou & Miller, 2012). Because this process is dyadic in nature – partners adjust their media use in response to one another, and relationships are constituted by the type of communication within them – individuals cannot *make* others use media in a particular way, even in the context of a relationship. For example, struggles over how and when to text is a common source of conflict in new romantic relationships (Miller-Ott & Kelly, 2016). It is more accurate to say that people use media in way that signals the type of relationship they would like to have with their partner (e.g., think flirtatious texts). People use media to implicitly or explicitly convey messages about future types and modes of interaction (e.g., "let's meet up IRL") (Sharabi & Caughlin 2017b; Sharabi & Dykstra-DeVette, 2019).

With this caveat in mind, noting differences between media is as old as the study of personal media itself. In presenting past research and my own evidence below, I accept that it likely reflects already established patterns of use and characteristics of the modality (e.g., number of social cues).

As summarized in my review of enduring niches in Chapter 4, people generally see media that more closely approximate FtF conversation as being in a different class, especially compared with modalities that inspire patterns of use that are very different from FtF interaction. Throughout the world, voice calls and video chat are often reserved for moments when longer, more engaged conversations are desired or more intimate or important information is exchanged (Duran & Kelly, 2017; Eden & Veksler, 2016; Madianou & Miller, 2012; Tillema et al., 2010). When keeping in touch with friends over long distances, telephone calls replace the lost FtF contact (Ruppel & Burke, 2015). Voice calls also tend to show positive effects similar to FtF conversation (Kross et al., 2013). Throughout the course of a week, having intimate phone calls is associated with change in well-being (Hall, 2017a).

Although they offer benefits, voice calls and video chats are seen as more work than other online communication (Baron & Campbell, 2012) and a signal of greater relationship closeness (Yang et al., 2014). When comparing the two, voice calls are perceived as less burdensome than video chat, and have the excellent ability to cut through the asynchrony and uncertainty of text messages, rendering them a quick and efficient way to clarify communication between partners (Eden & Veksler, 2016) or to stem conflict (Madianou & Miller, 2012; Scissors & Gergle, 2013). But when convenience is important and the message is informational in nature, voice calls can be seen as too time consuming, an interruption, or simply unnecessary (Baron & Campbell, 2012; Quinn, 2013; Rettie, 2007).

Since the introduction of text messaging, both researchers and users have noted its efficiency and utility (Baron & Campbell, 2012; Eden & Veksler, 2016; Ling 2004; Rettie, 2007; Sheer, 2011). As mobility has taken hold, IM or chatting through social media has been viewed in a very similar way as SMS, surely due to their functional similarity (Eden & Veksler, 2016). These two modes are valued because of their utility while the user is otherwise engaged – they neatly fold into lived life with minimal interference and maximal convenience (Ling, 2004; Rettie, 2007). That is, given lower expectations of availability and synchrony than a phone call, people can carry on chat and SMS interactions via a mobile device without totally interrupting what they are doing. (Chapter 9 addresses how this affects co-present partners.)

As a holdover from the 1990s, email tends to be regarded by young adults (Eden & Veksler, 2016) and working adults (Kim et al., 2007) as an impersonal, professional, or official means of communication. This has undergone a massive change since the 1990s when it was seen as an important means of keeping in touch with loved ones, more akin to long-distance phone calls (Boase et al., 2006; Flanagin & Metzger, 2001). More recent research suggests email is reserved for important rather than urgent communication topics, but even then primarily with colleagues and or acquaintances (Tillema et al., 2010). Less than 14% of people chose email to discuss important matters with close friends and family (Tillema et al., 2010). In data collected in my recent article on mobile entrapment (i.e., Hall, 2017a), the most common response for using email to contact close friends and family was "never." Similar to Tillema et al.'s findings, my research found that when participants did use email for personal correspondence, it was usually on a monthly or semi-monthly basis. I would also suspect that long, elaborate letter writing is even rare among those who use email to keep in touch. This is a good example of how a medium *could be* used in a very personal way, but that pattern of use can change as a consequence of better or preferable options.

Finally, there is widespread agreement that social media use – specifically public posts or status updates, likes and one-click acknowledgments – is a low effort, efficient means of sharing information with a large group of people (e.g., Baym, 2015; Eden & Veksler, 2016). Depending on the degree of overlap between the first fifteen and social media friend or follower network, social media can be used as a means of quickly conveying a great deal of information with a tight group of others compared with other modes of communication. However, this efficiency comes with trade-offs. Announcing important information in this way is insulting to close friends, such as not telling close friends about a wedding engagement before announcing it on social media (Bryant & Marmo, 2012). Even conveying less important information through social media has risks. Frequent social media updates are associated with less closeness between relational partners (Burke & Kraut, 2014), even between particular friends (McEwan, 2013). Attending to the content of the post, it appears that more superficial media updates are associated with less satisfaction and liking between friends (Rains et al., 2016).

Ruppel et al. (2017) examined experimental studies comparing self-disclosure FtF and CMC communication and found that video and text-based CMC has less self-disclosure than FtF communication. Ruppel and colleagues caution, however, that research does not provide sufficient information on self-disclosure in the context of ongoing relationships because the majority of research on self-disclosure studies new acquaintance interactions. As Utz (2015) found in a recent study of self-disclosure on Facebook, when self-disclosure is more intimate, it leads to stronger feelings of connection, but only in private, directed social media messages. In public status updates, disclosure intimacy was associated with closeness only if partners were already close (Utz, 2015), which suggests that the relationship between the partners makes a considerable difference in the value of mediated message interactions.

2.2 Comparison by Psychosocial Outcomes and Need Satisfaction

Given the history of comparing whatever mode that is popular or ascendant with FtF communication, most comparative research does not clearly differentiate between more than one mediated channel at a time. Early studies point to the comparative value of FtF over telephone calls and email to feel included, to feel affection, and to stay in touch (e.g., Flaherty, Pearce, & Rubin, 1998; Flanagin & Metzger, 2001). Recent research suggests that the amount of FtF contact is more strongly associated with subjective well-being than contact by phone or internet (van der Horst & Coffe, 2012). In a representative sample of Americans, the amount of FtF time with friends and family both predicted increased life satisfaction and lower loneliness, but the amount of email and other internet-based modalities had no such positive effects (Stepanikova, Nie, & He, 2010). Similar results were found in a representative sample of Canadians where the number of offline friends had a positive association with life satisfaction and happiness, but the number of online friends did not (Helliwell & Huang, 2013). This is not to say that online communication is not crucial to maintaining relationships that do not have the benefit of frequent FtF contact. These findings only point to the comparative value of FtF contact and relationships over online contact and relationships.

More recent cross-sectional research comparing FtF with contact via text/ IM or social media has found that FtF communication is more capable of meeting individuals' needs for inclusion and closeness and is more able to build connection (Ahn & Shin, 2013; Liu & Yang, 2016). IM appears to be no more likely to meet relatedness needs than social media (Bayer et al., 2016; Liu & Yang, 2016). In initial interactions between strangers, FtF contact is more able to meet relatedness needs (Sprecher, 2014) and creates a more positive mood than IM (Sacco & Ismail, 2014). Finally, in my own work (e.g., Hall et al., 2019b), I found that social media use is associated with a decline in well-being later in the day, but only when individuals are alone at later times in the day. We interpreted those findings as suggesting that social media use (outside the context of a social interaction) does not satisfy belongingness needs.

There is a remarkable consistency across studies that suggests that FtF communication has primacy over all other modes of communication when it comes to meeting relationship needs and generating affective well-being and connection. This has led some researchers to claim that FtF communication is different (in a statistical sense) from all other forms of communication (e.g., Vlahovic et al., 2012). Across a large spectrum of responses from young adults, FtF is also *perceived* as more adaptable to a wide range of emotions, communication goals, and relationship partners; it is still considered the best form of communication by 83% of young adults (Duran & Kelly, 2017; Eden & Veksler, 2016). This finding echoes the perceptions of young internet users twenty years ago, who also privileged FtF interactions (Flanagin & Metzger, 2001). When romantic partners recognize that some topics are best discussed in person, meaning they grant special privilege to FtF communication, they are closer and more satisfied in their relationship (Caughlin & Sharabi, 2013). Although nearly ten years has passed since this observation was made, I concur with Tufekci (2010), who wrote: "face-to-face interaction has inimitable features that simply cannot be replicated or replaced by any other form of communication" (p. 176). At least, not yet.

2.3 For *That* Relationship Yes, but on Average No

But what does it really mean that people on average self-report and perceive greater levels of closeness, connection, relatedness, and affective well-being during FtF exchanges compared with all other modes of social interaction across relationships and contexts and studies? Allow me to summarize:

- It does *not* mean that mediated social interactions are unable to be superlative in quality or that they are unable to convey important meaning. It *does* mean that interactions via media are of lesser quality from FtF interaction *on average* beyond statistical rates of chance across years and across studies.
- It does *not* mean that certain relationships, such as long-distance friends or romantic partners, cannot use mediated communication to keep their relationships in good health. For centuries, people have believed that mediated social interactions are important for maintaining long-distance relationships. From handwritten letters to telegrams to telephone calls to email to Facebook, each of these technologies carried personal messages of care and concern, updates on major life events and goings-on. They all can carry the relationship-sustaining message, "Though far away, you are with me." Communication re-creates and nourishes long-distance relationships into continued existence.
- It does *not* mean that new relationships cannot be found and cemented through media. The incredible success of online dating proves otherwise.
- It does *not* mean that a person cannot have a special, unique, or even transcendent experience when communicating online with someone. This is particularly important for those who are stigmatized and feel alone within their geographically proximal communities.

In accord with SCOT, some relationships may establish patterns of mediated interaction through media that are important to the relationship partners because they sustain the particular nature of the relationship. An undergraduate in my upper-level course told me that online gaming with friends back at home helped keep the routines of friendship alive while he was away at college. Personally, I use Words with Friends to keep in daily contact with my father, whom I see and talk to less frequently than I wish. The Scrabble-like game recreates our FtF games in my home growing up and keeps me in touch with him. A greater attention to the type of relationship being maintained through media might reveal even more findings of this nature. For example, Vlahovic et al. (2012) found that IM and text exchanges were more pleasant in the context of friendship than they were with family and romantic partners. Yang et al. (2014) found that international students relied on email and video chat at much higher rates than American students.

The confusion about what privileging FtF communication means is made worse by the fact that many correlational studies do not control for the preexisting nature of the relationship. Experience-sampling studies that measure partner type (e.g., Vlahovic et al., 2012) and experimental designs that account for relationship stage (e.g., Sacco & Ismail, 2014; Sprecher, 2014; Utz, 2015) offer partial solutions to these problems, but they are among the minority of study designs. In their meta-analysis of self-disclosure through CMC, Ruppel et al. (2017) point out that even when studies use data collected from multimodal, preexisting relationships, the nature of these relationships (e.g., closeness, type) is rarely explored and measured. When studies collapse all communication across relationship partners, it further obscures the role of the relationship in predicting outcomes. Statistically speaking, any longitudinal or cross-sectional study that does not attend to *who* is on the other side of the message when measuring communication essentially (and problematically) conflates mode with partner type and/or closeness.

This means that although more FtF communication may be associated with more connection, it does not demonstrate that this is not due to a greater frequency of communication that is FtF with close relationship partners. It is quite likely that whom you are communicating with explains more variance in the quality and connection than the mode of communication (Baym et al., 2004; Hall, 2018a). To test that very idea, I present the results from two of my own data sets.

2.4 Comparisons by Mode

Table 5.1 summarizes findings from two data sets – the first collected in 2015 and the second in 2018 (Merolla & Hall, 2018). In the first data set, 116 college students and working adults received five short surveys at random times throughout the day for five consecutive days (i.e., an experience-sampling design). In the second data set, 127 adults received five short surveys for seven days. In both cases, the first question was, Have you had a social interaction in the past ten minutes? If they had, they were asked what mode they interacted through. The response options were slightly different between studies (social media was an option only in 2015, video chat was an option only in 2018). Then they were asked what the nature of the relationship with the person on the other end was. This was measured in two different ways between studies. In 2015, it was four categories of relationship, from close friend and family to stranger, but in 2018 it was on a seven-point scale of how established the relationship was. Finally, everyone was asked follow-up questions about how connected and positive they felt (i.e., closeness, affective well-being).

2.5 Frequencies and Means

The results in Table 5.1 support the conclusion that FtF communication stands apart – people feel less lonely, more connected, and more positive after FtF interaction when compared with any other mode of interaction. There is one exception to this – video chat, which is both connecting and associated with good feelings at similar rates.

TABLE 5.1 Comparisons of loneliness, closeness, affective well-being, and relationship type by mode of social interaction

Mode	n Interactions	Loneliness[a] M	SD	Closeness M	SD	Affective well-being M	SD	Relationship type[b] %1	%2	%3	%4	Established[a] relationship M	SD
Face-to-face	3,231	1.87	1.30	4.95	1.49	75.28	17.88	51	24	18	7	5.87	2.01
Voice call	417	2.16	1.53	4.62	1.59	72.09	21.22	67	13	12	9	5.10	2.45
SMS/text	688	2.12	1.42	4.50	1.45	71.67	19.34	57	32	12	0	6.45	1.32
Social media[b]	48			4.50	1.44	69.04	15.23	21	42	29	8		
Video call[a]	34	2.30	1.69	5.76	1.48	82.84	14.36					6.41	1.58

Note: Loneliness, closeness, affective well-being, and established relationships measured on seven-point scales, affective well-being on 100-point scale (where 100 is feeling extremely good and 0 is feeling absolutely awful).

[a] Video chat interactions asked only in 2018 study; loneliness felt after a social interaction only reported in 2018 study (n = 1,845); 2018 established relationship measure: 1 = not at all established relationship, 4 = somewhat established relationship, 7 = established relationship.

[b] Social interactions through social media asked only in 2015 study; 2015 relationship type categories: 1 = close friends/family, 2 = friends/family, 3 = acquaintances, 4 = strangers.

There is a pattern to the types of people participants talk to through each mode. FtF communication is a means of communicating with close others and strangers alike (see also Boase et al., 2006). This also reinforces Ruppel and Burke's (2015) conclusion that FtF communication operates independently from patterns of online media use. This diversity can be seen in Table 5.1, which demonstrates that we communicate FtF with other people in somewhat established relationships often, but there is a lot of variability in how established those relationships are (i.e., a high standard deviation).

Channel comparisons often reveal some interesting quirks about patterns of communication. For example, voice calls are made both with our most intimate partners *and* with strangers. I expect this is a carryover from the days when one's phone number was the only publicly available means of contact. Intriguingly, participants used the phone to communicate with both strangers and close partners at the highest rates compared with the three other channels.

Consistent with other research about the role of texting and IM-type chat programs, close friends and family exchange SMS and chat messages, but this mode is a frequently used means to communicate with friends at intermediate levels of closeness (Duran, Kelly, & Rotaru, 2011; Liu & Yang, 2016; Quan-Haase & Collins, 2008). It is also interesting that it is *not* a means of socially interacting with strangers (0 percent). Rather, participants were more likely to communicate with people in established relationships when texting and chatting (i.e., the highest percentage for that category).

Finally, the last two modes were both comparatively rare, and they were used to communicate with very different types of people. For the few people who had social interactions through social media, it skewed toward less established relationships – particularly acquaintances. By contrast, video calls were reserved for established relationship partners, and generated very positive feelings.

2.6 Statistical Results

These data offer the unique chance to resolve the question, Do we feel better and more connected when we communicate through a particular mode because of something about the way we use it or because of whom we are communicating with? There is good evidence that interactions with closer relationship partners are more satisfying and important to our well-being than interactions with less close partners, independent of what things we talk about (Hall, 2018a). So, this debate about what mode we use versus whom we communicate with is quite important.

To answer this question, all 4,434 interactions for all 243 participants were analyzed using multilevel modeling (MLM). I first ran the analyses without controlling for relationship type. These analyses confirmed the means reported across the top of Table 5.1. Specifically, FtF communication was associated with significantly less loneliness, more closeness and more connection, and more positive feelings (i.e., affective well-being) when compared with voice calls, text or SMS interactions, and social interactions through social media (which did not measure loneliness). The MLM analyses showed that the other three modes were not significantly different from one another in terms of relatedness and well-being.

As for video calls, they were associated with greater closeness and well-being, but, intriguingly, more loneliness as well. This may be a product of trying to connect with a close partner who lives far away (Madianou & Miller, 2012; Vlahovic et al., 2012; Yang et al., 2014). Perhaps it feels good and builds connection to see the person via video, but it might make the participants miss the other person even more, knowing that they are not actually together (Neustaedter & Greenberg, 2012).

Once controlling for relationship partner statistically (i.e., included in the MLM analyses), the results barely changed at all. FtF communication was still associated with more relatedness and greater well-being compared with voice calls, text or SMS, and social interactions via social media. Voice calls, SMS/text, and video calls were still associated with more loneliness, even controlling for how established the relationship was. This confirms past study results that suggest FtF contact (measured in number of minutes) is associated with happiness across a variety of different relationship partners (Vlahovic et al., 2012) and that FtF contact has a stronger association with liking and closeness than contact through any other online medium (Sprecher, 2014).

However, there were a couple of small changes in the results after controlling for the closeness of the interaction partner. Voice calls became indistinguishable from FtF conversations in terms of well-being, probably because voice calls were most often made with close friends or family (67%). This finding does seem to support classic research that telephone calls are clearly superior than text-based communication for showing closeness, care, and companionship (Dimmick et al., 2000) and more similar to FtF interactions (Baym et al., 2004; Boase et al., 2006).

2.7 But Wait, What Did They Talk About?

Another issue that has bedeviled any attempt to make modality comparison claims is the content of communication. In my CBB theory research, I have developed an approach built around the episode of the conversation (e.g., Hall, 2018b; Hall & Davis, 2017) based on classic typologies of episodic communication (Goldsmith & Baxter, 1996). A communication episode is not strictly the content of the interaction, but instead a meso-level concept based on what a conversation does, is about, or is for. Two frequent communication episodes are joking around and school or work conversations. An episode of joking around is marked by the levity and relaxed nature of the conversation – akin to Goffman's (1963) *focused social interactions* in that conversation is engaged in for its own sake. The other type of episode (i.e., work or school talk) is instrumental in nature and is typical and routine in shared institutional contexts (Small, 2017). While strangers could engage in work talk (e.g., some jobs require conversation between customers and employees, who are strangers), the purpose of the work or school talk is shaped by broader institutional purposes.

I replicated the above analyses (i.e., controlling for relationship partner type) to explore mean differences by mode of communication for both joking around and for work/school talk. Unsurprisingly, people felt less lonely, happier, and more connected when joking around than when talking about work or school. Both communication episodes were marked by more connection and less loneliness when FtF and on the phone when compared with SMS or texting (video frequencies were too infrequent to be able to statistically compare). However, well-being during work and school talk was equal to the other two modes of communication when texting, but well-being was lower when joking around.

These results suggest that the benefits of greater well-being FtF are partly dependent on the type of interaction. CBB theory would predict that episodes that are likely to satisfy the need to belong (i.e., joking around; Hall, 2018a) are deployed for the sake of interpersonal bonding. These results also confirm that humor has a strong influence on people's happiness, regardless of modality (Vlahovic et al., 2012).

2.8 Having Social Interactions Is Better than Being Alone, but Using Social Media Is Not

It is worth pointing out that all of the ways of socially interacting are associated with more closeness, more well-being, and less loneliness than at moments when participants reported they were alone. Both studies asked people how they felt if they had not been in a social interaction when contacted. The results comparing social interactions with all modes and being alone suggest that having an interaction, no matter the modality, is better than being alone in terms of those three outcomes.

In my 2015 study, I also asked people whether they had used any social media whatsoever (e.g., looking at notifications, browsing) in the last ten minutes. Whether they had used social media had no association with relatedness and affective well-being at any point in time. This null effect did not matter whether people had had an interaction or had not had an interaction in the last ten minutes. Unlike all mediated social interactions, using social media does not influence connection and well-being when alone or when in an interaction. Essentially, using it is no better than being alone and not using it.

SECTION THREE: LAYERS OF ELECTRONIC INTIMACY

Patterns of media use between relational partners give rise to and are influenced by normative meanings of different modes of communication. These normative meanings reflect how, when, and why a mode of communication is used, but also reflect the relationship between the sender and receiver. For example, people, not the telephone companies, developed rules and norms of telephone use that dictated how a person answered the phone or ended a call, when it was appropriate to call, and why a person could call (Fischer, 1992). These rules also dictated who called whom, especially when calls were expensive or when a nascent romantic relationship was arising. In past eras, people wrote a posted letter to those they cared for the most, and perceived receiving a posted letter as a signal of relationship value (Fischer, 1992). Many people keep letters they received from loved ones throughout their lives, even to be passed on to the next of kin. The point is, the mode of communication has long matched the type of relationship partner.

Recently, this trend – that medium matches the relationship – has been given a catchy name: the "layers of electronic intimacy" (Yang et al., 2014). In this section, this idea and the research behind it are addressed, as it seems to me to be one of the more heuristic models that integrates partner type and modality usage.

3.1 What Are the Layers?

Fisher (1992) observed that throughout the twentieth century, telephone calls were often reserved for one's closest friends, and this continued to be true 100 years later (Baym et al., 2004; Flanagin & Metzger, 2001). Just as in the age of the landline, people tailor access to and from others on their mobile phones based on their relational importance (Barkhuus & Polichar, 2011; Lee et al., 2019). But as the options for communication multiplied, it had become an empirical question as to how these varying options map on to relationship closeness.

With data gathered via focus groups during the early stages of Facebook adoption (i.e., 2008), Yang and colleagues (2014) suggested that different stages of relationships require different types of communicative goals. In early relationships uncertainty reduction is important, but as relationships develop communication becomes more frequent and, eventually, more intimate. They found that relationship partners ascend through these layers of intimacy. In 2008, after meeting somewhere (most often FtF), participants used Facebook or Instagram to learn more about someone (see also Duran & Kelly, 2017; Standlee, 2019). Further communication was initiated on IM chats, texts, or social-media-enabled chat programs. Sometimes people made voice calls before planning a future intentional FtF meeting, but sometimes not. In reviewing this order with students in my own courses, some suggested that FaceTime or another video chat program may be preferred over voice calls at this later stage, but they generally agreed with this pattern of development.

At more casual levels of friendship and romance, superficial self-disclosure is appropriate, and modalities with more social cues (e.g., video chat) are considered to be a bit presumptuous. Thus, public profiles on social media are useful for learning more and developing attraction (Duran & Kelly, 2017; Standlee, 2019). As partners get closer, the instantaneous and more exclusive feelings associated with chat, texting, and IM allows partners to feel closer and more intimate (Ramirez et al., 2015), but still allow for selective self-presentation and a sense of control (Sheer, 2011). Finally, because voice calls and video chats are more similar to FtF communication (although more energy intensive and a bit awkward; Baron & Campbell, 2012; Rettie, 2007), they are considered much more intimate and are reserved for more developed relationships (Boase et al., 2006; Eden & Veksler, 2016).

Liu and Yang (2016) followed up on this idea with a meta-analysis that combined the results of twenty-two studies gathered across the world. Working with the idea of media niches, they suggested that texting and voice calls were not distinguishable; they had overlapping niches. This supports prior research suggesting that voice calls and text exchanges overlapped over ten years ago as well (e.g., Boase et al., 2006). The next outer layer of relationship closeness tended to correspond with social networking sites and IM. Finally, online gaming, often with strangers or acquaintances, was on the outside circle. As a caveat, Liu and Yang (2016) cautioned that there were few studies that included online gaming for the sake of comparison.

3.2 Do Layers of Personal Networks Map onto the Layers of Electronic Intimacy?

Another way to approach the above idea is to consider the exclusivity of media use. For example, if it is true that voice calls or SMS are mostly likely reserved for closer relationship partners, then it should follow that patterns of use of those media should show a smaller network of others. Recent research confirms such a conclusion: the size of the network maps onto modality.

Two separate massive studies of voice-call patterns (e.g., Ling et al., 2012, 400 million messages; Miritello et al., 2013, 20 million customers and 9 billion calls) confirm that the size of the voice call network is small – about three or four people. Just as would be expected if the layers of electronic intimacy argument is true, people appear to restrict their voice communication to a small group of important people – their core network. This also appears to be true in times of transition, where people would be most likely to form new relationships. Over a period of eighteen months, as participants transitioned into college, voice calls were reserved for about three or four important others

(Saramaki et al., 2014). Even if new close friends were made, the total network size was stable. This pattern of results is further supported by two other studies, which suggest voice calls are for close partners for working adults in Korea (Kim et al., 2007) and for young adults in England (Aledavood et al., 2015).

Ling et al. (2012) also report that the layer for SMS messages is slightly larger – about five to seven people. Other studies seem to suggest that texting is particularly important in maintaining friendships, particularly for young adults (Hall & Baym, 2012; Ling, 2010). As pointed out in Chapter 1, the "first fifteen" subsumes the core network of five to seven individuals, and includes more friends. SMS is used to keep a small friendship network intact (Kim et al., 2007), particularly among young adults in the evening hours (Aledavood et al., 2015). Ninety percent of all users had a voice-call network of fewer than twenty, and 80% of all users had a text message network of fewer than twenty (Ling et al., 2012). Taken together, these findings confirm Ling et al.'s (2012) conclusions about voice calls and texting: "the mobile phone is an instrument of the intimate sphere" (p. 295).

There is good reason that people turn to other, less effortful media to maintain relationships in the next layer of relational intimacy (aka forty to fifty friends and family; Dunbar, 1996). In a nationally representative sample of Americans, Hampton et al. (2011) reports that there is no association between core discussion network size and use of social media (e.g., SNS, photo sharing, blogs), which suggests social media are not used to maintain such relationships in isolation. When individuals had larger discussion networks, they were more likely to use IM. Similarly, Tillema et al. (2010) found that people with more numerous friends and family tended to rely on more forms of media (e.g., email, telephone, SMS) to maintain those relationships. IM has been noted before as a means of maintaining a less close group of friends, especially in college (Ramirez & Broneck, 2009; Valkenburg & Peter, 2009), which suggests that IM (or in contemporary times Instagram Direct or Facebook Messenger) may be used to keep in touch with a somewhat larger network (Hampton et al., 2011; Park et al., 2012). However, Miritello et al. (2013) reports that the larger the number of unique others (size of network), the more time a person typically spends making voice calls, but they are shorter calls. Because voice calls are time intensive and prevent multicommunication (having several conversations at once – a noted feature of chat programs and IM), there is a direct trade-off of voice-call length and network size.

Future research should consider the implications of research by O'Hara et al. (2014) and Ling and Lai (2016), who suggest that group texting programs and chat applications (e.g., GroupMe, WhatsApp) may offer a key dwelling space for broader friendship groups. The question as to whether program use to support group communication helps to maintain that forty-to-fifty circle of friendships, rather than just another means of reaching the first fifteen, is a crucial area of future research.

Finally, one of the key features of social media is the ease of communication with a large group of others, including old or ceremonial friends, distant kin, and casual relationship partners. As Hampton et al. (2011) found, Americans with larger discussion networks tended to use photo-sharing programs in 2008 to keep in touch with distant kin. There is ample evidence that social media in general, and SNSs specifically, help to maintain large networks of relatively weak ties (Quinn & Papcharisi, 2018).

3.3 Where Is FtF Contact Located in the Layers?

There are two ways to answer the question of where to locate FtF contact in the layers. Mediated communication frequency strongly maps onto FtF frequency for close partners in general (see MMT in Chapter 3). However, whether partners are geographically close or distant is an important moderator of this association.

As this chapter points out, there is a strong tendency to use more media with closer partners. And there is a strong overlap between using media restricted for close partners (voice call and SMS) and FtF contact frequency (Miritello et al., 2013; Requena & Ayuso, 2018), even in times of transition (Saramaki et al., 2014; Small, 2017). As the interdependence perspective suggests, those whom we rely on the most to accomplish daily life also require the most management across channels of communication. As an important caveat to the claims of MMT (Ledbetter, 2015), it does not follow that those who have ample opportunities to interact FtF by nature just add more and more media as a matter of course. FtF communication frequency does not seem to promote online communication (i.e., social media, SMS) over time (Dienlin et al., 2017); its frequency seems to stand apart from other forms of communication (Ruppel & Burke, 2015). Indeed, partners create niches of media use within their relationships that are idiosyncratic to the relationship (Kim et al., 2007; Madianou & Miller, 2012; Ruppel et al., 2018). That is, people have segmented patterns of communication that are relationship-specific (e.g., one texts and instant messages with this friend; one calls and emails with that one). They socially construct the relationship with media.

It is important to remember that individuals have many social interactions with acquaintances and strangers (see Table 5.1), often at work or school, for which no other mode of communication is needed. Thus, it follows that with no interdependence, there is no need to add a channel of communication. As interdependence rises – for example, when doing a joint project – new media are likely added for the moment, but not necessarily for the long run.

In the case of geographically distant but important relationships, the FtF interaction frequency drops dramatically. For those who live far away, less than one FtF interaction per month is very common (Tillema et al., 2010).

Now and in in the past, mediated communication has been a lifeline for these relationships. However, even within the category of a long-distance relationship, there is a strong correlation between frequency of FtF contact and mediated communication use (Boase et al., 2006; Tillema et al., 2010). The people you make a concerted effort to call, write, text, and video chat are likely the same people you'd like to *visit* in-person (Ruppel & Burke, 2015).

As one more additional caveat, long-distance relationships can develop idiosyncratic ways of communication that do not neatly map onto the above layers of intimacy. Yang et al. (2014) and Vlahovic et al. (2012) found that international students relied on Skype and other video chat programs to have "real conversations" because they were cheaper than phone calls. Madianou and Miller (2012) document examples of internationally dispersed families who use email to ask for money so as to hide embarrassment. Similarly, the use of email to send long, private messages was a practice found only in participants far from home (Yang et al., 2014), which carries on a long tradition of using email to keep in touch (Baym et al., 2004; Flaherty et al., 1998). There is a lot of variation in the ways that people use media to maintain long-distance relationships; people constantly substitute channels in and out as opportunity and constraint affords them (Ruppel et al., 2018)

SECTION FOUR: CONCLUSIONS

One last caveat to the layers of electronic intimacy concept is that it does not take into account the degree to which social interactions – through media or FtF – are elective or obligatory.

As geographic mobility rises and social networks become less fixed to a place, individuals must elect to keep in touch with others. The concept of networked individualism (Rainie & Wellman, 2012), in fact, presumes an active, intentional, and skilled person at the center of their mediated network of others, skewed toward weaker ties. But it is worth pondering this fact for a moment: each voice call, text, instant message, and status update requires the individual to *choose* to maintain a relationship. This is vastly different from the types of social interactions that are very much a part of individual's daily routines at work, home, and school that are obligatory (see Chapter 10). Simply put, many of our social interactions outside the home that are FtF are with people who just happen to be there, which allows for a certain presumptiveness that lowers barriers to sociality and routine interaction (Small, 2017). People are around, and it is easy to interact. As far back as the work of Rook (1984), there was a recognition that this routineness and ease of contact were critical features in building community and reducing loneliness. It is endemic to dorm life in college and the formation of friendships at work. The important point here is that compared with sharing a space with someone (or a whole group of others), mediated communication is optional and intentional, and probably more energy intensive too. Thus, the idea of networked individualism presumes that to maintain relationships, people must take up conscious action to do so. Yet there are many people who simply do not call, text, or write each other. And perhaps many, many more who do not keep in touch at all if we set aside the incredible ease of social media use.

This suggests that routine, presumptive social interactions built into everyday life may have some important and unique roles to play in keeping relationships in existence. And because they *have to* occur, they likely keep people in touch where they otherwise might not. I would guess that beyond social media, there are very few examples of maintaining these relationships of obligation or convenience through alternative modes of contact (e.g., SMS/chat, voice call).

Finally, there is good evidence that email, voice calls, and, for some employees, video calls or social media use constitute distinct niches of inter-action (Kim et al., 2007; Madianou & Miller 2012). These niches, and the multiplexity of media within them, suggest that high degrees of use and the number of media used may map better onto interdependence than closeness. What I mean is that communication via FtF, voice calls, video conferencing, email, and Slack that a workplace requires for their employees starts to look very similar to the amount of media used to maintain people's most intimate relationships. But, rather than intimacy, this multiplicity is likely a hallmark of interdependence. In fact, the pressures to be responsive to workplace demands can be so high that individuals have to adjust their patterns of mobile phone use to restrict access to those modes of communication when away from work (Barkhuus & Polichar, 2011). The obligation to be available creates a unique stress that must be managed in this day and age (see Chapter 8).

As Arnold (2003) foretold, mobile connectedness is Janus-faced. It creates new freedoms and creates new obligations. It is a tether and a bridge to others. Although social and relationship-specific norms certainly play a role, at the center of these dialectical tensions is interdependence. As we are more interdependent with others, all forms of connectedness – mediated and otherwise – follow. But so do the obligations of responsiveness and access.

6

Three Ways of Seeing Social Media

This chapter is dedicated to a constantly evolving set of platforms that are collectively called social media. These platforms vary in form and function and are constantly changing to anticipate and respond to user preferences and stay ahead of the fierce competition. Thus, it is challenging to compose a chapter on social media that will not be out of date before this book is even finished being written. The goal of this chapter is to define what makes social media distinct from the other modes of communication I have discussed so far. In doing so, I will describe three forms of communication made possible through social media. These are three ways of seeing what is happening when we use social media: social media as the social news, social media as the archive of the self, and social media as bridging social capital.

SECTION ONE: DEFINING SOCIAL MEDIA

1.1 What Are Social Media?

Although there is no single agreed-on definition, social media are typically defined by a set of platform features that enable searchable and publicly distributed content (Ellison & Vitak, 2015). Users create the content that becomes "social media," and the transmission of that content is decentralized, which means users, to varying degrees depending on platform, decide on what is shared and reshared (Stoycheff, Liu, Wibowo, & Nanni, 2017). Social networking sites (SNSs) (e.g., Facebook) are the most ubiquitous and identifiable form of social media (Gramlich, 2019), but microblogs (e.g., Twitter) and photo- and video-sharing platforms (e.g., Snapchat) are also social media (Ellison & Vitak, 2015; Stoycheff et al., 2017). Scholars have long noted that there is a challenge inherent to studying social media in that naming a platform (e.g., Pinterest) is an incomplete picture of what it can do (or will do in the future). Furthermore, what social media *can* do may not resemble how people typically or predominately use it. Because technology changes rapidly and platforms copy the most popular features of their competitors, without a careful description of how a platform functions, just naming the platform and saying that "people use it" or "people enjoy it" tells us very little about what users are doing within its virtual ecosystem.

Social media platforms, particularly Facebook, are actively competing to be a hub for *all* modes as well as a primary entry point for engaging with the internet as a whole. Thus, it is more likely than not that platforms will continue to add new modes of communication to their menu of options. One approach to managing this challenge is to be more explicit about the features and functions of social media when we research it (Larsson, 2015).

1.2 Differentiating Modes from Platforms

The Introduction of this book explained Baym's (2010) conceptual dimensions for understanding and differentiating personal media from one another. In that chapter, I advocated for adopting a mode + feature approach to studying personal media. Therein, I argued that some modes of communication, particularly email and IM-style chat programs, can and should be separated out from the providers (e.g., America Online) or platforms (e.g., Instagram) that offer(ed) such functions. In their review of research on social media, Stoycheff et al. (2017) recommend a similar distinction between directed, low reach modes of communication in contrast to social media. For the purposes of this book, all chat programs – regardless of the platform from which they originated or the device on which the program is installed – can and should be researched and understood under the umbrella of a single modality. In the case where there are features of chat programs unique to some platform or app, these should be studied in conjunction with the modality. For example, Snapchat's feature of being ephemeral (i.e., difficult but not impossible to archive) makes it distinct from other chat programs. Yet I would argue that this feature of Snapchat still constitutes the SMS mode. Such an approach does not diminish the unique features of a platform or app; the ephemeral and photo-centric aspects of Snapchat deserve further investigation on their own (e.g., Bayer et al., 2016).

Furthermore, in describing media niches in Chapter 4, I suggested that there are modes of communication that have endured over time and are likely to continue to do so. Three merit recall here. High synchrony, high social cues, and low reach modes of communication, such as voice calls and video chats, are a class apart not only from other forms of communication in function, but also in patterns of use and typical communication partner (see Chapter 5). Medium synchrony, low social cues, and low to medium reach modes of communication, specifically text-based mobile communication, stand apart as well. Whether tied to a phone number, as in texting, or tied to a smartphone application, such as WhatsApp, I argued that this mode was distinct and warranted separate investigation. Because it matters whether the mode was used to converse with one person or many, its reach is an important distinction among chat programs. But again, text-centric chat programs constitute a singular mode, and features that distinguish one modal option from another deserve attention on their own.

Another important factor in separating out these three modes of communication was the recognition that these modes were all much more exclusive and private in nature (low on the public dimension). They may vary in searchability (or having a record), permanence, and number of social cues. Chat programs deserve to be studied as modes of communication in themselves, whether they emerged from America Online, a mobile phone provider, or a social media platform.

1.3 Social Interaction as a Unit of Analysis

Another way to distinguish between modes of communication is to consider the social interaction as a critical unit of analysis. In my past work (i.e., Hall, 2018b), I attempted to answer the question, When is social media use social interaction? I found that when forms of social media use were lower reach and more synchronous, they were more likely to be considered social interaction by users. In a series of three studies, the most common example of mediated social interaction was sending and receiving direct messages in rapid succession to and from a known other – in other words, an action very similar to a text, a chat message, or an email (to a lesser extent). So, if we exclude these forms of communication when we study social media, what remains?

Although features vary by platform, the two central activities of social media are browsing and user-driven broadcasting. Browsing is scanning the available, personally curated and/or system-curated updates, tweets, videos, or photos of other users. Currently, the central hallmark of browsing is scrolling, especially on a smartphone. When users pick up their mobile device and scroll, scroll, scroll through the available content, they are browsing.

Broadcasting is posting, sharing, or uploading content through the platform. Broadcasts give browsers content to browse, but they are comparatively infrequent. Neither browsing nor broadcasting is conceptually similar to social interaction, nor are they considered to be social interaction by users (Hall, 2018b). Rather, both are a form of social attention, people watching, or virtual surveillance.

There are a few distinct ways of using social media that prevent easy categorization from the perspective of social interaction. Specifically, acknowledgment and direct responses to posts are conceptually akin to social interaction (Hall, 2018b). Broadcasted posts or pictures that are acknowledged through a like/favorite/thumb's up or down button or emoji are called "lightweight" or "one-click" acknowledgments (Burke & Kraut, 2014). Direct responses, particularly in the form of words, are considered weightier responses as they take more time and are more personal. (Other media content (e.g., memes, GIFs, emoji) are sometimes considered more substantial and substantive than one-click acknowledgments (Kelly & Watts, 2015), but more research is needed to explore the degree to which this is true.)

These two common responses (i.e., one-click versus directed messages) are not equivalent in terms of effect on relationship (Burke & Kraut, 2014) or in terms of the definition of social interaction (Hall, 2018b). Directed communication (i.e., comments, wall posts) between relational partners is more common among close friends (Bryant & Marmo, 2012), is associated with greater tie strength over time (Burke & Kraut, 2014), and is clearly interactive in the sense of people responding to one another (Hall, 2018b). By contrast, one-click acknowledgment does not strengthen relationship ties (Burke & Kraut, 2014), perhaps because likes/favorites are grouped anonymously and presented as a total count and for some platforms is merely quantification for its own sake rather for the sake of interpersonal communication (Nesi et al., 2018). Acknowledging a shared post without directed comment is not a social interaction because it fails the condition of exchange and focused attention by both partners. Personally, I think it is fruitful to consider one-click acknowledgment as a digital greeting or head nod, such as while walking past familiar others in a crowd (see Chapter 1).

Finally, resharing and reposting are two of the central features of many forms of social media, but also tend to happen among casual or acquaintance relationships (Bryant & Marmo, 2012). Furthermore, this action itself may say little about how the one who shares the original post or message regards or feels about the original poster. On Twitter, for example, retweeting is not the same thing as endorsement or agreement. Many retweeted messages are composed by opinion leaders and celebrities (or their social media agents) and are not socially interactive by nature.

Given that so little of social media use can be considered social interaction (again barring directed messages enabled through chat/texting programs), how can we approach the study of social media from this book's perspective?

1.4 Mass Personal Communication

Just because these ways of using social media are not social interaction, it certainly does not mean social media is not social. Posting messages or photos can be deeply personal, even if not necessarily interactive. Browsing the content of photos or videos of friends and family may indeed foster a sense of connection. One perspective that tries to reconcile the difficulty of characterizing less interactive uses of social media is the mass-personal perspective.

O'Sullivan and Carr (2018) point out that social media defies easy categorization as it contains characteristics similar to both mass communication and interpersonal communication. To resolve this, they theoretically develop the conceptualization of mass-personal communication. This concept varies based on two dimensions: the personalization of messages and the exclusivity of audience (i.e., reach). Posts, pictures, tweets, and other types of sharable content vary by the degree that the content of the message appears to be personalized by the user. The degree to which it is personalized intersects with the perception of the poster's audience. Acknowledging that social media users have, at best, a vague conceptualization of the reach of their post (see Bernstein et al., 2013), O'Sullivan and Carr (2018) concede that the perception of the size and composition of the audience (i.e., one's imagined audience) matters more than the actual audience. The personalization of the message, then, varies by the perception of who will see or read it rather than who actually sees it. People have only a vague idea of how many people see their social media posts, much less the identities of those who saw it but did not respond (Bernstein et al., 2013). The ever-changing algorithms of the social media platforms do not help us out in the least as they change whose broadcasts we see and who sees our broadcasts.

Similar to the reasons I offer above, O'Sullivan and Carr (2018) characterize direct messages and dyadic chat options, including old-school private chat rooms, as more akin to social interaction and interpersonal communication. Additionally, other social media, such as YouTube videos, podcasts, and listserv messages that are public impersonal messages, are options of communication that I excluded in the Introduction and that O'Sullivan and Carr (2018) also exclude from the mass-personal category. Thus, the mass-personal domain excludes public communication, which is also not within the scope of this book, and excludes forms of communication that I identify as social interaction. O'Sullivan and Carr (2018) argue that the niche of communication that fits into the mass-personal domain includes social media posts, one-click acknowledgments, and Twitter mentions – all of which are examples of mass and personalized messages.

This perspective dovetails nicely with the general focus of this book; mass-personal communication is what remains when we consider mediated social interaction through social media as an independent mode of relating. So, how can we understand relating through mass-personal communication?

SECTION TWO: THE SOCIAL NEWS

In two important articles written at the dawn of SNSs, Donath (2008) and Tufekci (2008) both recognized that the one of the central appeals of social media is the all-too-human curiosity about what other people are doing. As an added draw, SNSs offer the chance to be the object of observation by others. Donath (2008) identified its basic pleasure: "endless novelty in the flow of new people and new information, and the knowledge that someone is paying attention to you" (p. 247). Tufekci (2008) argued that users' lack of awareness that they use social media to watch people underscores its centrality. That is, users rarely recognize that this is what they are doing, and instead insist that they are just passing the time. As addressed in Chapter 1, we are fundamentally social animals, and we seek information about and connection to other people. We crave the *social news* – information about the goings-on of others. Social media offer a high reach, low effort way of satisfying that craving.

As I addressed in Chapter 2, one important externality, or unexpected effect, of widespread seeking and sharing social news on social media is that it constrains users' ability to stop looking at it and sharing on it. As recent revelations of Facebook's inadequate and unethical responses to data breaches by Cambridge Analytica became known (Frenkel, Confessore, Kang & Rosenberg, 2018), several of my friends publicly announced that they had decided to quit the platform outright. Although many responses were supportive of this conclusion, there was a strong trace of anxiety as Facebook friends began to recognize there was simply no other way to read the social news without reconstructing their entire network somewhere else, such as on some other platform. The externality of a desire to know the social news is a dependence on what functions as the newspaper. And that is what Facebook will continue to count on to stem the tide of defectors.

Orchard et al. (2015) forecasted the difficulty of departure and the collective investment users have in social media's continuing existence. They argue that Facebook can be viewed as a collective virtual ecosystem, where the needs of the community take precedent over the needs of the individual. Because each member of the network invested so much time in and personal content to the collective, their continued use becomes an obligation to the community as a whole. The authors suggest that this balancing of needs manifests in a sense of discomfort when a member considers quitting or disengaging with the site.

Why do we think the social news is so compelling that we will continue to share our personal data and information with social media corporations who monetize our identities and when we are somewhat dissatisfied with its influence on our lives?

2.1 Our Social Brains

One holiday tradition in the United States and United Kingdom that is currently surviving the social and mobile media revolutions is sending out holiday cards and photos through snail mail. Americans have sent more than 1.6 billion holiday cards each year (Vejnoska, 2016), and the five-year average suggests that this number is not in decline. This ritual of selecting comely family photos (or dog photos) and/or writing an updated letter about the goings-on of each member of the family (sometimes penned by the dog) is the prototype of the *social news* from the pre-internet era.

In my own home, my parents sent both photos and letters about my family. The cards, photos, and letters we received from others piled up and sometimes were hung decoratively during the holidays. I know some families who hang photos of those near and dear adjacent to the stockings on the mantle. The written letters were read once or maybe a few times before the season was over, but ultimately all were filed away (maybe in the trash can after updating the address book). Many households' holiday season includes a ritual of sending and receiving a slow trickle of social news.

As I discussed in Chapter 1, human beings have evolved to be socially engaged and concerned with what is going on with other people. We are deeply interested in human affairs in general, and more interested in the nitty-gritty details the more we are emotionally close to someone. In Lieberman's (2013) fascinating book *Social: Why Our Brains Are Wired to Connect*, he presents compelling evidence that the default state of the brain is not resting; it is recounting social events that have happened or have yet to happen. In other words, our nonoccupied brain is a social brain. The human brain is a social computer, analyzing social events, attempting to anticipate or solve social problems, and examining the self in relation to the views, thoughts, and actions of others (Lieberman, 2013). To feed the computer, we need more social news.

Humans have also evolved abilities to make rapid and accurate inferences about others' personalities, capacities, and intentions effortlessly outside our conscious awareness (Haselton & Funder, 2006). Watching others and making judgments about them – who they are, what they are doing, and what they are like – is so natural that it is extremely difficult to stop doing so. Consider that the innate ability to judge others' personalities with remarkable accuracy is so intrinsic to human nature that there is little between-person variability in this skill (Haselton & Funder, 2006).

We want to know about other people; we are constantly thinking about other people; and we are effortlessly assessing others' intentions and characteristics. Given all of this attention, the mere presence of others strongly influences our behavior, even more so if the audience is composed of people with whom we have a relationship or want to have one (Schlenker, 1980). The best example of this is when you are in public, you present a public self that is tailored to the norms of that space. When a friend passing by gets our attention or says hello, we awake from enacting our public face (sometimes with a start) and refocus our self-presentation on that person. Once we are alerted to the presence of someone we know, our behavior changes and a distinct and tailored self-presentational effort kicks in.

Once in conversation, we quickly shift our attention to what other people are talking about and what our response to their words will be. This attention to the conversation is definitional to the act of social interaction. Social attention signals that you care about what your partner has to say, and that they are worth your time and attention both in comparison to what another person could be saying and compared with another use of time. Listening to what other people are saying is a key characteristic of social bonding.

2.2 Gossip Is a Part of Human Nature

We love gossip but we have a love–hate relationship with loving gossip. I suspect that a great deal of the hate part of that equation is directed at malicious and judgmental gossip – and rightly so. Due to these negative connotations, identifying talking about other people as gossip is problematic, but it is also the most intuitive and convenient shorthand for that speech act (Goldsmith & Baxter, 1996). So, I will continue to use it here to refer to talk about other people without regard for the valence of that talk.

Consider that most conversations between friends start with taking turns asking, "How are you?" Once this is done, conversation quickly turns to telling stories about the goings-on of others, particularly mutually acquainted others. Whether gossip includes talking about the self and our relationships with other people or it refers only to talking about a mutually acquainted third party who is not present, gossip is among the most common types of conversation (Dunbar, 1996; Goldsmith & Baxter, 1996; Hall, 2018a). Gossip is also a cross-cultural phenomenon that has deep historical roots as well (Dunbar, 1996; Goldsmith & Baxter, 1996). It is a way of knowing what is going on in the social world, and, as such, it is a valued resource.

From a relationship perspective, gossip serves as a means of maintaining or developing a relationship between communicators by situating speakers in a community of known and knowable others. Communication partners use knowledge about their networks to enact their relationship between one another (Goldsmith & Baxter, 1996). Dunbar (1996) suggests that gossip is a form of social grooming through speech.

Both Tufekci (2008) and Donath (2008) adopted this idea in their early analyses of SNSs. As anyone who has engaged in a conversation among a group of people has surely noticed, to be attended to by others (i.e., to hold the floor) is a competitive act. Social attention, especially in a noisy space, is a form of social connection – we give attention to the person whom we either seek to be close to or find more interesting than other people (and this is often the same person).

By adopting a gossip and grooming approach, early perspectives on social media (Donath, 2008; Tufekci, 2008) made three important points: (1) people share social information to be seen and heard, (2) the ability to gain social attention (through comments, likes, etc.) is a deep draw of social media, and (3) this link between posting/sharing and acknowledging/responding is a relational act. Keeping track of the mundane changes in people's lives, through photos and text, is functionally similar to sending and reading holiday cards; it brings the relationship into the present and is a testament to its ongoing nature.

As a final point, there is a long history of complaining or worrying about the banality of what is shared in mediated exchanges (e.g., Crystal, 2008), particularly social media. Although many people have fruitfully pointed out that mundane maintenance through personal media is an essential form of relationship maintenance (e.g., Hall & Baym, 2012; Tong & Walther, 2011), this obscures a more important point. Much of the content of _spoken_ communication is also terribly dull and observational in nature (Alberts, Yoshimura, Rabby, & Loschiavo, 2005). In fact, when crafting content to be shared through social media, people seek to convey something interesting, humorous, or pleasing (Pennington & Hall, 2014; Utz, 2015). Thus, any criticism that much of what is shared on social media is boring or inane should be tempered by the recognition that nearly all spoken talk is that way too. As someone who has spent hours and hours watching and reading the transcripts of conversations among research participants, I can tell you that very little of the content of conversation when it is taken out of context is objectively interesting to anyone (probably not even to the people in it!).

If the content of social media can be fruitfully thought of as the social news, what is an offline corollary of broadcasting, browsing, and some acknowledging on social media?

2.3 Virtual People Watching

When we are out in public, we are always aware that others are present and can observe the self (Schlenker, 1980). This awareness does not require mutual acknowledgment by co-present other(s). In other words, you do not have to know exactly who is looking at you to know you can be seen. At this point, the private self or self-as-ego becomes the public self (Schlenker, 1980). A colloquial term for this dynamic is _people watching_. The more aware we are of being seen, the more individuals modify their self-presentation, especially when social attention begets mutual observation and acknowledgment (Schlenker, 1980).

This sort of social attention through social media has been called social surveillance (Marwick, 2012) or virtual people watching (Joinson, 2008). Marwick (2012) points out that both virtual people watching and a high awareness of being virtually observed are core characteristics of online communities. Indeed, broadcasts are partly motivated by a desire to remain digitally visible to friends (Trottier, 2012). I would argue that social media inspires an enhanced form of public self-awareness – people come into life and are even living because we observe them as such – enhanced because being seen is the only way to "exist" on social media. The importance of self-documentation is reflected in phrases such as, "Pics or it didn't happen," where events are real or complete only when shared through social media (Humphreys, 2018).

Karakayali and Kilic (2013) also see virtual people watching (or "analytic labor," using their terminology) as a central component of social media use. They suggest that watching and evaluating others is such a given of social media use – people become defensive when the behavior is questioned. The inherent enjoyment of looking at others is somehow taboo ("but everyone is doing it"). This is tied to the poor nomenclature: words like "creeping" or "lurking" used to describe virtual people watching are labels so hopelessly outdated and negatively biased as to be ridiculously unhelpful.

Marwick (2012) and Karakayali and Kilic (2013) are much more on point when they recognize that an inquisitive stance toward others is exactly what is intended by the poster/sharer when they post/share. People want that attention. By indicating that they are paying attention (through likes/comments/etc.) to other people's social media contributions, users acknowledge the importance and visibility of the post itself.

Taking it a step toward relationship maintenance, keeping in touch via social media requires both the seen and the seer. As a user skims her social media feed, she may simultaneously read her friends' content, comment on it, and broadcast her own content to other people's feeds, using this information to improve her mental model of unfamiliar other's identities, actions, and relationships (Levordashka & Utz, 2016). The consumption of social news offers users a sense of "ambient awareness" of the goings-on of others. This awareness develops peripherally, not through deliberately attending to posts or pictures or intentionally exploring other users' profiles (Levordashka & Utz, 2016). This type of awareness has relational consequences too. By keeping tabs on people who are relative strangers through ambient awareness, users often feel that they know the person's personality and are more inclined to approach them in the future (Levordashka & Utz, 2016).

Although seeking information about another person with little risk of detection may be a distinct affordance of social media (Marwick, 2012; Trottier, 2012), people watching, both virtual and in person, is an extension of social tendencies of keeping tabs on others (McAndrew & Jeong, 2012), which has long been a central part of everyday public life (Marwick, 2012).

2.4 Social Media Use as a Social Snack

Well before the advent of social media, there was a long-standing tendency to surround oneself with pictures, letters, or precious objects from loved ones.

Recent research has examined this behavior from the perspective of "social snacking" (Gardner, Pickett, & Knowles, 2005). People who feel inadequately connected to others may "snack" on symbolic reminders of their social connections until they can engage in FtF interactions. Snacks can include rereading emails or love letters, reminiscing, and looking at photos (Gardner et al., 2005). Without opportunities to interact FtF with loved ones, social snacking protects individuals from the feeling isolated (Gardner et al., 2005).

Although it is not well known the degree to which people snack on the posts and photos of loved ones when feeling disconnected or as a way of stemming loneliness, it is consistent with the CBB theory (Hall & Davis, 2017) (see Chapter 3) that they would do so. Symbolic communicative behaviors, such as writing or seeing a photo, are highly energy efficient compared with FtF interaction. The tendency toward energy conservation may encourage social media users to snack on the symbolic reminders of their connection to others, even if that act of viewing has no meaningful influence on the relationship partner. From the perspective of CBB theory, social media use is a low energy and enjoyable communicative behavior. Consistent with this position is the fact that one of the most salient features of social media for both detractors and advocates is its *ease* of use. The audience of these communicative acts can respond positively (e.g., through a "like") with very little energy output. Similar offline disclosures to a similarly sized audience would require considerably more energy. Thus, one part of the bigger picture about why people enjoy consuming the "social news" is that many browsing behaviors on social media entail characteristics similar to social snacking.

To answer this question, Knowles, Haycock, and Shaikh (2015) explored "whether exposure to Facebook can stave off the pangs of social hunger, or if instead, it exacerbates one's social needs" (p. 313). They found that when individuals were experimentally induced to feel momentarily excluded, they doubled their Facebook use. And, by doing so, their feeling of having their social needs boosted was satisfied. These findings line up with those of Burke and Kraut (2014), who found that "[q]uietly taking in the mundane details of another's life also works to enhance closeness" (p. 9).

SECTION THREE: THE SOCIAL ARCHIVE

The second metaphor for understanding what people are doing when they use social media to relate to one another is focused on the self. If browsing can be best understood as reading the social news, then maintaining and sculpting one's profile can be best understood as creating a social archive. The profile owner is the central character of that archive, and the ongoing history of connection to others conveniently organized and made searchable by social media makes plain the social archival nature of social media use. In other words, the social media profile is a visual snapshot of one's present and past self. To explain the social archive metaphor for relating through social media, I will start by how social media assists in the representation of the self, and then in the representation of the self in relation to others.

3.1 Representing the Self

Research on CMC has long recognized that digital media offer users a wide range of opportunities to craft a highly controlled impression of the self. One of the primary assumptions of social information processing theory (Walther, 1996; 2015) (see Chapter 3) is that CMC offers the opportunity to selectively self-present through language selection or message construction. Taking advantage of the features of text-based CMC (e.g., low synchrony, control of message composition), users can create a favorable self-presentation that is often more strategic, controlled, and positive than in FtF settings.

From the early days of social media, researchers recognized the potential for the medium to play in both impression management and impression formation (Tong, van der Heide, Langwell, & Walther, 2008; Walther, van der Heide, Hamel, & Shulman, 2009). In creating and maintaining a profile, social media users engage in online impression management, wherein one actively engages in creating, maintaining, and modifying an image that reflects one's ideal self. The construction of a profile has important social consequences for the profile owner. Social media profiles are often used to gather information about new acquaintances (Standlee, 2019; Utz, 2010; Yang et al., 2014). This makes profile contents particularly important for new social media contacts who do not have access to offline information to form impressions. Social media profiles have a particularly strong influence on impressions of long-lost friends, or acquaintances who have few or no chances to meet in person.

All public behavior, from our attire and cosmetic choices to our eye contact and posture, are public acts of self-presentation (Goffman, 1959). Yet what social media profiles offer changes the presentation of self as a matter of degree and kind. For example, Nesi et al. (2018) argue that some social media (e.g., Snapchat, Instagram) steer users to value visual (rather than textual) representations of the self. The importance and concern users place on crafting an attractive image is likely much higher on more visually geared platforms. Although the picture profile/image is a well-maintained part of many SNSs, other social media rely much more on text to convey impressions of the self (e.g., Twitter). Although there may be different salience placed on different aspects of the self, depending on the features of the platform, one consistent theme emerges in terms of self-presentation: people seek to balance their self-presentational efforts between attractive and accurate (Rettberg, 2018).

3.2 The Accurate and the Ideal

The idea that CMC and some forms of social media allow for a weak or even nonexistent link between the online and offline self has been with us since the 1990s (e.g., Stone, 1995). Yet research has called into question whether this has led to more strategic, more inaccurate, or more deceptive profiles online versus offline. Challenging the central presumption of social information processing theory, Chayko (2018) suggests that online self-presentation is strategic, but not necessarily more strategic than in-person presentations of self. Just because profiles and text messages are more manageable and tailored online, due to significant overlap between online and offline worlds, profile owners' allowance for ideal self-construction is low. In other words, although users may be tempted to enhance their self-presentations, friends and family who are both offline and online keep users' self-presentations in check. Misrepresentation on profile pages can have serious offline consequences: even those near and dear can be castigated for misleading/dishonest online self-portrayals (DeAndrea & Walther, 2011). Therefore, online impressions are typically managed within the parameters of a user's offline personality.

When a small group of friends compared the personality reflected in Facebook profiles with their offline perceptions of that friend, profiles were judged to be accurate, although slightly enhanced (Vazire & Gosling, 2004). A recent meta-analysis confirms that social media profiles do indeed convey an accurate impression for most personality characteristics (Tskhay & Rule, 2014). Thus, there is significant social pressure for profile owners to construct a desirable and attractive profile, while attending to the social sanctions against misrepresentation or lost opportunities for new relationship development by not presenting oneself accurately.

3.3 Who Am I?

Sometimes I may aim to impress or entertain an audience, or to put something deeply significant into words or images, but more often I am narrating or visualising my experiences so as to remember them better, or understand them better.

—Jill Rettberg (2018, p. 441)

Although questions about self-presentation in terms of selective self-presentation and accuracy have received considerable research attention, the social archive speaks to the idea that social media profiles reflect a narrative of the self. Just as holiday cards sent to friends and family provide a narrative of the growth and change in the family, social media updates provide an ongoing revealing of the self – relationships, celebrations, tribulations, jokes – all the glorious mundaneness of a lived life. We must remember that this action is still performative in that it creates a claim of the self that we are reliant on others to verify and support. Just as Goffman's (1959) dramaturgical perspective suggests, online self-presentation is a claim to a desired self, but this claim is contingent on the reception of the audience. Communication online and offline has both a self-advertisement function (e.g., look at me, what I have done, who I am) and a persuasive component in that it is to influence others' perceptions of us. Let us not imagine that online self-presentations do not have a self-verifying function – offered up for audience approval – any less than offline presentations of self. This is the sense in which Chayko (2018) suggests that people *post themselves into being*.

As in offline contexts, there is good reason to believe that this narrative sense of self is strongly influenced by the composition of the audience. O'Sullivan and Carr (2018) persuasively argue that mass personal communication has a greater potential to influence individual's self-concept and shift one's identity than other types of online self-presentation exactly *because* of the overlap between offline and online worlds. Those who respond to posts and pictures often know the poster, and by publicly responding, they are bolstering this claim to self. Leary (2001) argues that much of self-presentation is done for the sake of audience approbation and acceptance, which again is deeply rooted in research on online self-presentation.

Rettberg (2018) and Humphreys (2018) pull back the lens further when considering how social media is a social archive when they compare contemporary visual and textual online representations of self with the diaries and self-portraits from past eras. In both cases, we seek to represent ourselves to an audience; other times we are presenting our present self to our future self. The audience of our self-portraits can be very limited, perhaps just to intimates, just as letters home were shared among pioneer homesteaders in *My Antonia* or diaries were shared among friends in the nineteenth century (Humphreys et al., 2013). In that spirit, Rettberg (2018) also suggests that selfies are far from a new phenomenon; long ago, people made faces and hammed it up when taking photos in old photo booths with friends and lovers. Photographs and posts are essentially processes of knowing the self in relation to others (Humphreys, 2018). Consider that most tweets are self-referential, but in 40% of cases tweets about the self include references to the self in relation to others (Humphreys, 2018).

Embedded in the concept of social media as a self-archive is the complex interplay between reflecting the self and defining the self both in terms of one's internal conception and in terms of public reception. In stating who one is through a picture or a post, a social media user makes a public commitment to a certain identity, which is a type of a promise to the audience (Goffman, 1959). No doubt people are motivated to show an attractive side of the self but are also trying to shape and mesh the self already known by the audience offline with the self they wish to claim online (Vazire & Gosling, 2004). Although users may be aware and intentional about trying to curry favor from the audience, Rettberg (2018) argues that many posts are more for the sake of the writer than the viewer. As Marwick (2012) pointed out, social media are characterized by both watching and being watched; this is certainly a publicly available and archived self that is distinct in this moment of history. What is also particular to contemporary times is the diversity of audience. The audience on social media is often made up of acquaintances, kin, and friends from different domains in life and, for some forms of social media, nearly anyone in the world with internet access. The varying nature of the audience complicates a simple presentation of self.

3.4 Who Am I to You (and You and You and You)?

Goffman (1959) described "audience segregation" as the attempt to segment one's viewing audience from another audience (p. 49). He suggested that we would prefer to see and be seen in the original context where a relationship was formed, rather than have all of these audiences in one place. This concept has been identified as "context collapse" in the social media world (Bernstein et al., 2013). There are three parts to context collapse that make it challenging to avoid: the mixing of social worlds, the nature of the imagined audience, and the lack of control we have of audience response.

As Parks (2017) argues, social media have created a situation where there are many more impressions and many more audiences to manage than before. Now that grandma and old college friends and current workmates are all "friends" on the same platform, it is challenging to meaningfully segment one's audience, especially if we consider the formative act of impression formation that is the construction of a profile. I would suspect that the move toward other platforms that are more private and away from platforms that are more public (e.g., away from Facebook and toward Snapchat) is sometimes motivated by a weariness and wariness that accompanies managing a context collapse. Taking a person-as-corporation approach, Rainie and Wellman (2012) suggest that people should treat their online identities as brands to be managed and monitored, which requires a segmented identity to different audiences.

Second, we have only a fuzzy picture of who are audience is. Ellison and Vitak (2015) offer this useful metaphor: posting on a SNS is like speaking to an audience behind a curtain; through their responses (e.g., like, comment) you get only a partial picture of its reception and who even heard it. The less the actual audience is known, the more user is reliant on an imagined audience, and what is imagined may be as influential to what is posted as an actual audience (Litt, 2012). Because of this fuzzy picture of audience, people are constantly monitoring what others are doing and how others respond to posts to manage context collapse (e.g., What are people doing here? What will people like? Is it okay to post this?) (Karakayali & Kilic, 2013). We figure out the norms of self-presentation by watching others' behavior and audiences' responses to that behavior.

This challenge of context collapse is magnified when audience members respond to one another. I recently commented on Facebook on the topic of Kansas state politics' influence on public education, which affects my job and my family directly, and found myself watching an ugly exchange between an office colleague and a friend from college who lived in another state. They went at each other while I was offline, so I was not fully aware of the unpleasantness of their conflict until all of that mess was on public display in response to my original post. In response to this battle, one of those people unfriended me.

This is an example of the consequences of context collapse that people wish to avoid, but have limited means of achieving. Instead, it is more often the case that audiences have no clue about which social circles are intersecting during such exchanges. Having limited control over the behavior of others on one's own posts or pictures, the hope is that civility will prevail when social circles collapse. Although social media platforms have features that allow creating groups, lists, and circles to prevent context collapse when one posts, these groupings are not reflected to the audience itself, which leaves the relationship between one person and another obscured (Quinn & Papacharissi, 2018).

3.5 Representing Our Relational Self

The representation of one's social network through social media is both personal and public. That is, part of the appeal of social media is that it represents our relational self and relational history to ourselves (Humphreys, 2018). Through social media this relational identity is communicated to the social network as a whole, even if just represented as the number of friends or followers. In reviewing theories of the self, Schlenker (1980) points out that the relational self has long been a central component of the self. The question of Who am I? is often responded to with relational responses – in my case, I am a father, a husband, a son. Social media publicly present this relational self well beyond this list of intimates I offer above, and extends its public presentation far beyond people who even qualify as friends. And the value of this presentation of the relational self to the user is significant.

Karakayali and Kilic (2013) make a compelling case about how the preservation and representation of past relationships are critical components of the online profile of the self: "almost all informants maintained that old friendships have a unique place in their lives. In particular, they noted the lasting effects of sharing something in common at a special period in their lives" (p. 179). In this fashion, the representation of past relationships has a narrative quality that lends itself to storytelling and reflection, even if those narratives are told only in the user's own memory (Chayko, 2014). Relationships preserved through connections on social media are commemorative, to be honored as scarce commodities because they involved a shared history and survived the test of time (Karakayali & Kilic, 2013; Quinn, 2013). Past and present ties are integrated into a narrative about the relational self on social media that offers salient reminders of identity personally constructed by the user's engagement with the media (Humphreys, 2018; van Kruistum et al., 2014). This helps to offer the user a continuity of self – particularly a relational self – that is a major component of identity construction.

From the days of Friendster (an early SNS), one of the most attractive features of social media was the ability to reconnect with people from one's past (Tufekci, 2008). Social media is remarkably efficient compared with prior versions of keeping up with friends from long ago, when people had to rely on gossip, chance encounters, or reunions to keep informed about their old friends. The moment of reconnection through social media is often met with excitement, but an excitement that quickly wanes after initial contact (Karakayali & Kilic, 2013; Quinn, 2013). Charting the course of development of these old ties, Ramirez et al. (2017) report that 74% of participants studied had reconnected with someone in the past year, with adults reporting a much higher rate of reconnection (85%) than college students (many of whom had yet to lose contact with friends). People who use social media more actively are more likely to reconnect, and the friends who are reconnected with are often same-gender friends with whom participants were once close. That is, we are not reconnecting with people we barely knew in the first place. However, once these lapsed friendships are reestablished through social media, they begin to recede into the background of intimacy once again. Pennington's (2015) analysis demonstrates that these lapsed friendships are indistinguishable from acquaintances both based on individual's self-reported closeness and based on the content of their public communication through Facebook. People are loath to let go of these old ties for a variety of reasons (Karakayali & Kilic, 2013), and the efficiency of social media to preserve relationships shrinks the costs of doing so to nearly zero. But seen as a major part of an archive of self, I would suspect that this laissez-faire attitude about removing old ties is partly due to the value that they offer to the continuous construction of the relational self.

Although there has been limited work on how audiences view the users' network as a whole (except to say that people with more friends are accurately perceived as more extroverted; Hall, Pennington, & Lueders, 2014b), there is one relationship that has received considerable research attention in terms of its presentation of a relation to an audience: the romantic partner. For adolescents and young adults, the presentation of the relationship as "Facebook official" (FBO) is a marker of relationship stability and exclusivity, particularly for young women; it is an intentional act of relational declaration in the context of a social group (Lane & Piercy, 2017). This act may be quite important for couples in long-distance romantic relationships, as the nature and stability of that relationship may be difficult to see by those in both partners' geographically close social networks (Johnson et al., 2017). This form of identity construction transforms a private process into a public announcement – one that is often received with cheers, heart emoji, and congratulations messages from one's social network (Lane & Piercy, 2017). Facebook users recognize that making a relationship FBO is a meaningful act as a sign of commitment, done, in part, to make the relationship visible and knowable (Johnson et al., 2017; Lane & Piercy, 2017). It demonstrates to people who otherwise might not know the couple what the couple is like or how they feel about each other. This, however, puts strain on the couple to police each other's public presentation of the relationship. As Fox and Frampton (2017) suggest, couples feel a need to present their relationship as flawless on Facebook even when it may be in turmoil privately.

3.6 Representing a Personal History

As a final component of the self archive metaphor, social media are a means of representing one's own personal history. People have long used journals and photo albums to commemorate meaningful experiences, vacations, and personal journeys to themselves. Although these often were objects available for viewing by others, they provided a more important purpose: to be representations of one's own history. Social media have made this incredibly convenient and efficient in the sense that keeping one's profile active is the act of creating a personal history in itself. We are composing our own photo journal in real time.

Facebook is capitalizing on this by offering new features that suggest that users post a Facebook-created commemoration, "On This Day," of posts from the previous year, or post a "friendship anniversary." Humphreys (2018) sees this as a process of reckoning, where users make sense of this digital record in relation to their identity now and in the past. This is not dissimilar to picking up an old photo album or reviewing old journals in terms of what it does for the self, but this act has the added value of making it social and commemorative because the content of the suggested posts is representative of a relational self that is borne on the platform itself.

To broaden the scope somewhat, it is important to point out that the choice of platform to enact one's identity is also a way of representing oneself. The ability to create or maintain a personal website was once a challenging thing to do, requiring particular expertise and internet savvy (something that Myspace capitalized on in its heyday). People used personal websites to construct their identities, usually quite accurately (Marcus, Machilek, & Schütz, 2006), but being able to create a website was an expression of identity in itself. In more contemporary times, Goodreads and Spotify also build in an archival service in tracking which books and music people enjoy (Rettberg, 2018). These are also self-constructive acts (Vazire & Gosling, 2004) that convey identity and employ the symbolism of the platform (e.g., a book lover, a music lover) to represent oneself.

SECTION FOUR: BRIDGING SOCIAL CAPITAL

4.1 What Is Social Capital?

The idea that one's relationships are an important resource has a long history in the study of social networks in general (Wellman et al., 1988) and in the study of online networks particularly (Fu & Lai, 2020; Stoycheff et al., 2017). Social capital gained through social media is the collective informational, material, and emotional resources available because of one's position in the network (i.e., the number and character of network ties). Typically, social capital is divided into two types: bonding and bridging social capital. Bonding social capital is most akin to social support, particularly emotional support. There is a great deal of conceptual and operational overlap between bonding social capital and emotional support. Bridging social capital is thought of as access to novel information, resources, or opportunities. These two concepts map very strongly onto types of relationships – close relationship partners are typically a primary source of bonding social capital, while more distant acquaintances, even arguably strangers, are a source of bridging social capital.

Online social networks have long been closely tied to social capital. One of the earliest bulletin board systems, called the WELL, largely replicated offline ties among technology workers in the Bay Area, and was explicitly maintained for the purpose of bridging social capital, such as looking for new career opportunities (Stevenson, 2018). Scholarship on social media has followed suit. In their quantitative summary, Stoycheff et al. (2017) found that scholarship on social capital is the most dominant approach to social media research, accounting for 39% of all studies. Understanding social media as bridging social capital is a long-established and important way to understand what it is and does.

4.2 Bridging Social Capital

In their valuable meta-analysis of 50 studies with 22,290 participants, Liu, Ainsworth, and Baumeister (2016) explore the association between social media use and both types of social capital. This meta-analysis was followed up with a larger meta-analysis (63 studies, 35,000 people), including online media use of various types (Domahidi, 2018). They conclude that the evidence for social media use facilitating more bridging social capital is quite strong (Liu et al., 2016). That is, users who report having more bridging social capital are more intense users of a SNS (which is typically Facebook). This analysis was reinforced by Domahidi's (2018) conclusion that the majority of online media use (i.e., internet generally, online games, blogs, chats, email) have no association with both bridging and bonding social media. Only online discussion forum and SNS use were associated with these social resources, pointing to their distinct value compared with other online media for social capital.

The two activities most strongly tied to the sense of greater social capital are seeking information and replying to posts (Liu et al., 2016). This makes sense; if you want to have access to information (which is the essence of bridging social capital), you probably need to solicit it through asking for it and to encourage reciprocity of information exchange by responding to others' requests. This builds a norm of reciprocity among casual friends and acquaintances. Responding to other's posts is associated with bridging social capital, but those exchanges need to be reciprocal to be valuable (Burke, Kraut, & Marlow 2011).

This conclusion squares nicely with a three-wave, nationally representative, longitudinal study of Norwegian social media users from 2008 to 2010 (Brandtzæg, 2012). They report that the highest degree of bridging social capital is with those who use social media in a variety of ways. So, it is not enough to just have an account on social media or to spend time on it; it takes active and ongoing use to foster bridging social capital (Domahidi, 2018).

It is worth noting that there are features of social media that facilitate bridging social capital. Quinn and Papacharissi (2018) offer four such characteristics: (1) Social media keep the effort of broadcasting and browsing exceedingly low in comparison to offline corollaries for keeping in touch; (2) social media create pressure to share/post and log in, which enhances collective investment (Orchard et al., 2015); (3) social media have built-in algorithms that promote maintenance and keeping in touch (e.g., birthday greetings); and (4) profiles on social media are living and persistent address books, which may even surpass the phone number or email address in access and longevity (see also Ellison et al., 2014; Standlee, 2019).

4.3 Bonding Social Capital

The evidence for bonding social capital gained through social media is weak. Ellison and Vitak (2015), who are major social capital researchers, suggest that SNS use is unrelated to bonding social capital. In Liu et al.'s (2016) meta-analysis, the effect sizes for bonding social capital were very small and largely contingent on self-disclosure by the users and the portion of close friends and family on the SNS. A study by Facebook researchers themselves supports such a conclusion: Burke et al. (2011) report that "frequent Facebook users tend to be already rich in bonding social capital, and their use of the site does not directly increase the value of those relationships" (p. 8). This also lines up with other lines of inquiry that suggest that socially active people are likely socially active both online and offline (Hall et al., 2019b; Requena & Ayuso, 2018; Twenge et al., 2019).

In summary, the feeling that one has received social support, particularly emotional social support, on social media is largely contingent on self-disclosure and having strong relationships with others who are on the site (Ellison et al., 2014; Liu et al., 2016; Manago & Vaughn, 2015), but these benefits may be simply unrelated to social media use itself because these strong ties are almost certainly offline sources of support as well (Domahidi, 2018).

4.4 Do Social Media Uniquely Contribute to Social Capital?

Answering the question of whether social media uniquely contribute to social capital is strongly tied up in the challenge of studying the multimodal nature of modern relationships. In the case of bonding social capital, the answer seems to be probably not, but for bridging social capital I would respond with a tepid *maybe*.

In the case of bonding social capital, the research suggests that using social media to solicit and receive social support may not matter, and there is some evidence that it may hurt the relationship indirectly. If we return to the arguments of Chapter 1, the first fifteen relationship partners are the most important people in our lives. It is hard for me to imagine circumstances where all of those fifteen significant others are maintained *only* through social media. Research on friendships and social media suggests that more posts by one friend are associated with less closeness between friends (McEwan, 2013) and that "real" friends are expected to make an effort to communicate outside social media (Bryant & Marmo, 2012). Rather, it is much more likely that several modes of communication are necessary to maintain and keep close friends (Domahidi, 2018; Quinn & Papacharissi, 2018). So, there may actually be no value added to perceptions of bonding social capital by using social media more, and using social media as a primary means of seeking emotional social support in the absence of or as a substitute for other social interaction may be detrimental to the relationship.

For bridging social capital, the evidence that the social capital gains are worth the time and/or energy investment is a bit stronger. This is partly due to the remarkable ease of maintaining weak ties. The strongest evidence is that social media activity bridges social capital not so much by reaching out to attract new ties, but rather by strengthening and enriching relationships with people one has met offline (Liu et al., 2016; Manago & Vaughn, 2015). These benefits may be enhanced for people who energetically use social media to maintain a social network that can only be found on social media itself (Ellison et al., 2014). This lines up nicely with Stevenson's (2018) observation that in the early days of online engagement, keeping up with business contacts through posting and sharing on the WELL was a particular boon to bridging social capital for those in the nascent tech industry. In some ways, this is just what professionals call "social networking."

This conclusion should be accepted with the caveat that very few studies actually compare bridging social capital cultivated offline with bridging social capital made possible through social media. The evidence is not so encouraging for saying that the time and effort is worth it. Brandtzæg (2012) found that SNS users and non-SNS users did not differ *over time* in bridging social capital, but SNS users felt more loneliness over time. Domahidi's (2018) meta-analysis concurs that users and nonusers do not differ in perceived social resources in general. Karakayali and Kilic (2013) point out that people may still maintain unpleasant or disappointing relationships through social media for the sake of future material and/or informational benefits, which suggests that cultivating bridging social capital comes with potential costs. Indeed, Hampton, Lu, and Shin (2016) suggest that awareness of undesirable, major events in the lives of others made possible through digital media can be a source of psychological stress (see Chapter 8). But perhaps the most damning evidence comes from Domahidi's finding that online media use is unrelated to offline social capital in general.

The idea that the gains in bridging social capital are greater than the lost time or lack of intimacy associated with socially grooming weak ties online may be unfounded. Future work would do well to simultaneously study the benefits of social capital and the costs of caring and knowing about other people's lives, especially when they are less-than-positive relationships, as well as the costs of time and energy. This work should recognize that bridging social capital certainly exists, offline independent of social media, to better disentangle the purported benefits.

SECTION FIVE: CONCLUSIONS

Once we account for the modes of communication enabled by social media that are extensions (often competitors) for other technologies (e.g., chat programs, email), we can begin to understand what value social media offer relationships. The three metaphors for understanding what social media are – social media as the social news, social media as an archive of self, and social media as bridging social capital – bring into focus that social media use is both personal and relational, both instrumental and affective, and both participatory and leisurely. From the lens of how people relate through technology, the window into the lives and loves of others whom we *choose* to watch is an extension of the all-too-human desire to know and share the goings-on of others. It is an extension of the project of self-construction, particularly, a relational-self. Social media facilitate the maintenance of relationships that represent the narrative of the self and make possible the sharing of knowledge and information. As the SNS and its users have matured (Gramlich, 2019), the question has shifted: Is using Facebook to maintain relationships, again, independent of other modes of contact, a good thing for our sense of well-being and growth as people?

Writing in *The Atlantic*, Julie Beck (2019) calls Facebook the place where friendships go to "never quite die." She writes that because of Facebook these vestigial friendships "live an extended half-life far beyond their nature life space, hobbling on, an inch from death, in the form of likes and invitations to multi-level marketing groups and news-feed photos of children you've never met and don't care about." Although Beck concedes that the majority of communication on SNSs is among close ties, the ambient awareness of the goings-on of others continues to keep these weaker ties in our consciousness, but she queries: To what effect?

It is extremely challenging to account for the multimodal and always-on nature of important personal relationships while at the same time comparing social media–based and non-social media–based social capital (see also Domahidi, 2018). I would argue that we simply do not know whether the value of maintaining these vestigial relationships is a net cost or a net benefit for our own well-being and social capital. Although I would speculate it would depend on the individual and what else they might do with their time, this important question is left to future research to investigate.

7

Five Enduring Tensions in Personal Media

There must be some word today / From my boyfriend so far away/ Please Mr. Postman look and see / If there's a letter for me.
                    —"Please Mister Postman," The Marvelettes (1961)

It's good to hear your voice, you know it's been so long / If I don't get your calls, then everything goes wrong / Don't leave me hanging on the telephone.
                    —"Hanging on the Telephone," The Nerves (1976)

Call-waiting, phone in another time zone / How do you say I miss you to / An answering machine?
                    —"Answering Machine," The Replacements (1984)

Longing for a response has always been a part of keeping in touch with those we love. With a posted letter, delivery delays the response. Once the return letter is received, the confirmation of the reception of the original letter and the response to it are one and the same. Voice calls tie reception to response – if the receiver takes the call. Answering machines, voice mail, and missed call notifications leave a trace of the attempted connection, but do not guarantee a returned call. Until Apple added read receipts to iMessage in 2010, senders could not tell whether a text was received and read by the intended recipient. Mass-personal media (e.g., blogs, social media) have dramatically broadened the size of the audience, but as the audience grows, the ambiguity of reception has risen along with the number of people in the audience who see it but do not respond.

This chapter is dedicated to navigating the issues of message reception, attention, and response in the digital age. To situate this conversation, I will introduce dialectal theory (Baxter & Braithwaite, 2007; Baxter & Simon, 1993), which suggests that there are ever-present and inherent forces in human communication that are mutually dependent yet pushing in opposing directions. These dialectical tensions create a tug-of-war between the opposing sides. Dialectics exist both in the message itself and in the relationship between communication partners. In this chapter, I examine and explore dialectics inherent to contemporary personal media use:

- Hyper-coordination versus micro-coordination
- Personalized messages versus generalized messages
- Contributing to the conversation versus virtual people watching
- Intentional attention versus incidental awareness
- Routine access offline versus limited access offline

These tensions are inherent to interpersonal relationships that are formed and maintained through media, and often result in counterintuitive outcomes. For example, task coordination through CMC requires some degree of relational communication, but too much relational communication crowds out and distracts from task talk. As social media users know well, there is nothing to see if no one is posting or sharing, but would anyone post or share without a responsive audience? Just as in FtF interactions, the self-presenter and their audience are dependent on each other. Dialectical theory offers a useful lens from which to see how coordination, personalization, responsiveness, awareness, and access are essential components of signaling and building intimacy through personal media. None of these can be fully understood without understanding the opposing force on the other side of the dialectic.

SECTION ONE: WHAT ARE DIALECTICAL TENSIONS?

From the perspective of the social construction of technology (Chapter 2), patterns of media use are not inherent features of the technological device or platform, but are emergent properties of use. Media technology may steer users toward particular types of actions, but it is users who bring media affordances into being (Evans et al., 2017). In the context of communicating within personal relationships, the patterns of media use are also influenced by the characteristics of the relationship and the purpose of the interaction. That is, people use media to accomplish particular goals, and these goals are shaped by the relationship between interaction partners. Elements of this fact are inherent to the communication interdependence and layers of electronic intimacy perspectives in that both recognize that particular media are reserved for particular relationships (see Chapter 5). However, there is another pertinent issue here: people socialize for different reasons and with various goals both within a modality and within a relationship. One way to consider this variability is to consider it as a tension within the process of communication itself.

Dialectal theory characterizes relationships as interdependent and ongoing. Like Duck's (1994a) approach to relationships, social interaction is at the center of the dialectical theory. Everyday talk creates space for relationship creation and sustenance, and through talk the dialectical tensions are revealed (Werner & Baxter, 1994). The theory conceptualizes the processes by which relationships find balance within tensions that are both holistic and opposing (Baxter & Braithwaite, 2007; Baxter & Simon, 1993). In other words, the theory assumes that dialectical tensions are unified in that each component of the tension is dependent on its opposite. For example, relational dependence can be understood only in contrast to independence, and without dependence, independence would cease to have meaning. The dependence–independence dialectic, which has been understood as both integration–separation (Werner & Baxter, 1994) and freedom to be both dependent and independent (Rawlins, 1992), is at the core of relationship maintenance (Baxter & Simon, 1993). People seek to be unified in communion and they seek to have their autonomy honored within the relationship. This tension, along with openness–closeness and stability–change, are the three traditional tensions of dialectical theory. However, the central tenets of dialectical theory can be extended to other tensions in relationships and within talk (Baxter & Braithwaite, 2007). This chapter explores five such tensions when relating through technology.

SECTION TWO: HYPER-COORDINATION VERSUS MICRO-COORDINATION

2.1 Hyper- and Micro-coordination in the Era of Texting

The early aughts were a critical period of mobile phone adoption. With increasing adoption, texting frequency grew dramatically, particularly in Europe (Ling, 2004; Rainie & Wellman, 2012). Yet new users did not universally embrace this rise in connectivity. The freedom to be unreachable was rapidly disappearing as presumptions of access grew (Licoppe & Huertin, 2001). This tension closely resembles the dependence–independence interpersonal dialectic (Baxter & Simon, 1993). The constant push toward dependence and pull away toward independence are fundamentally concerned with what it means to be integrated with another person yet able to maintain individuality. New cell phone adopters found themselves in touch with another person in new and compelling ways but also tethered and leashed by this new technology. Along with Licoppe, Ling (Ling 2004; Ling & Yttri, 2002) developed a theory of this tension in the emergent SMS environment, arguing that mobile devices allow for micro-coordination and hyper-coordination.

Although it may be difficult for anyone who grew up with a mobile phone to imagine, the changes brought about by mobile access were dramatic. Mobile connectivity meant that plans were no longer set in stone; you could contact the other person and alter things as needed. Constant connectivity meant events and plans could be rescheduled or better timed, and specifics clarified in the moment (Ling, 2004; Ling & Yttri, 2002). Compared with getting stood up, mobile access meant fewer hurt feelings and confusion when plans changed unexpectedly or someone was unexpectedly delayed. In further developing this idea, Ling and Yttri (2002) note that mobile devices allowed for "nuanced instrumental coordination" (p. 139), especially for individuals in interdependent relationships who are planning and executing many goals at the same time. Little updates, reminders, and check-ins make up the core of SMS communication between romantic couples (Barkhuus & Polichar, 2011), and this type of communication is characteristic of micro-coordination.

By contrast, the hallmark of hyper-coordination is the use of mobile phones for increased relational communication. Just as childcare pick-up plans can be coordinated, in-the-moment joy and upset can be shared and managed with a romantic partner throughout a day, integrating the emotional states of geographically distant partners. This meant relationship partners were no longer completely alone in their own thoughts or feelings or in their ability to share in another's thoughts and feelings.

Both micro- and hyper-coordination were made possible through mobile connectivity. Ling (2004) recognized that expectations of access and responsiveness do not in themselves dictate the content of communication, which can be instrumental as well as emotional. With fewer barriers to continuous coordination, both instrumental and emotional communication skyrocketed between geographically separated partners.

It is consistent with dialectic theory that micro- and hyper-coordination occur simultaneously. That all communication has a content dimension and a relational dimension is a classic axiom of communication theory (Watzlawick, Beavin, & Jackson, 1967). That is, messages convey information but also imply the state of a relationship. Extending that argument to the present mobile moment, all mediated communication has elements of micro- and hyper-coordination (assuming the message has at least some receipt and relevance for the receiver). Indeed, the presence of both types of talk – instrumental and relational – has long been a feature of internet-based communication (Baym, 2000).

The more mobile devices are used to maintain relationships, the more heightened expectations of access there are (Hall & Baym, 2012). At any moment, a mobile user can reach out to someone else and receive validation for any particular thought or feeling. Undoubtedly, smartphone-enabled social media programs have further extended the network of friends and family one could feel obliged to be accessible to (Hall, 2017a). Constant access, bolstered by heightened expectations of responsiveness, becomes a form of emotional labor – not just with close relationship partners but with a broad network of others. This obligation is Janus-faced (Arnold, 2003); it establishes closeness and brings about entrapment (Baron, 2008; Hall & Baym, 2012).

2.2 Coordination and Interdependence

It is important to note that these two sides of the dialectic presume some level of interdependence, but not necessarily intimacy. Long-distance coordination of instrumental tasks is a central purpose of many twentieth-century communications technology. Indeed, instrumental communication was one of the primary purposes of the internet. Coworkers who are interdependent engage in a great deal of time-sensitive, electronic communication. During the rise of the Blackberry, an early mobile device that had a more functional keyboard than its mobile phone competitors, employees often reported a great deal of stress arising from endless contact with the workplace (Middleton & Cukier, 2006). Smartphone access has taken this expression of workplace interdependence one step further. Mobile devices continue to invade personal sanctuaries from work and can be experienced as an infringement on private or domestic spaces (Barkhuus & Polichar, 2011). This experience is not limited to workplace communications. In Ling and Lai's (2016) recent work on micro-coordination, they note that many undergraduate students feel overwhelmed by the sheer number of instrumental messages from teammates, members of student groups, and study partners. The task talk, updates, and reminders are all examples of micro-coordination.

Furthermore, Ling and Lai (2016) provide ample evidence that expected access and responsiveness for instrumental purposes (i.e., micro-coordination) often give rise to relational talk. For some users, this switch to noninstrumental talk (e.g., gossip) encourages them to pay more attention and chime in. This ironically contributes to a muddle of expressive and instrumental talk in the subsequent cascade of messages (Ling & Lai, 2016). This makes it hard for message recipients to discern what to attend to and what to ignore if they just want the "bottom line." The hundreds of messages from a single close friend studied by Hall and Baym (2012) has now become hundreds and hundreds of undirected, general notifications from clubs, teams, study partners, and friends on a smartphone. This suggests that smartphone chat apps (e.g., GroupMe) have made it difficult to avoid the cascade of messages that are imbued with elements of both micro- and hyper-coordination, even in the absence of ongoing interdependence. More textual communication with more, less intimate partners contributes to mobile entrapment over the course of a week (Hall, 2017a). Without mindfully opting out and potentially missing out on relevant updates entirely, these zombie groups slouch along trying to eat the attention of users' brains well past the period of functional interdependence.

2.3 The Irony of Connection

Between close relationship partners both micro- and hyper-coordination result from and create ongoing interdependence. Coordinating dinner plans and brief affectionate messages and emoji are often contained in the same text. Thus, it is quite likely that mundane mediated maintenance (Tong & Walther, 2011) within close relationships has characteristics of both types of coordination at the message and relational levels of analysis. Quick thoughts and check-ins are likely quite welcome between close partners, even contributing to a sense of satisfaction between friends (Hall & Baym, 2012; Licoppe, 2004). Indeed, group texts within a small group of friends (fewer than five) can generate a sense of coziness where people can "really connect" (Ling & Lai, 2016).

As dialectical theory would predict, the connection brought about by mobile devices between relationship partners is ironic (Arnold, 2003), even among relational intimates. Rising expectations increases dependence and overdependence in relationships, which influence relational satisfaction both positively and negatively (Baron, 2011; Hall & Baym, 2012). Duran, Kelly, and Rotaru (2011) found that participants who reported higher expectations of availability saw themselves as more restricted and trapped. One participant commented, "We would argue about whose turn it is to call the other one, or he would act mad that I didn't text him enough or didn't call when I was out at night with friends" (Duran et al., 2011, p. 33). More coordination within the relationship can benefit and undermine relationships, just as dialectical approaches would predict.

SECTION THREE: PERSONALIZED MESSAGES VERSUS GENERALIZED MESSAGES

3.1 Personalization of Messages

Foreshadowed in the bulletin board systems (BBS) in prior decades, the dramatic changes to the media landscape of the 1990s greatly expanded ways of socializing (Delwiche, 2018; Stevenson, 2018). In 1994, Justin Hall (no relation) normalized the idea that "web logs" could be used for personal expression and self-construction. His emergence as the first micro-celebrity of the online world demonstrated that the internet could be used to share personal messages with a large and unknown audience. People wanted to express themselves, and others wanted to read about it.

By contrast, chat rooms, IM programs, and email were all fundamentally different in that the messages were typically directed to one person or a small group of others. While listservs and mass emails were used to share content that was not necessarily directed at any individual, members usually opted to receive those messages from the message author(s) (or perhaps were under professional obligation to receive them). In contrast to both internet-based technologies, personal telephone calls were nearly always one-on-one affairs. The communication within them was highly personalized – it was meant for and responsive to the other person on the line. Thus, on this dimension, IM and email had (and still have) much more in common with a telephone call than the blog, listserv message, or even a social media post.

Message personalization is associated with both the reach and the interactivity of the medium (Baym, 2010) (see the Introduction). As reach increases, the ability to personalize declines. One simply cannot fashion a message that is personalized to every person in a large audience. Social theorist Latanè (1981) argued that as a general rule, the impact of the message is inversely proportional to the size of the audience. The larger the audience, the less each person assumes that the message is meant for them and feels any sense of responsibility to respond to it. Although low reach does not guarantee a highly personalized message, expectations of personalization by the audience and ability to personalize by the speaker both increase with lower reach technology.

Similarly, interactive media facilitate social interaction and personalization. The features of such media steer users toward one-on-one communication, often by increasing social cues as well, such as in the case of voice calls and video chats. Those two characteristics (i.e., reach and interactivity) are core concepts for understanding personalization.

3.2 Mass-Personal Theory

Personalization is also central to mass-personal theory (O'Sullivan, 2005; O'Sullivan & Carr, 2018), and it has been conceptualized as message personalization by Bazarova (2012). The message sender determines the degree of personalization of the message, and it is the degree to which the message is directed toward and tailored for a particular recipient. On the other side of this continuum would be messages shared on the BBS, where the audience was unknown in composition and where it was unclear whether the message was received. On social media platforms (when settings are set to "private"), broadcasted messages have an audience that is restricted to friends and followers. Thus, it is somewhere in the middle in terms of message personalization. Although that audience can be exceedingly large (think about the millions of followers of LeBron James), the audience is still identifiable and recipients could be tracked (depending on the platform and settings).

As discussed in Chapter 6, this book is focused on what O'Sullivan and Carr (2018) call (mediated) interpersonal communication. Highly personalized messages are the hallmark of pure conversation, or social interactions engaged in for the sole purpose of communicating (Duck, 1994a). All personal phone calls and video chats are fully personalized. It would be exceedingly weird (and maybe impossible) to have a conversation with someone on the phone without tailoring and directing the message in response to the person on the other end of the line.

Personalization plays an important role in relationships maintained through texts and group chat programs (Kelly & Watts, 2015; O'Hara et al., 2014). Emoji and memes convey a sense of shared experience and identity. This is particularly powerful when joking around and being playful (Kelly & Watts, 2015). A connection forged through shared humor is a powerful connection.

When messages are sent to an increasingly larger and/or increasingly unknown audience, perceptions of the recipients may not square with the speaker's intended degree of personalization (O'Sullivan & Carr, 2018). As Baym's (2018) analysis of musicians and their fans reveals, fans often feel that a song spoke to them personally or even was meant for them at certain times in their lives. Sometimes they write to the musician wanting to share that feeling. In that case, I would argue that the fan's email to the musician is personalized, but the musician's song is not – no matter what the fan thinks or feels. Although I agree that the audience member's perception is important, when I speak of personalization, it is from the point of view of the message composer.

As a dialectical tension, message personalization has meaning when it is in contrast to a generic message. As Duck (1994a) has argued, when we speak toward another person's individuality and history, we establish a relational force that draws from past communication and points to its continuance. Personalized messages are backward facing in the sense that they draw from what is already known about the audience member(s). Generic messages show no such knowledge or awareness.

SECTION FOUR: CONTRIBUTING TO THE CONVERSATION VERSUS VIRTUAL PEOPLE WATCHING

4.1 Browsing Social Media

In contrast to message personalization, the third dialectic is focused on the audience responsiveness to the messages. This picks up the concept of interactivity (Baym, 2010) in that highly interactive media require a contribution by sender and receiver. This dialectic also engages reach, replicability, and searchability. Media that are broadcasted to a large audience and media that are more permanent and archived encourage users to scan, sort, search, and select what they want to respond to. These features of media enable users to engage in the far end of the dialectic: virtual people watching. Messages wait for you to come to them (although they are increasingly pushed into your attention on the smartphone via notifications). This presentation of content to be browsed encourages scanning and scrolling, but never extinguishes the possibility of contributing to the conversation. Being high reach, highly replicable, and highly searchable are characteristics of many types of social media, and these characteristics engender particular patterns of use.

As addressed in Chapter 6, the majority of time spent on social media is not spent socially interacting but is more like people watching. Several studies have confirmed that browsing is the most time-consuming social media activity (Ancu, 2012; Tosun, 2012). In a three-wave study of nationally representative Norwegian respondents (2008–2010), Brandtzæg (2012) found that most users typically browsed but did not post. In my recent work (i.e., Hall, 2018b), I found that over 50% of social media time was spent passively consuming information others had shared. Furthermore, browsing took up an increasing portion of time as participants spent ten compared with five minutes on social media (i.e., Facebook, Instagram, Twitter). Thus, when people spend time on social media, they rarely contribute content, instead preferring to browse others' posts, photos, tweets, or snaps.

This is by no means a new trend. The early precursors to social media showed a marked tendency toward "lurking" or, more accurately, passively consuming broadcasted information (Delwhiche, 2018; Stevenson, 2018). As dialectical theory presumes, both speaker and audience play an important role in sustaining a mediated space or community. Users who shared personal and instrumental information on BBSs may have led the conversation, but other users kept it going by acknowledging it and threading it into ongoing text-based conversation (Delwhiche, 2018). Although open communication and seeking connection with others were celebrated by those who built virtual communities within the BBS (Stevenson, 2018), there were many members of the community who enjoyed seeing what others had shared, but did not share themselves. The audience has always had a crucial role to play.

The majority of people who made up online discussion groups in the late 1990s were also passive consumers of others' posts (Baym, 2000; Nonnecke & Preece, 2001). Their reasons for doing so should sound familiar to our own experience with social media: they enjoyed reading the conversations between and shared stories of other users, but did not feel they had anything to contribute. Read from the perspective of gossip and the social news (see Chapter 6), we may enjoy hearing about what is going on with other people even if we do not have anything to add today. This trend continues on into the present: a recent analysis of Reddit offered a 90-9-1 rule: 90% watched what was going on without contributing, editing, or liking; 9% provide edits, up votes, or likes; and only 1% of users contribute new content (Buntain & Golbeck, 2014).

Rather than maligning the noncontributors as "lurkers," I believe that reading the social news is a central part of the social experience of social media. We *need an audience* to see our contributions (Donath, 2008). Using social media to get caught up on the social news from both specific individuals and cliques of friends or groups is a central function of social media and promotes awareness of the goings-on of others (Karakayali & Kilic, 2013; Levordashka & Utz, 2016).

It is important to keep in mind that among social media platforms (e.g., Facebook, Twitter, Instagram), the types of responses and the expectations of responsiveness vary (French & Barazova, 2017). That is, whether a sender anticipates some sort of mediated response depends on the norms of the platform. French and Barazova (2017) found that one-click acknowledgments were expected at twice the rate as directed comments in general, but social media users expect more "likes" on Instagram and more direct comments on Facebook and Instagram compared with Twitter. Twitter showed weaker expectations of responsiveness in general, as its platform-specific norms are more informative than social.

4.2 Whether to Respond as Reach Shrinks

This issue of choosing not to respond to messages is relevant to group texting applications (e.g., GroupMe, WhatsApp). The flow of messages among group members can be simply overwhelming: the "signal-to-noise ratio" is difficult to manage (Ling & Lai, 2016, p. 847). Hundreds of messages, complicated by off-topic conversations, asides, jokes, and other commentary, make it exceedingly difficult to figure out the main point or conclusion of the thread. This is an excellent example of a dialectical tension in that the more that people feel the need to contribute and respond to a message thread, the more it may push others to not contribute and respond. Indeed, back channels of communication between smaller groups or dyads sometimes are formed so as to *not contribute* to the volume of responses (Ling & Lai, 2016).

Although we know very well that observing what others have to offer is a long-standing and important component of building an online community, we know very little about how the audience regards threaded conversations between members of the community (O'Sullivan & Carr, 2018; Walther et al., 2010). This idea may inspire future work on virtual eavesdropping and evaluating and/or learning the communication norms from the threaded public conversations of others online. Figuring out what people do and do not say and what is positive or negatively received is a key component of contributing to the social news in an acceptable fashion. This all has implications on impression formation and management as well (Walther et al., 2010). How does all of this public behavior influence impressions of both the original poster and their commenters? To what degree are we known by the content of messages composed by (some) of the company we keep?

Other examples of the tension emergent from the contributing versus watching dialectic can be seen in online spaces where there is a mid-sized to large audience. Work email conversations can break down when too many responses overwhelm others' ability to understand what is going on. The person who decides to respond to every single email may deter other people from chiming in, even when their input or response is valuable or needed.

Again, this is a good example of how a vigorous push to one side of the dialectic can threaten the erasure of the other.

Finally, the size of the group likely further deters future responsiveness *after* someone has responded. Again, classic social psychology research on audience size (i.e., reach) and message influence suggests that people will choose to slough off responsibility for responding to a request when others are around, assuming that others will step up to take responsibility if they just keep quiet (Latanè, 1981). This suggests that even among smaller or mid-sized message groups, contributing to a conversation by any one member may have the effect of decreasing contributions from the rest.

4.3 The Prior Two Dimensions Taken Together

If we think of the prior two dimensions in tandem, high personalization and high target responsiveness (i.e., point A in Figure 7.1) might be characterized by a phone call or video chat where people are highly responsive to one another and engaged in the conversation. Of course, we do not always give our full attention to our conversation partner, and as speakers we often share our own scripted stories or anecdotes that are somewhat depersonalized. My work with Andy Merolla (Merolla, Hall, & Bernhold, 2019) found that when people are distracted in both mediated and FtF social interactions, they feel less connected and more isolated. Distraction seems to detract from the connection that conversation engenders. Although it is accurate to say that high personalization and high partner responsiveness are more likely with high synchrony, high social cues, low reach, and highly interactive media, interactions on such media are not without the possibility of distraction, which may decrease both speaker personalization and partner responsiveness.

On the other side of the continuum (i.e., low responsiveness and low personalization) (i.e., point B in Figure 7.1), we find listservs, blogs, mass emails, and social media posts that no one comments on and no one acknowledges even with a single click. The responsiveness to those type of messages could be low either when the portion of the audience who responds is low or when the amount of the response is low (e.g., a few one-click acknowledgments or a single comment). If Latanè (1981) is correct, the reach of the message itself may contribute to the likelihood of low personalization and responsiveness. It is important to point out that these sorts of occurrences rarely qualify as social interaction at all (Hall, 2018b; O'Sullivan & Carr, 2018), thus to some degree they are outside the scope of this book. Communications in this quandrant rarely have any meaningful impact on relationships, that is, if their effect can be measured at all.

A blog that is heavily shared, retweeted, commented on, and even elicits direct contact in response would be in the low personalization, high responsiveness sector (i.e., point C in Figure 7.1). In both cases, these events may not actually qualify as social interaction, except in the case that there is some

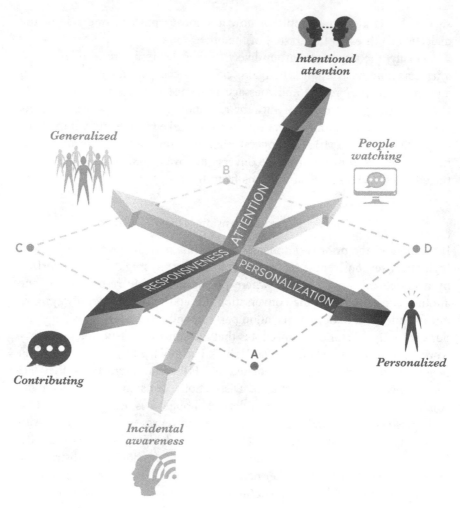

FIGURE 7.1 Enduring tensions: personalization/responsiveness/attention

back-and-forth engagement with the original message poster (Hall, 2018b), which there may be. Nonetheless, partner responsiveness meets an important precondition of social interaction.

At the other corner (i.e., point D in Figure 7.1), messages could be highly personalized but the partner responsiveness could be nonexistent. Such an event presents the mix of anxiety and longing expressed in the songs at the beginning of this chapter, and are part of the process of waiting for a response from the earliest records of people sending messages (Farman, 2018). Did they get my letter? Did they get the message I left on the answering machine? If so, why aren't they responding? These experiences are often fraught with uncertainty and anxiety because the message sender does not know whether there is anybody out there listening.

SECTION FIVE: INTENTIONAL ATTENTION VERSUS INCIDENTAL AWARENESS

5.1 What Is Incidental Awareness?

Message responsiveness and attention to the message are not the same thing. The degree to which they go hand-in-hand is a function of the particular social norms of the medium and the relationship between the people at the two ends of the exchange (Lee et al., 2019). This tension is not solely a function of media reach, replicability, or social cue; instead, it is highly influenced by the existing relationship with the sender.

Consider the concept of ambient awareness. This occurs when an awareness of a person – their personality and their interests – develops not directly through social interaction, but peripherally through repeated observations through social media (Levordashka & Utz, 2016). We may not deliberately attend to anyone in particular on social media, but through repeated consumption of what they share, we gain ambient awareness of what they are all about. This awareness is likely dependent on the human ability to quickly form impressions of others. Indeed, a small portion of followers of any given Twitter account gains ambient awareness of the person behind the account (Levordashka & Utz, 2016). Thus, even in conditions of zero message personalization and zero target responsiveness, some degree of awareness of other people emerges. Though our attention is diffused among those who tweet, as ambient awareness increases, these once-strangers seem more approachable (Levordashka & Utz, 2016). Thus, through incidental awareness, nonpersonalized communication increases the likelihood of future connection with someone we have never directly interacted with.

While ambient awareness is generally considered a positive side effect of social media consumption, the cost of caring is a negative instance of the same phenomenon (Hampton et al., 2016). Among the events shared on social media, many are unpleasant – a job loss, a personal hardship, a midlife crisis. Awareness of negative events in the lives of our online social network may trigger sadness, guilt, or anger in us, even if we do not actively respond to that person's social media posts or engage with them in other ways. It also may make us feel beholden to more closely watch for updates on their situation, thus producing anxiety through anticipation of some resolution that may never come or may never be shared. While this effect was stronger for close ties, Hampton and colleagues (2016) found that people in general, and women in particular, felt greater stress when they were more aware of the negative life events shared by others through media.

Both examples mean that incidental awareness has an effect on the audience, even when the information is neither personalized nor gained through direct interaction.

The modern media landscape fosters an awareness of a wide variety of information (e.g., interests, experiences, opinions) shared by members of one's social media networks (Hampton, 2016). By spending time browsing, reading, and watching, but also by seeing who responds to what in what way, this awareness becomes a crucial component of online community building. It may, in fact, be an essential criterion of what constitutes an online community (Baym, 2000; Walther et al., 2010). We learn not only what is going on with others, but also how attentive and available others in our network are to one another.

This underscores an important point; rather than just "lurking," virtual people watching is an extension of our love of the social news and is a valuable way to learn the social norms of an online community. Virtual people watching has an effect on the audience.

5.2 What Is Intentional Attention?

On the other side of this dialectical axis is intentional attention. This is the attention we give to particular messages or to particular others. Treating this as a separate dimension from responsiveness is appropriate because there are many times where people attend quite actively to a message but do not wish to respond, are waiting to respond, or do not feel a response is even necessary (Lee et al., 2019). People read and reread emails, texts, and social media content, even when they do not have an opportunity or means to respond. For messages that provoke uncertainty, a careful, thoughtful response may take time. Thus, the lack of a quick response (or one at all) may not be a good indication of the importance of the message or the depth or quality of the eventual response. Consider the fact that both in the past and in the present, taking time to create an intentional and thoughtful response through media contributes to the delay in message transmission (Farman, 2018). The delay of response is not a clear indication of the attention given to the message, which means that it is not the same as audience responsiveness. In their innovative study, Lee and colleagues (2019) even found that while people were more attentive to messages from close friends and family, they were not necessarily more responsive to them – that seemed to depend on the co-present contextual demands.

Again, this dimension is bound up in the concept of media that are socially interactive (Baym, 2010; Hall, 2018b). Intentional attention is also built into the voice calls and video chats that we *elect to answer*. Once the call is taken, message responsive and attention are tightly connected on such media. Interestingly, several researchers (Arnold, 2003; Licoppe, 2004; Rettie, 2007) suggested that as texting became widespread, many users began to avoid phone calls altogether. Maybe preferences had switched toward short targeted messages or away from long or drawn-out conversations, or perhaps people never really liked phone calls that much to begin with (Fischer, 1992). Whatever the case, as reported in Chapter 5, this trend of decreasing voice calls has continued in the last decade as well. This could reflect a broader shift in preferences or an outcome predictable from the perspective of CBB theory; people would likely shift to a low-energy medium (i.e., texting) as it increased in availability and decreased in cost.

Whatever the case, compared with voice calls, texting gives people the ability to not attend and to not respond right away, which suggests that people may prefer to have the option to offer their intentional attention when it suits them or as the context demands (Lee et al., 2019). As norms for delayed response through texting developed, it became clear that one of the noted benefits of texting was that it allows people to respond as they are able and willing (Arminen, 2005). Thus, it puts less pressure to be immediately responsive than a voice call, and allows people to slip out of the tether and toward the freedom side of the dialectic that mobile phones first promised (Arnold, 2003).

By disentangling responsiveness from attention, it becomes clear that people are often quite attentive to information they are not responding to immediately. This offers a means of managing increasing obligations of responsiveness in terms of whom we respond to, how we respond, and how much or how often we respond.

5.3 To Whom Do We Give Our Attention?

This issue of choosing to attend to one message over another is relevant to a great deal of media that do not entangle responsiveness and attention. The degree to which people feel that a message or a stream of messages has any relevance for them or has reason for even existing is poorly understood in research. What is it that influences people to send messages or to attend to them in a group chat setting? People are annoyed by the volume of messages and notifications, but admit to being too lazy to bother opting out (Ling & Lai, 2016). I suspect that there is something more than laziness inspiring attention to messages from these zombie groups.

Consider that in a social media environment, personal and emotional posts are frequently offered by acquaintances, especially those seeking social support or acknowledgment (Quinn & Papacharissi, 2018). If seen as an example of hyper-coordination in social media, some level of interdependence is implied. But to whom do we feel responsive toward? How do those responses shape our interdependence with others? How do we regard conversations between others in the thread – with annoyance or interest? Does knowledge of or responsiveness to messages fostering hyper-coordination on the social media platform create costs for the viewer? Micro-coordination of shared activities or events is simply not the primary focus of weak tie relationships (Ling & Yttri, 2002). Instead, the hyper-coordination of the emotions, thoughts, and happenings of increasingly larger networks of others through "likes" and comments will likely follow with each new form of media enabled on a smartphone. How people will manage this dialectal tension as the number of messages from close and distant ties increases?

As a relational phenomenon, I would argue that attention to mediated messages is a sign of relational interest or potential. We attend to messages from people we care about the most both in person and in mediated environments (Lee et al., 2019). When the message composer is unknown to us or someone we know only vaguely, I would suspect that we attend more to messages that we find personally relevant or suggestive of a person whom we might like to get to know better. Because it is possible to accurately detect personality through email names, online profiles, and social media posts and profiles (Tskay & Rule, 2014), when we respond, we may be responding because we find the personality behind the message attractive or similar to ourselves (Grebe & Hall, 2013). On online dating sites, personalized, directed messages may help to elicit a response. Learning about and potentially meeting a new partner can occur only if the partner responds to the message. Often (48% of the time), those introductory messages try to convey similarity between sender and receiver (Sharabi & Dykstra-DeVette, 2019). Once contact is established, asking more questions, seeking similarity, and reducing uncertainty all predict first date success (Sharabi & Caughlin, 2017b). These examples from IM and online dating suggest that attention to the message is an important precursor to message responsiveness. In essence, we give our attention to that which we (might) love.

5.4 In Combination with Other Dimensions

High personalization/high responsiveness (front quadrant in Figure 7.1): Although voice calls and video chats frequently offer me this experience, I can recall moments while texting when I felt fully immersed in interaction – high in all three dimensions. I am attending closely to each message coming in, usually composing a response while receiving new messages. Each message I write is personalized and given my full attention. Although neither completely synchronous nor high on social cues, the experience is compelling and memorable. Thus, it is not just the modality that brings life to these dimensions, but the way they are used.

The alternative occurs when my attention is split or when I am distracted. Although I am still responding to and personalizing my texts or email messages, I may be misreading the meaning of the message sent or perhaps my response is too glib, inattentive, or poorly composed. It is hard to be responsive or to personalize messages when one's attention is split or when one is preoccupied.

High personalization/low responsiveness (right quadrant in Figure 7.1): The initial stages of courtship conducted via text is a great place to see how social attention and personalization could both be high, but responsiveness be low. There is a mountain of lay wisdom about the speed with which someone should contact or respond to a potential romantic interest via media. It used to be focused on how soon to place a voice call, but now a great deal of courtship takes place via text. The more romantically interested someone is, the more effort they may put in crafting careful responses and thoughtfully considering the meaning of past messages. However, both of these intrapersonal actions delay the response. Additionally, not wanting to seem too eager may further delay responses someone would, in fact, very much like to make.

Another example of attention, but not response, as a sign of relational interest is to consider romantic partner monitoring through social media. Everyday surveillance for the sake of romantic partner monitoring is common (Tokunaga, 2016b). People use social media to learn more about a partner without them knowing they have been seen (i.e., low responsiveness, high attention) (Duran & Kelly, 2017; Fox & Frampton, 2017).

On the other side of the continuum, ghosting or blocking someone occurs when the messages received are personalized, but from an unwanted other. Both the responsiveness and the attention to the message are quite low. However, this also creates a delay in response, which adds to confusion, which is inherent to waiting for a reply. By nature, a lack of response, especially to a personalized message, is ambiguous. Thus, this dimension is plagued by the uncertainty of the meaning due to the lack of response itself.

Craiglist's Missed Connections posts are one final example of highly personalized messages, often sent into low responsiveness and low attention environments. People use this free online space to reconnect with someone they briefly met offline. In an insightful article on the content of such posts, Bevan, Galvan, Villasenor, and Henkin (2016) point out how writers praise the beauty and sociability of the missed connection post, which often provides personal and attentive details in hopes of finding and getting a reply from the missed connection. Bevan et al. (2016) were unable to determine the successfulness of such posts because partner responsiveness is not visible on the site. Nonetheless, you have to admire the optimism of posting such yearning, personalized messages.

These examples point out that just because a partner does not reply does not mean they aren't interested (but it doesn't mean they are interested, either).

Low personalization/High responsiveness (left quadrant in Figure 7.1): We might call this *intentionally opting in*. There are several online environments where messages have low to moderate degrees of personalization and audience members respond with varying degrees of responsiveness.

Consider Twitch.tv, where gamers showcase their skills by streaming themselves playing video games. The audience for these content creators can respond to the streamer, but they can also communicate with one another within a text window accompanying the game stream. Although the live-stream has the potential for social interaction, it is a curious form of mixed modality. In real-time streams, the content creator (i.e., the person playing the game) can respond verbally to text-based comments and emoji of audience members who are identifiable by their handles. Arguably, this is a situation where the messages are generally not personalized; however, it affords the possibility of content creators and other audience members to respond to each other directly. When the streamer continues to respond generally (rather than to a particular post by the audience), this is a good example of the streamer using a medium in a less personalized way despite an attentive and active audience.

In the social media environment, a generic and undirected tweet could go viral or gain a multitude of responses and a great deal of social attention. By nature, many social media posts and pictures fit the bill of low personalization. Ones that receive a great deal of attention and responses (i.e., highly quantifiable) are low on personalization but high on the other two dimensions.

Alternatively, the audience might not give much attention to things they one-click acknowledge. Like many people, I have found myself "liking" the post of a person at the top of my Facebook feed who has just received an accolade or experienced a happy event. I join my response with the hundreds of others, but I may quickly forget what happened to this person and give no more thought to their happy day.

Again, these two possibilities are examples of how high responsiveness to a less personalized message in the social media environment may not be equally representative of social attention or social interest. As I mentioned in Chapter 1, this is another case in which we should not confuse the quantification of response as a good indication of interest, approval, or relational connection.

Low personalization/ low responsiveness (rear quadrant in Figure 7.1): Undoubtedly, a great deal of listserv messages, mass emails, and social media posts fit the dimension of low responsiveness and low attention. No one cares and no one responds.

In the case that people care very much, but are simply not responding to nonpersonalized messages, the author may be quite taken aback. I have heard of cases of bloggers who stop sharing their ideas online because they have not seen a sufficient response to merit continuing. Once they stop, their previously unseen audience responds in dramatic fashion – singing their praises and appreciating their work.

Again, this dynamic speaks to the ambiguity created when attention and responsiveness are not in alignment.

SECTION SIX: ROUTINE ACCESS OFFLINE VERSUS LIMITED ACCESS OFFLINE

6.1 The Erasure of Geographic Distance

One of the most important ways communication within relationships has been transformed by media is the erasure of geographic distance. More than at any other time in human history, geographic distance is no longer a barrier to social interaction. The current menu of personal media options has nearly completely erased all of the traditional boundaries between individuals. I say "nearly completely" with two caveats in mind, the first being access. Despite incredible market penetration of mobile media and wireless internet connectivity in the United States and other industrialized countries (Rainie & Wellman, 2012), access to technology is still a major barrier to reaching people you might wish to communicate with. In a revealing study on mobile phone use in Colombia, Velasquez (2018) found that when deciding whether to purchase a mobile phone for their teen, parents often had to balance the costs and risks associated with owning one (e.g., robbery) with the desire to reach their teens when they were away. Work-arounds were often found to reach their children through a combination of media, including traditional landline telephone calls. Depending on the area of the world, a particular service or platform may not be available at all. Showing the power of making do (Chapter 2), families find creative means of gaining access to one another (Madianou & Miller, 2012).

This constant potential for communication makes friendships and romantic relationships more flexible than ever (Johnson & Becker, 2011; Johnson et al., 2017; Ruppel et al., 2018). There is no question that the current personal media landscape, including wireless access and high-quality video streaming, are vastly cheaper and more seamless than CMC options ten or twenty years ago. Geographically distant friendships can be maintained with greater ease than before (Ruppel et al., 2018). Furthermore, social media have transformed people's ability to keep in touch with a large network of friends and family despite frequent moves across the country (Ramirez et al., 2017).

In part because of these options, young adults maintain long-distance romantic relationships (LDRRs) quite often; 75% report having been in a such a relationship at some point (Stafford, 2015). These relationships are heavily dependent on mediated social interactions, from text and phone calls (Tong & Walther, 2011) to social media (Johnson et al., 2017) and video chat (Neustaedter & Greenberg, 2012). Through these means of connection, LDRRs can sustain similar levels of closeness and satisfaction as geographically close relationships (Stafford, 2015). Partners carry on mundane mobile maintenance through texting and make a voice call to coordinate tasks or talk in greater depth (Neustaedter & Greenberg, 2012). One of the greatest benefits of video chat, among the modalities, was the feeling of being able to hang out with the other person, to see them, and to share day-to-day experiences like watching TV, eating dinner, and even falling asleep or waking up together. All of this points to the extensive use of mediated social interactions to keep a relationship sustained. Indeed, when the frequency and duration of mediated social interactions drop off, LDRRs often experience decreases in closeness that may end the relationship (Tong & Walther, 2011).

6.2 Long-Distance Relationships Require People to Build Interdependence

While recognized for its historical exceptionality, it is important to temper this enthusiasm for the possibilities of maintaining relationships over geographic distance by recognizing that – somewhat ironically – relationship maintenance is more elective and perhaps less interdependent as a consequence. Rainie and Wellman (2012) celebrate the atomized, geographically free, choice-driven nature of mediated personal networks. The concept of *networked individualism* refers to the way that people are increasingly at the center of their own voluntary and far-reaching network of ties. If their analysis of the present moment is accurate, it is incumbent on long-distance friends, family, and romantic partners to build interdependence through media. This is, indeed, quite an important skill set in the digital age we live in (Caplan, 2018).

This issue is given more attention in Chapter 8, but for now consider how much more difficult it is to establish interdependence between relationship partners – romantic partners, friends, and family alike – who are geographically separate compared with those who are frequently co-present. If relationship interdependence is the driving force that motivates patterns of media use and integration of media is associated with closeness in relationships (Caughlin & Sharabi, 2013; Ruppel et al., 2018), it is difficult to establish interdependence without routine, predictable, and daily communication. Because mediated interactions are elective and social interactions that are geographically proximal are more obligatory and routine by nature, couples have to work harder, mindfully, and habitually to keep in touch when separated geographically.

To do this, long-distance relationships must construct and reinforce predictable patterns of social interaction (Quan-Haase & Collins, 2008). There is something quite intimate in knowing someone's daily schedule (Humphreys, 2018). There is evidence that this work may be primarily reserved for our most important relationships, and rightly so. Core network members are the closest and most enduring relationships in a person's life (see Chapter 1). At least a few of them are unique – one's parents and children are irreplaceable and one's LDRR partner can be exclusive. There are dramatic examples of the importance of media in maintaining those relationships: mothers and grandmothers of Filipina migrant workers who first went online to see their children and grandchildren via a webcam, joined Facebook to see family pictures, or started texting to be close to their kids (Madianou & Miller, 2012); international students who leave Skype on for hours while they go about their business to create a feeling of routineness and "real conversation" with family far away (Yang et al., 2014; Vlahovic et al., 2012); and young adults who make a voice call in the evening to mimic the routine, evening check-ins with parents that they enjoyed when they lived at home (Aledavood et al., 2015). For modalities that require more synchrony and engender greater social presence, such as video chat, LDDRs developed routines to simulate "a couple living together" to keep their relationship in good health (Neustaedter & Greenberg, 2012, p. 4). This mirrors families spread out over the world who rely on video chat and voice calls on particular times and days to foster routine connection (e.g., Madianou & Miller, 2012; Platt et al., 2014). All of these examples point to how the *absence* of important others shapes personal media use in crucial ways.

6.3 The Barriers to Long-Distance Communicative Interdependence

I find it curious that proponents who celebrate the reduction of geographic barriers do not focus much on whether and why people do not call, text, or reach out. Consider that even among the first fifteen most important relationship partners, more than monthly contact with people who do not live in the same house is rare (Tillema et al., 2010). That is, although people could keep in touch through media, in practice, they do not. I suspect that just as in the era of the telephone and posted letters, some people are just not very good at maintaining relationships from afar (Fischer, 1992).

Part of this has to do with the other side of the interdependence dialectic – the availability of others who are geographically close. When people develop interaction routines and become reliant on others to manage day-to-day tasks and activities, the need and desire to keep in touch with geographically far others likely declines. Following the overall dialectic tension, it seems quite likely that these efforts to create routine connection may result in less communication with geographically proximate others. In a study of the adoption of texting and voice calls among adolescents, Thulin and Vilhelmson (2005) found that more frequent mediated communication tended to increase connection felt with long-distance others, but the total amount of communication with others remained constant overall.

Furthermore, individuals may not wish to be accessible at certain times, and are not equally responsive in terms of length of response or attentiveness (Licoppe, 2012). In fact, one of the challenges during early stages of romantic relationships is sorting out norms of mobile and social media use – how responsive, how accessible, how lengthy the response should be (Miller-Ott &

Kelly, 2016). Although the barrier of reaching people may be removed – that is, people *can* call, text, connect to others at any time – individuals often choose to be unreachable, unavailable, or inattentive, thus reestablishing boundaries (Licoppe & Heurtin, 2001). Among parents and college-aged kids, there are challenges to knowing when someone is available to take a call (Platt et al., 2014). Even if the interruption is welcome, a person may not be able to talk.

Some of the dark side of LDRRs is evident in this dialectic as well. Because of a greater reliance on media, there may be more conflict or disagreement as to how to use media and more partner guarding (i.e., surveillance) through social media (Johnson et al., 2017). The public presentation of the couple's identity through social media can be a particular source of stress as couples in LDRRs attempt to demonstrate their "couplehood" to audiences that are often quite distinct for each partner (Fox & Frampton, 2017). Because their identity as a couple is tied up in the use of media, they must present their identity as a couple and their relationship with co-present others carefully.

SECTION SEVEN: CONCLUSION

There is no question that the options for connecting with others are radically different in scope and nature than they were forty years ago. Yet the fundamental need to connect with one another and find available and responsive partners remains, no matter the modality of connection or amount of media options. The five tensions addressed in this chapter reveal that some characteristics of more traditional forms of social interaction are still present and important no matter the modality, but this new media landscape has changed the nature and pattern of links between them. Unlike in FtF interaction, in mediated social interactions partner reception is not a given, and a lack of responsiveness does not mean that attention is not being paid. These challenges and disconnects create new tensions in the navigation of our social lives because they increase uncertainty and require greater intentionality. To manage the integration of our relationships among and between various modalities, we must be more intentional and mindful in our communication choices. Social routines must be built and uncertainty about partners and connections must be managed in this age of multimodality, to a greater extent now than perhaps ever before.

8

Digital Stress

Both those who study technology and those who are active users of it are deeply concerned about the role of smartphones and social media on personal and societal health and well-being.

Consistent with the arguments of Chapters 1 and 2 of this book, the relationship between technology use and well-being is not linear and unidirectional, especially in the context of communication within personal relationships. For reasons I review in this chapter, I believe that although there are meaningful stressors that accompany the use of personal media, the experience of digital stress is not *caused* by media itself. These stressors can be understood at the intersection between the fundamental tendency to seek connection and individuals' patterns of media use enabled or encouraged by a platform's or a device's functionality. Technology does not *do* things to us (Chapter 2), but patterns of technology use and the internalized experiences of what it means about our connection to others can contribute to digital stress.

Underlying these debates is the all-too-human struggle to stay present and build nourishing relationships with others. This chapter looks at how digital stress interferes with our ability to get these fundamental needs met.

I start by reviewing the evidence that social media, in particular, and technology, in general, *causes* harm. Then I present five possible sources of digital stress that represent the subjective negative experiences that can accompany personal media use.

SECTION ONE: IS SOCIAL MEDIA BAD FOR YOU?

1.1 It's Not That Bad, If It Is Bad at All

Two decades ago, there was widespread concern about the harms of the then-newish internet (e.g., Nie, 2001), but these concerns dissipated as people became more familiar with the technology and began to realize the various social and instrumental ways it could be used. Summarizing research from that time, a large meta-analysis confirmed a negligible association between internet use and well-being ($r = -0.04$) (Huang, 2010). As mobile and wireless technology developed, the target of our public anxieties shifted.

Contemporary debates about the harms of personal media use have zeroed in on two particular sources: social media, particularly Facebook, and the smartphone. A meta-analysis of cross-sectional studies reporting on the association between Facebook use and loneliness, including more than 9,000 Facebook users, reported a small association ($r = 0.13$) (Song et al., 2014). A systematic quantitative review concluded that the association between SNS use and depression is positive, but often influenced by the type of user and types of use (Baker & Algorta, 2016). The use of multiple social media platforms is associated with increased risk of depression and anxiety (Primack et al., 2017). A recent meta-analysis of time spent on social media, including nearly 20,000 participants from sixty-one studies, found a weak negative association between time on social media and well-being ($r = -0.07$) (Huang, 2017). When positive and negative indicators of well-being were separated, time spent on social media seemed to have no association with positive outcomes (e.g., life satisfaction) and a weak association with negative outcomes (e.g., loneliness) (Huang, 2017). As these studies report cross-sectional and not experimental effects, the next question is, What is the evidence of social media *causing* loneliness, lowered well-being, and increased stress?

Unfortunately, the answer is that there is not much experimental evidence, and the evidence that does exist is decidedly mixed. Abstaining from Facebook for forty-eight hours increases feelings of disconnection (Sheldon et al., 2011), but also increases life satisfaction (Hinsch & Sheldon, 2013). Another study found that, compared with abstaining from Facebook for five days, staying on Facebook showed an *increase* in life satisfaction and *decrease* in perceived stress (Vanman, Baker, & Tobin, 2018). One study found that a single week of abstinence from Facebook resulted in an increase in life satisfaction and positive emotions (Tromholt, 2016), but another showed no significant reduction in stress (Turel, Cavagnaro, & Mesi, 2018). Stieger and Lewetz (2018) studied a single week of social media abstinence situated between two four-day periods, which allowed the researchers to check how well-being changed as people switched onto and off of social media. Social media abstinence, however, produced no changes in positive or negative affect from a baseline (Stieger & Lewetz, 2018). Another study found that limiting Facebook, Instagram, and Snapchat to ten minutes of use of each program per day for a period of four weeks decreased loneliness and depression from baseline, but produced no change in anxiety or well-being (Hunt, Marx, Lipson, & Young, 2018).

In my own work (Hall, Xing, Ross, & Johnson, in press), I tracked people for four weeks and asked some people stay off social media the whole time, some people to stay on social media the whole time, and some to switch back and forth for weeks at a time. However, we found no benefit of abstinence when participants were required to stay off all of the four most common social media platforms (i.e., Facebook, Instagram, Snapchat, Twitter). In other words, using or abstaining from social media had no effects on loneliness, affective well-being, and quality of day. Our null effects are consistent with Stieger and Lewetz (2018), who also asked participants to abstain from several types of social media, and Hunt et al. (2018), who found no change in well-being over four weeks. This suggests that there is no real benefit to getting off social media.

I would point out that the only study (Vanman et al., 2018) that used biological measures of stress (i.e., salivary cortisol) found that Facebook abstinence decreases stress ($d = 0.41$). However, participants seemed to be unaware of this benefit. That same study reported that participants *perceived a decrease* in stress whether continuing to use or abstaining from Facebook, even though only the abstainers' biological data suggested they were actually less stressed.

Studies exploring the effect of social media use on well-being over much longer periods of time have also been mixed. A recent three-year longitudinal study (Shakya & Chistakis, 2017) of the association between Facebook use and well-being found that the number of clicked links and "likes" predicted lower physical and lower mental health one year later. Researchers from Facebook (Burke & Kraut, 2016) found that the number of direct messages sent through Facebook from strong social ties was associated with increased well-being over time, but other forms of Facebook use were unrelated to positive outcomes. Focusing on adolescents, Twenge, Joiner, Rogers, & Martin (2018a) found significant associations between the screen activities of adolescents in general (including, but not limited to, the use of social media) and self-reported depressive symptoms and suicidal ideation. But these conclusions were controversial. Responding to Twenge et al. (2018a) directly, a longitudinal study including adolescents and young adults showed that social media use did not predict depression, but depression predicted future social media use, and more strongly for adolescents than for young adults (Heffer, Good, Daly, MacDonell, & Willoughby, 2019). Another recent study focused on adolescents describes the longitudinal effects of social media use as "tiny – arguably trivial" (Orben, Dielin, & Pryzbylski, 2019, p. 10227).

I would caution that despite attention-grabbing headlines about the inevitable harms of social media use, especially on adolescents, the research evidence is mixed. At worst, the effect is negative and very small. At best, there are no causal harms or benefits from using social media.

1.2 How You Use It Matters

Consistent with the SCOT perspective, how people use social media seems to influence what they get out of it. Passive use (e.g., browsing, not interacting) is associated with decreased well-being, while active use (e.g., posting updates, sending private messages) shows no effect (Hall, 2018b; Verduyn et al., 2015). This suggests that active use of social media leaves the user no better or worse than they were before. A recent experimental test of this association suggests that typical patterns of use influence the effects of taking a social media break (Hanley, Watt, & Coventry, 2019). People who post, upload pictures, comment on others' posts and pictures, and privately message each other through Instagram and Facebook stand the most to lose by abstaining from social media. People who primarily scroll and browse have the most to gain from abstaining. Notice that the first set of behaviors might qualify as social interaction, and the second is not social interaction at all (Chapter 1). Thus, if you use social media to socially interact, you lose out more if you take a break from it.

Also notice that unlike in the case of social media, there are no studies that I could find that look at texting abstinence, voice call abstinence, or video chat abstinence. It seems that neither is there a public worry about the negative effects of those modalities nor does it seem that researchers are interested in studying the effects of abstaining from them (in Chapter 9, I review the evidence of the harms of co-present device use). However, it was not always this way. Fischer (1992) suggests that Americans once believed that telephones were ruining people's lives and making them isolated.

Summarizing research from the online era before social media (i.e., 1996–2005), Caplan (2018) suggests that people who experienced problematic internet use were often drawn to the social functions of the internet: chatting, meeting new people, and seeking social support. Around that same period of time, another study suggests that those who seek new romantic relationships online may struggle with intimacy in FtF romantic relationships (Scott, Mottarella, & Lavooy, 2006). Unfortunately for those who relied on online intimacy, they were often unsatisfied with the romantic relationships that stayed online (Scott et al., 2006). Both findings suggest that solely online means of relationship building, for both romance and friendship (Mesch & Talmud, 2006), are interpersonally unsatisfying and may even promote problematic uses of online media.

As research designs become more sophisticated and research labs move past self-reported measures of technology use and stress, I hope researchers begin to explore the effects of technology use in relation to several modalities at once, in the context of preexisting relationships in general and taking into account differences between multimodal and online-only relationships. It seems quite likely to me that relationship qualities (e.g., partner closeness and whether the relationship is online only) play a considerable role in understanding whether the modality is a net benefit or a net cost to individuals' well-being.

1.3 How You Perceive It Matters Too

Diving deeply into research on smartphone and mobile use broadly speaking (i.e., not only social media use), it appears that the amount of mobile use itself is not a good predictor of well-being. Rather, it is the stress and anxiety accompanying the connection demands (Thomée, Härenstam, & Hagberg, 2011) or the perception that the load is unmanageable (Misra & Stokols, 2012) that best predicts negative outcomes. The stress of availability through mobile phones is associated with lower present and future well-being (i.e., stress, depression), but this stress is only weakly associated with frequency of use itself (Thomée et al., 2011). Considering various forms of media use, the total amount of media connection is inconsistently associated with well-being (LaRose, Connolly, Lee, Li, & Hales, 2014; Reinecke et al., 2017). Yet when media connectivity is perceived to be uncontrollable or overwhelming, it negatively predicts well-being (Misra & Stokols, 2012; LaRose et al., 2014; Reinecke et al., 2017; Thomée et al., 2011).

This is where digital stress comes in. The raw amount of personal and social media use is not a good indicator of how one is affected. Instead, it is whether the use of technology feels unmanageable or overwhelming, anxiety provoking, or upsetting. It is the subjective experience of media use that really matters.

SECTION TWO: SOCIAL NEEDS, REGULATORY PROCESSES, AND DIGITAL STRESS

2.1 Two Social Systems and Finite Time and Energy

As discussed in Chapter 3, CBB theory (Hall & Davis, 2017) presents two social systems that regulate the patterns of sociability within people's days. First and primary is the fundamental need to belong, which pushes us to engage in social interactions and other communicative behaviors in order to form and maintain meaningful, enduring relationships (Leary & Kelley, 2008). Both mediated and FtF interactions can nourish relationships (Hall, 2018b; Hall & Merolla, 2020). CBB theory does not suggest that mediated interactions are not capable of nourishing our need to belong or playing a crucial role in relationship maintenance. However, in Chapter 3, I discussed why I am skeptical whether forms of social media use that do not qualify as social interaction (e.g., passive browsing) can nourish our belongingness needs (see also Pollet et al., 2011; Sheldon et al., 2011). It should also be noted that modalities are not equivalent in the effects they have on relationships (see Chapter 5). Yet I do believe that most people perceive that social media use is quite social and that it is a useful way to maintain relationships.

The second social system described in CBB theory is the homeostatic social interaction system as described by the social affiliation model

(O'Conner & Rosenblood, 1996). This model offers the basic observation that we do not endlessly seek social connection; sometimes we wish to be alone and sometimes we wish to be in the company of others. People will steer their days to balance these two desires (Hall, 2017b; O'Conner & Rosenblood, 1996). Once people get their belongingness needs satisfied, they are more likely to be alone later in the day (Hall, 2018a). People who typically feel that their social needs are met when they are alone are happier, emotionally healthier people (Hall & Merolla, 2020).

Following the logic of CBB theory, these two systems are affected by a third force: the conversation of energy. Time and social energy are finite; thus, people are pressed to look for more efficient ways to get those needs met, and social media is truly a low-energy expenditure medium; passive browsing is no more energy intensive than being alone and not interacting (see Chapter 3). Thus, I expect that passive social media use is partly a result of trying to balance these three forces – people seek a low energy means to try to get a quick hit of social need satisfaction (Hinsch & Sheldon, 2013; Wang et al., 2012), and no type of personal media is as efficient as social media browsing.

2.2 This Is Where Digital Stress Comes In

As I have argued throughout this book, one of the challenges of the smartphone era is managing the constant access to one another and building routines of mediated social interactions that are both practically achievable and relationship nourishing (see Chapter 10). Unfortunately, these goals are not the goals of the designers of social media and smartphones (Harris, 2014). Corporations compete for our attention and time through online media. As we become further wedded to our smartphones for managing the tasks of day-to-day life, it is becoming increasingly hard to find an escape from those social and nonsocial demands on our time and attention. Digital stress is partly a manifestation of our attempt to regulate the satisfaction of belongingness needs with the manifold opportunities to connect through technology. We struggle to sustain habits of connection that balance the inherent dialectic of interdependence and independence when relating through technology (Licoppe, 2012).

A recent study illustrated how social media features and device functionality influence our ability to get our needs met. This clever study had participants turn off read receipts, hide their phones when they were not using them, and turn off ringtones and vibrations to find out what effect these features had on participants' pressure to be available to others (Halfmann & Rieger, 2019). When participants reduced these technological connection cues (Bayer, Ling, & Campbell, 2015), they felt more able to meet their own goals and more able to feel free and in control of their lives throughout the day. However, turning off those technology-based cues had no effect on participants' ability to feel close and connected to others. This suggests that, rather ironically (Arnold, 2003), people use smartphones to socially connect, but all of those reminders, buzzes, and notifications have little bearing on our ability to feel connected. As Reinecke (2017) summarized: "the constant presence of the online environment makes it hard to get a break from the challenging and potentially straining effects of Internet use" (p. 237). This pressure to be available has social origins amplified by technology, but the internalization of the obligation may not actually help us feel connected. The pull of technology (e.g., notifications) interferes with our sense of control of our lives and does little to engender connection.

Consider another irony that accompanies the social pressure to be constantly available. My research on entrapment (Hall, 2017a; Hall & Baym, 2012) suggests that availability stress is an outgrowth of efforts to figure out relational norms of mobile dependence for relationship maintenance. Our mobile media habits are often social connection practices as well, formed when we internalize expectations to communicate with and be responsive to others. But this pressure to be available is a double-edged sword: it is associated with relational satisfaction and dissatisfaction in friendships (Hall & Baym, 2012). Indeed, ease of access is perceived to be the best *and* the worst thing about mobile devices (Baron, 2011; Weinstein & Selman, 2014).

2.3 What Is Digital Stress?

The navigation of device and platform functionality, the learning and internalization of norms, and the formation of technological habits can be challenging and taxing. As Chapter 2 illustrated, we are always under pressure to learn how to use new devices, new platforms, and new apps, which leaves us trying to make do with what we already have (see also Primack et al., 2017). In short, navigating the use of technology is stressful. Digital stress has been defined as the "stress resulting from a strong and perhaps almost permanent use of information and communication technology ... that is triggered by permanent access to an inconceivable amount and diversity of (social) content" (Hefner & Vorderer, 2016, p. 237). The term refers to notifications from devices or platforms and the actual use of media platforms (Thomée et al., 2011) and the resulting stress or anxiety (e.g., Reinicke et al., 2017).

My colleagues and I (Steele, Hall, & Christopherson, 2020, p. 17–18) define digital stress as the "subjective experience of an event, condition, or stimulus (i.e., a "stressor") in the context of the individual's social and relational contexts and coping resources" (pp. 3–4). This definition allows for the possibility that people are stressed by their media use, no matter how much or how little they actually use it. Although we expect that the amount of media use probably contributes to stress, it is the subjective response to the experience of using technology that matters the most (Hefner & Vorderer,

2016). Think of it this way: digital stress is opportunistic; it takes advantage of us when we try to do too much with technology.

SECTION THREE: FIVE TYPES OF STRESS

Many qualitative and quantitative studies have talked about digital stress, but they use a wide variety of terms to refer to similar or identical constructs (Steele et al., 2020). Our team counted at least nine different types of digital stress in the literature. Below, I offer a summary of the four types of digital stress that we propose (Steele et al., 2020), and one additional type of digital stress developed by Hampton et al. (2016) that I feel merits inclusion in this conversation.

3.1 Availability Stress

Ever since the widespread adoption of the mobile phone, the demand to be available has been a source of stress (Baron, 2008; Hall & Baym, 2012; Licoppe, 2012; Mihailidis, 2014). Social media, in particular, and increasingly chat apps (e.g., WhatsApp, GroupMe) offer a near-constant stream of communicative input that one may feel obligated to be responsive to (Ling & Lai, 2016; Lo, 2019). This pressures mobile device users to respond to and be available to others. For example, Thomée et al. (2011) identified availability demands as a predictor of stress and depression in adult mobile phone users. Among adolescents, Reinecke et al. (2017) identified social pressure as a significant predictor of communication load. Many college student Facebook users reported pressure to "stay connected to friends no matter the place or time" (Fox & Moreland, 2015, p. 171). Particular features of a platform (e.g., "seen" or "read" functions that are becoming increasingly available across platforms) can accentuate stress by heightening the obligation to respond (Ling & Lai, 2016; Mai, Freudenthaler, Schneider, & Vorderer, 2015). When read receipts are enabled, if you read a message, you might feel as if you have to respond to it so as not to upset or offend the sender.

Availability stress is likely greater in certain modalities than others. The synchrony and mobility dimensions of some media (Baym, 2010) may enhance the social pressure to be constantly available. When a platform or program is more synchronous, the transmission of digital messages is nearly instantaneous. When media are more available (i.e., high mobility), users are accessible no matter where the user is geographically and what else they are doing. Licoppe (2012) calls this the "crisis of the summons," pointing out that wherever we are and whatever we are doing, communications from the device demand our attention.

Consistent with the SCOT perspective (Chapter 2), availability stress is not merely a product of technology; it emerges from social norms of use. Nesi et al. (2018) note that the dimension of availability is tied up with internalized expectations of availability. Thus, this type of stress is not strictly a function of media but a response to societal, relational, and personal norms surrounding availability and responsiveness. Indeed, each relationship (e.g., friendship, parent–child) develops its own norm of availability (Baron, 2008; Hall & Baym, 2012; Miler-Ott & Kelly, 2016; Platt et al., 2014). When a smartphone buzzes or lights up, its owner does not know whether it is an urgent message from mom or a romantic partner or a former classmate weighing in on an Instagram photo (Lee et al., 2019). Noting that the use of several social media platforms is a risk factor for depression, Primack et al. (2017) speculate that constant learning and relearning of these expressive and availability norms may contribute to negative outcomes. Thus, developing norms of use within relationships and within each platform or modality may contribute to availability stress in itself.

3.2 Approval Anxiety

Approval anxiety is the degree of uncertainty and anxiety about others' responses and reactions to one's posts, photos, or messages and to the composite of one's digital footprint (i.e., one's digital profile) (Steele et al., 2020). CMC research has long recognized that digital media allow users to craft a highly controlled impression of the self. Theories such as SIPT and the hyperpersonal model speak to how this process influences relationship development through media (see Chapter 3). We also think (Steele et al., 2020) that approval anxiety is influenced by age and social development. The need for peer approval and social validation in adolescence creates a fecund environment for social comparison, reflected appraisal, and feedback seeking. On several social media platforms, particular features, such as quantifying the number of one-click acknowledgments, likely draw attention to the degree to which users get the feedback they seek. This may contribute to more approval anxiety: the association between time on Facebook and self-reported depressive symptoms is mediated by users' social comparison behavior (Steers, Wickham, & Acitelli, 2014).

Approval anxiety is likely most salient when constructing a profile or sharing new digital material, or in the context of understanding or interpreting new relational partners or communicative exchanges with uncertain outcomes (e.g., chatting with a potential romantic partner). Many users on online dating platforms describe the process as tiring and exhausting, plagued with repeated moments of uncertainty and social judgment. Offering oneself up for approval and judgment through profiles and photos carries the risk of experiencing approval anxiety and stress.

Personal media that are more public, more searchable, and more permanent are likely to be places where approval anxiety is higher by nature.

Social media have all three of these characteristics, compared with other modalities. Partly because it is so public, so searchable, and so permanent, people feel they have to create a desirable and attractive profile (see Chapter 6). At the same time, profiles cannot be misleading because there are consequences of misrepresentation, such as lost opportunities for new relationship development (Hall et al., 2014b). People must avoid appearing conceited or full of themselves, while at the same time seeming sexy, interesting, engaging, and successful. It is exhausting just listing the inherent challenges of managing this impression.

Thus, approval anxiety likely is tied to the performative, public, and permanent nature of social media posts and profiles (Weidman et al., 2012). Personal media that render shared content more permanent and public seem likely to lead to more approval anxiety than media that are ephemeral (e.g., Snapchat) or private (e.g., texting). When platforms such as Instagram encourage the sharing of photos (i.e., greater "visibility") or steer users toward public acknowledgment (i.e., quantifying their "likes" or "shares"), approval anxiety may be heightened. This appears to be partly the motivation behind the current consideration of phasing out quantifying metrics on Instagram.

3.3 Fear of Missing Out

The lay public knows what the fear of missing out (FOMO) is. We proceeded cautiously, defining this idea as "the distress resulting from the real, perceived, or anticipated social consequences of others engaging in rewarding experiences from which one is absent" (Steele et al., 2020, p. 19). You'll notice it is not exactly fear but the anxiety or upset that accompanies feeling left out or excluded. Digital media are both places where social interaction occurs and a means by which offline activities are presented for others' consumption. In other words, we share and post to be seen, and we voraciously people-watch to see what others are doing. Thus, our definition refers specifically to the positive experiences of others advertised through media, particularly experiences from which one is absent and others we know are present.

FOMO influences the associations among poor mood and depression and social media use (Barry, Sidoti, Briggs, Reiter, & Lindsey, 2017; Przybylski, Murayama, DeHaan, & Gladwell, 2013). That is, whether social media use is associated with well-being partly depended on whether people felt excluded by what they saw there.

Some modalities, such as one-on-one texting or chatting, direct users toward more socially interactive experiences (Baym, 2010), which tend to result in a stronger sense of relatedness than with social media use generally and browsing specifically (see Chapter 5). More directional communication (i.e., one-on-one or one-to-few) may decrease FOMO, because such patterns of use are fundamentally interactive and inclusive, especially compared with passive consumption or scrolling (see also Valkenberg & Peter, 2009, on IM). This also may account for why active social media use, which includes posting, commenting on others' posts, and sending direct messages, has a more positive influence on relationships (Burke & Kraut, 2014) and well-being in general (Burke & Kraut, 2016) compared with passive use. I would suspect that highly socially interactive digital media use is associated with less FOMO compared with less interactive forms of use because such forms of use limit the number of communication partners by nature (Hall, 2017a), which allows for the possibility of feeling more related and connected (Hall, 2018b) (Chapter 7).

As a feature of many mobile platforms, "visibility" may contribute to FOMO, particularly for young people. By mid-adolescence and continuing through young adulthood, peer networks have matched or outpaced parents and siblings in terms of relative social importance (Wrzus et al., 2013). When confronting scores of photos of attractive friends doing exciting and adventurous things with their other friends, but not including you, you may feel left out. Platforms that steer users to make their experiences more publicly available, quantifiable, and visible may be more likely to have users who experience FOMO-related digital stress.

3.4 Connection Overload

Unlike the previous three aspects of digital stress discussed above, connection overload is not explicitly social. Although the messages and notifications that contribute to individuals' overload are often social in nature, past research suggests that the visibility of this information is often a product of the platform and specific smartphone settings, not just the message frequency (Halfmann & Rieger, 2019). Connection overload stress occurs when the amount of information available exceeds the capacity of the individual to process or handle it (e.g., Hefner & Vorderer, 2016; LaRose et al., 2014; Reinecke et al., 2017). We define connection overload as the "distress resulting from the subjective experience of receiving excessive input from digital sources, including notifications, messages, and posts" (Steele et al., 2020, p. 20). In other words, perception of being overloaded *is* digital stress, but the number of notifications, messages, or texts received is not – it is just use.

In defining connection demands in terms of objective units (e.g., number of log-ins, followers, notifications, texts received), LaRose et al. (2014) found a *positive* association between connection demands and the psychological well-being of participants. However, when participants' subjective experience of connection overload was taken into account, the model suggested that poorer mental health was associated with greater connection demands. Similarly, Reinecke et al. (2017) examined the association between "digital stress" and psychological health in a sample of college students, using a measure of communication load that incorporated both the subjective experience of receiving excessive input and objective data of emails and messages sent and/or received. Consistent with earlier findings (e.g., Misra & Stokols, 2012), results indicated that communication load was positively associated with perceived stress and was indirectly associated with higher burnout, depressive symptoms, and anxiety.

Some platforms and apps produce more notifications and alerts than others, such as synchronous and quantifiable platforms and apps. For example, Ling and Lai (2016) suggest that many users of WhatsApp feel exhausted by the amount of content they have to scroll through. This may overload users' cognitive and attentional systems, resulting in the experience of digital stress, particularly when users enable multiple platforms and applications simultaneously (LaRose et al., 2014; Primack et al., 2017).

3.5 Cost of Caring

The final type of digital stress – the cost of caring – was introduced in Chapter 7 and not covered in my work with colleagues (i.e., Steele et al., 2020). Although past research on *technostress* focuses on people's perception of how stressful a technology is, or how responsible a technology is for negative feelings or consequences, Hampton et al. (2016) suggest that people may be unaware of how media affect them. This differentiates the cost of caring from the other four forms of digital stress. Hampton and colleagues (2016) describe the cost of caring the following way: "digital media provides heightened awareness of network life events in the lives of both close and more distant acquaintances. An awareness of undesirable, major life events in the lives of others can be a source of psychological stress" (p. 1268). The heightened awareness of the lives of others, made possible by the broadcasting and archival features of social media, can upset us.

Furthermore, social media draws our attention into weak ties, creating persistent contact with people we would have otherwise lost touch with – contributing to a greater volume of events to be aware of. Knowing the unpleasant or downright awful things that are happening to friends and acquaintances may increase feelings of obligation to offer social support, or could trigger guilt, anger, and helplessness. Essentially, the cost of caring is the flip side of the social support gained through social media.

Employing a large, nationally representative sample of American adults, Hampton et al. (2016) explored how aware participants were of both positive and negative life events in the lives of members of their online social networks. Having those who were close ties who experienced more negative life events was associated with greater stress in general, particularly for women. This was also true about negative events with weaker ties, but to a lesser extent. Supporting the overall argument of this chapter, Hampton et al. (2016) found that there was no overall association between digital media use (i.e., email, texting, social media) and stress; this association depended on the awareness of others' negative life events. More media use contributed to greater awareness of stressors, particularly the stress encountered by closer ties.

Of the five types of digital stress, the cost of caring speaks to a very human predicament. In knowing and caring for others, particularly close others, we have an obligation to attend to them in times of need (Hruschka, 2010). Digital media of various types make broadcasting negative life events and learning about them easier than ever before. This also means that we become more aware of our obligations toward loved ones in their hour of need and are, unfortunately, more aware of our helplessness if geography and other barriers are present.

SECTION FOUR: CONCLUSIONS

There is an important caveat to the idea of digital stress: What causes what? Many researchers have questioned the causal direction between negative psychosocial outcomes and media use (e.g., Heffer et al., 2019; Song et al., 2014), instead suggesting that dispositional characteristics may create digital stress and media use. Valkenburg and Peter's (2013) differential susceptibility to media effects model suggests that dispositional and social characteristics (e.g., depression, quality of peer relationships) could moderate the effects of media on outcomes. Such an explanation would suggest that digital stress moderates the association between digital media use and negative outcomes, not because of the patterns of media use but because of individuals' dispositional characteristics giving rise to heightened or dampened digital stress overall.

This perspective is well developed by Caplan (2018) and Tokunga and Rains (2016) in their reviews of problematic internet use. One of the notable trends in this research that stretches back into the 1990s is that compulsive or excessive use of internet technologies is a much better predictor of the negative effects of media than is the amount of use per se. The individuals most likely to engage in problematic use are those who are looking to manage their moods or resolve an unmet need. Those who turn to media to alleviate loneliness or cope with anxieties are more likely to develop unhealthy patterns of media use. This may be indicative of those who do not have sufficient skills or relationships in their lives (Caplan, 2018), but is certainly not a product of the media themselves.

Thus, people may turn to online platforms and modalities to make up for what they lack socially and relationally (Caplan, 2018). Those who lack social skills or have failed to develop strong relationships offline may turn to online environments to try to compensate for that which they lack in their lives (Scott et al., 2006). This compensatory struggle may not make up for what is missing and may instead result in excessive use of digital media. This deficit account appears to be a good explanation for problematic SNS use, online gaming, and internet use in general (Caplan, 2018).

The *poor-get-poorer* hypothesis suggests that these online environments may worsen, rather than improve, outcomes for those who are initially less skilled and socially connected. Looking to Facebook to boost self-esteem or cope with loneliness may leave users feeling more of a burden or lonely. Caplan (2018) offers this summary: "Thus, social networking habits that originally developed to compensate for insecurity may end up leaving people feeling more excluded and worse about themselves" (p. 44).

When considering the (uncertain) benefits of social media abstinence, there is another important caveat to the published research. Namely, many people think media use generally, but social media particularly, is a waste of their time. People are at best ambivalent about their social media use – it is both harmful and helpful (Orchard et al., 2015). More than half of American adults have curtailed their use within a day or taken a break for days at a time (Gramlich, 2019), which suggests that the feeling that they ought to take a break is widespread.

Thus, when people participate in a study where they are required to stop using social media, the increase in well-being they self-report may simply be participants patting themselves on the back for cutting back on what they think is a bad behavior. If participants feel particularly successful in being able to abstain from social media use in a study on social media abstinence, especially for weeks at a time, it stands to reason that participants would report greater well-being, perhaps due to a sense of accomplishment. Even forgetting the idea of research for a moment, it is possible that we might perceive greater stress when reflecting and reporting on our media habits because we feel we are just wasting our time when on social media. So, if we admit to using social media for hours each day, we may report lower well-being because we feel we could be doing something better with our time.

That said, I believe that digital stress is real and that it is fundamentally tied to trying to live up to new challenges to our ability to stay connected and to facing the consequences of striving for such a goal. Mihailidis (2014) notes that adolescents "find it increasingly difficult to distinguish relationships that exist in their pockets from those that exist in their physical surroundings" (p. 59). Young adults in particular recognize that the mobile phone can be used to make oneself socially available, but also that in doing so one becomes less available to those around them. We have to build new social habits that incorporate media in a positive way, but the very act of learning and internalizing habits can be taxing. No doubt this is a challenging environment to navigate; people must find ways to increase the connective potential of media, learn uncertain and evolving social norms, and form new media habits that support personal goals rather than detract from them.

9

Social Displacement

> In 1926, the Knights of Columbus proposed that its group meetings around the U.S. discuss, among other topics, "Does the telephone break up home life and the old practice of visiting friends?"
>
> —Stanley Fischer (1992, p. 1)

From the telegram to the smart phone, the adoption of new technologies has inspired widespread fears of moral decline and social harm (Bryant & Fondren, 2009; Fischer, 1992). Two decades ago, the rapid adoption of internet technologies was accompanied by concerns about deterioration of personal relationships and communication within those relationships (Kraut et al., 1998; Nie, 2001). Called the "internet paradox" by Kraut et al. (1998), greater internet connectivity was seen as "inevitably" displacing FtF contact with close friends and family (Nie, 2001). This argument became known as the *social displacement hypothesis*. As social media use grew in the past fifteen years, similar concerns about its effect on well-being have arisen (e.g., Dunbar, 2016; Turkle, 2011), prompting a rigorous, but not unfamiliar, debate about the degree to which that anxiety is warranted.

This chapter examines the evidence of whether new media technologies replace FtF conversations, particularly those with close friends and family. Starting with the adoption of the internet in the 1990s and continuing into the present era, I focus on what effect, if any, the use of digital media has on FtF communication.

This chapter also addresses *co-present device use*, which is the influence of the presence of or use of mobile devices on interaction partners who are FtF. Although social displacement is concerned with how time spent on the internet, social media, or smartphones is borrowing time that would otherwise be spent in FtF conversation, co-present device use explores whether the presence or use of a mobile device decreases the quality of conversation, the experience of connection, or liking or being attracted to a co-present conversation partner.

SECTION ONE: THE SOCIAL DISPLACEMENT HYPOTHESIS

1.1 A Quick History of Social Displacement

Throughout the twentieth and into the twenty-first centuries, there is a recurring fear that new media will displace positive, prosocial activities (Bryant & Fondren, 2009; Chayko, 2014). The late 1990s offer an illustrative example. There was a widespread belief that social displacement via internet use was prevalent and harmful (Nie, 2001). People worried this new technology was driving a wedge between them and their friends and family. There was evidence that as individuals spent more time on the internet, they were spending less time having FtF interactions with close friends and family (Kraut et al., 1998). This association was called the "internet paradox" because increased communication opportunities through the internet use seemed to paradoxically lead to reduced social involvement (Kraut et al., 1998; Nie, 2001). The well-being of internet users was then thought to be diminished (e.g., more loneliness, social isolation) because of the subsequent reduction of high-quality social engagements.

However, this claim did not end up with much subsequent empirical support, even in research by the authors themselves (e.g., Kraut, Boneva, Cummings, Helgeson, & Crawford, 2002; Nie & Hillygus, 2002) and later by independent researchers (e.g. Tokunaga, 2016a). Overall, a meta-analysis found trivial evidence ($r = -0.04$) of the association between internet use and well-being (Huang, 2010).

Yet the worry of displacement carries on. Since its original formulation, the displacement hypothesis has found new life in the study of online discussion groups (Cummings, Butler, & Kraut, 2002), IM (Boase et al., 2006), and then-emergent SNSs (Parks, 2011; Turkle, 2011). This was particularly acute in the case of texting by teens. There was widespread anxiety that it was ruining their ability to communicate with one another, have relationships, or even speak or write normally (Crystal, 2008).

Beyond the anxieties associated with new media, this phenomenon taps into a broader cultural anxiety about relationships. There seems to be long-standing perception that relationships are not properly appreciated or are being degraded by emergent, nefarious cultural forces. Hruschka (2010) identifies a pervasive worry across cultures and over time that the term "friend" has lost its *true* meaning. Facebook's use of the term "friend" to denote mutual ties to individuals, corporations, or celebrities has provoked a similar anxiety that people, especially the young, don't know what it means to have a friend (for evidence to the contrary, see Chapter 1).

1.2 What Is the Evidence of Displacement?

Proponents of displacement often point to evidence that social media (or internet) use is associated with loneliness. As reviewed in Chapter 8, this association is weak, if it exists, and may get the causal direction reversed: there is more evidence that lonely or depressed people use more social media than there is that social media leads to loneliness or depression.

Proponents also harness evidence to support their case that only a small portion of social media ties are to actual friends. Indeed, a recent meta-analysis confirms that social media use is associated with more engagement with more-distant relationship partners (Liu & Yang, 2016). Therefore, more time on online media seems to mean more time with less close ties.

They also point out that the association between the number of FtF relationships and positive psychosocial outcomes is stronger than the association between online-only relationships and psychosocial outcomes. This argument has fairly strong empirical support (Ahn & Shin, 2013; Helliwell & Huang, 2013; Pollet et al., 2011; Shakya & Christakis, 2017). Because close relationships and FtF social interactions are more beneficial to well-being than online-only relationships and mediated interactions, I have to concede that the displacement of the former with the latter would probably lead to declines in well-being.

However, the most direct evidence for displacement comes from studies that confirm a negative association between social media use and the number of interactions with close friends and family (Ahn & Shin, 2013; Dunbar, 2016; Helliwell & Huang, 2013). This suggests that more social media use is associated with displacement.

These arguments are persuasive, but do not tell the full story.

1.3 What Is the Evidence against Displacement?

In addition to the caveated claims of the original proponents of displacement (e.g. Kraut et al., 2002; Nie & Hillygus, 2002), many independent researchers have found evidence contrary to what would be predicted by the social displacement hypothesis. In 2004, a nationally representative sample of Americans suggested that email did not displace voice call or FtF contact (Boase et al., 2006). Instead, people who used email more also had more social ties. One-third of Americans surveyed at that time perceived that the internet increased the number of strong and weak ties alike, which was three times the percentage of people who thought the internet diminished their social ties (Boase et al., 2006). In a classic study on IM, Valkenburg and Peter (2009) argued that CMC removes obstacles to personal disclosures with close relationships, so it enhances the quality of relationships. Longitudinal research from 2004 and 2005 suggested that the best explanation of the positive association between internet use and loneliness was that some people are more socially active and healthier psychologically than others (Stepanikova et al., 2010). This means that healthy people engage in more social activity both online and offline and unhealthy people engage in less. Thus, there is no trade-off between positive time with friends and family and internet use – the effects happen simultaneously with two different groups of people, not as a trade-off within the same people. Both Rainie and Wellman (2012) and Chayko (2014) conclude that internet and mobile technologies do not lessen or diminish human interaction. Specifically, CMC and FtF communication with close friends and family do not have either/or relationship; they have a both/and relationship with one another (which is the core argument of MMT; see Chapter 3).

1.4 Social Displacement by Social Media

In my own research (Hall et al., 2019b), I explored the question of social displacement by social media. The first study used a nationally representative longitudinal sample of Generation X (LSAY; Miller, 2014) to explore social displacement via social media between 2009 and 2011. This period of time was particularly important in the history of social media in terms of adoption and use. The number of Facebook users trebled and growth was particularly high for Gen Xers (Wilson, Gosling, & Graham, 2012), which is squarely in the age range of participants in the LSAY dataset. Growth in Twitter adoption and use was also particularly dramatic from 2009 to 2011. Our analyses revealed that there was not much evidence that social media adoption was associated with frequency of direct contact within or between years. Our findings did offer limited evidence of one component of social displacement – a negative association between early adoption of new technology and direct social contact in the future. However, Kraut et al. (2002) also found that the initial negative associations of internet use on family communication disappeared in their original sample and even revealed a positive association in subsequent analyses. LSAY data that we analyzed may have shown a similar trend during a similar time of rapid media adoption and use (i.e., internet 1998–2001, social media 2009–2011).

Whatever the case, our analyses did not support the social displacement hypothesis when it comes to the supposed harm of social media adoption and use. Change in social media adoption from 2009 to 2011 was associated with *positive change* in well-being in 2010. This finding supports the positive association between internet use and positive affect found in Kraut et al. (2002). People who were early adopters of social media experienced a boost in well-being.

Other research has found evidence directly in opposition to social displacement. Among Germans, active SNS communication was positively associated with FtF communication six months later – a conclusion in contrast to social displacement (Dienlin et al., 2017). Similarly, Facebook researchers have found a modest correlation between direct communication through Facebook (i.e., private messages, comments, wall posts) and other forms of communication (i.e., phone, email, FtF) (Burke & Kraut, 2014). This supports prior research that argues that personality or disposition likely accounts for the association between Facebook use and social capital (Burke et al., 2011; Requena & Ayuso, 2018).

You might notice that many of these studies are either over long periods of time (i.e., months, years) or are cross-sectional surveys. You might ask, What about displacement within a day? What if using social media influences us to seek out fewer social interactions later in the day? My colleagues and I (Hall et al., 2019b) found that social media use earlier in the same day neither predicted fewer FtF interactions nor predicted more interactions with less emotionally close others later that day.

Finally, there is evidence that social media may increase social contact when other opportunities to connect are not present. For those who do not keep in touch with their friends and family through other types of interactions (i.e., phone, email, FtF), Facebook communication may help to build connection (Burke & Kraut, 2014). Social media likely bring old friends into social awareness in a unique way, such as by reinitiating contact with old friends (Quinn, 2013; Ramirez et al., 2017). Often, these renewed contacts get together FtF or talk on the phone, which offers another pathway whereby social media use might promote other types of communication or build up relationships.

1.5 Okay, but Where Does the Time Spent on Social Media Come From?

At the center of the displacement debate is time. Both the original (e.g., Nie, 2001) and contemporary proponents (e.g., Ahn & Shin, 2013; Dunbar, 2016) of the social displacement hypothesis agree that the time spent on social media cannot be spent in other ways. There is recent evidence of increasing use of social media in terms of number of minutes (*The Economist*, 2016). Indeed, the average active Facebook user spends fifty minutes per day on the site, or approximately two full working days a month (*The Economist*, 2016). My own work tracking time spent using the four most common social media suggests that people spend about an hour and fifteen minutes each day using social media (Hall et al., 2019a). Given that there are only about seventeen waking hours in a day, giving up an hour-plus each day is a lot of time, especially over the course of a week. However, there is no clear evidence about from where that time is coming.

In Chapter 4, I discussed media displacement theory, which examines how media use displaces a variety of other ways to use one's time. There are surprisingly few studies that directly examine what social media use displaces. During a period of sustained growth in internet use (2003–2007), Robinson (2011) reviewed the association between internet use and a variety of activities using high-quality time diary data. Heavy internet use was associated with less time spent on a variety of nonsocial activities, including housework, driving, and working. A nationally representative sampling of Swedes from 2010 to 2011 also suggests that heavy internet use is associated with less time in child care, prepping meals, driving, and at work (Vihelmson et al., 2017). The principle of marginal fringe activities (see Chapter 3) suggests that time spent using social media is likely diffused across several activities.

In my own research (Hall et al., 2019a), we explored this question directly. We enrolled 135 participants in a daily diary study where some were required to give up social media for weeks at a time. Each day they filled out a time diary explaining how they used their time engaged in seventeen activities, including time on social media and on the internet. We were able to compare how people changed their time use as they switched from being on and off social media, and how people who abstained from social media used their time compared with those who stayed on it.

We found that when abstaining from social media, people mainly spent more time browsing the internet and working. Both those who switched onto and off of social media and those who abstained entirely compared with those who did not change their social media use confirmed that these were the two most displaced activities. Obviously, browsing the internet likely provides for similar entertainment and information-retrieval purposes as social media. Social media are likely displacing time spent using the internet, just as internet use displaced time using other media (Twenge et al., 2018b; Vihelmson et al., 2017).

The change in time spent working is consistent with past studies that suggest heavy internet use is associated with less time working (Robinson, 2011; Vihelmson et al., 2017). Whether an employee is allowed to do so, Americans consistently use social media at work (Olmstead, Lampe, & Ellison, 2016). Although this is not exactly "free" time (at least from the employer's perspective), use of social media likely fills gaps of time at work.

The final three activities that increased in frequency during periods of social media abstinence were domestic in nature: taking care of children, sleeping, and cooking/cleaning. Interestingly, all three activities were displaced by internet use (Robinson, 2011; Vihelmson et al., 2017), which again suggests that social media use is functionally similar to internet use. One mother in my study reported spending more time taking care of her children during periods of social media abstinence, but no other open-ended response offered us insight as to why time spent sleeping or cooking or cleaning the house might have been displaced by social media.

Our interpretation (Hall et al., 2019a) is that people use social media to avoid doing other things, essentially to procrastinate (Meier, Reinecke, & Meltzer, 2016). Just like taking a mental break at work, people may use social media to take a mental break from taking care of a child or cleaning up after one.

1.6 People Are Ambivalent about Their Media Use

I do not believe there is good evidence that internet-based personal media (e.g., IM, email), mobile media (i.e., SMS, voice calls), or social media (e.g., Facebook, Twitter) displace time spent in FtF conversation with close friends and family (see Chapter 5). Nor do I believe that media use leads to reduced well-being in general (see Chapter 8), and certainly not for the reason that use of media diminishes time spent in FtF contact. Given that there is a decided lack of supporting evidence for generations of scholarship, why is the social displacement hypothesis so persuasive and persistent across time?

One clue I think comes from the fact that for generations, people express a deep ambivalence about using media themselves and in regard to media's influence on society as a whole. People feel it is the best and the worst, wonderful and disastrous, liberating and imprisoning (Baron, 2008; Gramlich, 2019; Orchard et al., 2015; Weinstein & Selman, 2014). One study about how users regard Facebook found that the most common perception was that it is a superficial environment, not an integral part of offline socialization, and focused on distant friends to excess (Orchard et al., 2015). But the second most common theme from the same people was that Facebook was generally good, fun, and social and that it kept them "in the loop." Just as Fulk (1993) and Fischer (1992) foretold, the user experience with media is often ironic, even among the same people.

Another reason that people believe in social displacement is that many people believe that technology does things to them. Deterministic perspectives of technology have had a long life in public discourse on media and are firmly rooted in the emergence of the promise and perils of the both the internet and the mobile phone (Baym, 2015; boyd, 2014; Chayko, 2014). In fact, Nie's (2001) original arguments about the social displacement hypothesis were developed partly from public opinions on the topic, not empirical evidence. I think the contemporary belief that social media are bad for us keeps the social displacement hypothesis alive and well. I would predict that whatever new media we encounter, maybe virtual or augmented reality, will be met with skepticism and people will suggest it is to blame for a lack of quality time with friends and family.

Finally, I suspect that people that believe that if they were to stop using social media, they might keep in touch in other ways. Although the quantitative evidence does not support this, the most common theme from the qualitative evidence in my own study (Hall et al., 2019a) was that participants felt that staying off social media increased other forms of communication, such as texting, calling, or talking FtF. Furthermore, my study actually suggested that when people are able to use social media freely, they spend *more* time communicating with their less close relationship partners, which is completely the opposite of the social displacement hypothesis. So, it is curious that people seem to think that they communicate in different ways if they are asked to abstain from social media, but, on average, they do not engage in more or less mediated communication whether on or off social media.

SECTION TWO: CO-PRESENT DEVICE USE

The social displacement hypothesis is about time, but it views time spent using media as a zero-sum equation. The assumption is that one cannot do two things at once (an assumption shared in the American Time Use Surveys, conducted by the US Department of Labor). Co-present device use presumes that time using mobile media happens at the same time as FtF interaction. Quick glances at one's phone as well as longer periods of time staring at a screen while in another person's company count as co-present device use. People are rarely without their mobile devices; thus, the opportunity to use one's mobile phone in the presence of others is perpetual. Indeed, almost 90% of mobile device owners reported using their phones during their most recent social activity (Rainie & Zickhur, 2015). As countries throughout the world show increasing rates of smartphone adoption, co-present social displacement follows – in Thailand (Chotpitayasunondh & Douglas, 2018), in India (Davey et al., 2018), in Chile (Halpern & Katz, 2017), and in China (Wang, Xie, Wang, Wang, & Lei, 2017). Perhaps it isn't all that surprising that the lure of the mobile device is strong even with a person right next to you. But is it harmful for relationships and conversational connection? Although the evidence is slowly accumulating and mixed, the answer seems to be that the effects of co-present device use are negative in general, but they are bound up in the constantly evolving norms of media use both between partners and in various locations.

2.1 What If It Is Just Lying There?

One of the first experimental studies of co-present device use (i.e., Przybylski & Weinstein, 2013) reported that the mere presence of a cell phone during a get-to-know-you interaction diminishes FtF conversation quality. Another study, conducted a few years later, suggested that the mere presence of a mobile device while at a café tended to be a distraction for the mobile device owner (Dwyer, Kushlev, & Dunn, 2018). This distraction was associated with less enjoyment more negative emotions felt during the meal. Misra, Cheng, Genevie, and Yaun (2016) explored the effect of the presence of mobile phones in natural settings and found that the presence of the device was associated with less empathic concern, and this effect was stronger among close partners.

However, a preregistered replication (i.e., where the authors announce the question they will answer and the methods they will use on an online public site before they collect data) of Przybylski and Weinstein (2013) (i.e., Crowley, Allred, Follon, & Volkmer, 2018) could not replicate the original results. Intriguingly, Crowley and colleagues speculated that because having a mobile device present has become more normative, its influence on people in conversation diminishes. This is quite consistent with arguments from a domestication perspective – that once people no longer attend to media, it has fully become part of our lives, which suggests the norms have changed and stabilized (see Chapter 3). This explanation of changing norms continues to be an important factor in considering the influence of co-present device use.

2.2 What If You Are Getting to Know Someone?

Subsequent studies have focused not simply on the presence of a mobile device but on the frequency of use of it. The idea is that as people shift their attention toward smartphones, they take their attention away from their co-present partners – who probably notice it and evaluate using it negatively (Misra et al., 2016). Although negative effects on the process of relationship development (e.g., intimacy, liking) have been explored, of particular concern is that people's FtF interactions are of worse quality when people's attention shifts away from their co-present interactions and toward their mobile devices. Although this argument seems reasonable, the evidence in support of it is decidedly mixed.

In a clever experiment conducted through video chat (Sprecher, Hampton, Heinzel, & Felmlee, 2016), there were nearly no effects of checking Facebook and SMS during a get-to-know-you conversation on enjoyment and affect for either partner (i.e., the partner who is checking Facebook and SMS and the partner who is not). There was some evidence that those who could check social media or SMS messages felt less conversational engagement. What was particularly clever about this design was that because it was conducted through video chat, study participants could not *see* whether their conversation partner was checking Facebook or SMS messages. Furthermore, the design of the study attempted to increase the likelihood participants had a meaningful and intimate interaction; so, ostensibly, there should have been some influence of checking media (assuming such effects were present). Whether or not the device was noticeable continues to be an important new aspect of research (Caplan, 2018).

When checking one's mobile device was much more obvious, it indeed seems to reduce the experience of belongingness in the interaction (Chotpitayasunondh & Douglas, 2018) and reduces impressions of partner attentiveness and politeness (van den Abeele, Antheunis, & Schouten, 2016). Mobile use during conversation between people who know each other already diminishes conversational quality but does not affect liking (van den Abeele et al.,

2016). The idea here is that one distracted interaction does not fundamentally change one's liking of or relationship with a person, but it does affect the quality of the conversation.

It appears that co-present device use has two pathways toward diminishing the conversational experience. For the checker, it may make them less engaged or more distracted. For the other person, *noticing* the checking may result in a sour impression, increasing perceptions that the checker is inattentive and rude, which hurts the quality of the conversation. Of the two effects, the perceptions of the person *not* using the mobile device seem to be stronger (Caplan, 2018).

2.3 What If It Is Someone You Know Already?

How does in-the-moment and chronic co-present device use influence people in more established relationships? Twenty-five percent of married and 42% of unmarried respondents in serious romantic relationships reported that their partner was distracted by their mobile device when they were together (Lenhart & Duggan, 2014). This distraction appears to be related to some fairly negative outcomes. Misra and colleagues (2016) report that the negative effects of device use are worse in the context of familiar compared with less familiar partners. In romantic relationships, the perception that one's partner is chronically distracted by their mobile device is associated with less relationship satisfaction (Roberts & David, 2016), particularly for those married longer (Wang et al., 2017), and is associated with more frequent conflicts about the smartphone itself (Halpern & Katz, 2017; Miller-Ott & Kelly, 2016; Roberts & David, 2016).

Mobile device use breeds conflict about how it *should be* used, which leads to reduced relationship satisfaction. Using longitudinal data from romantic couples in Chile, more texting predicted future declines in relationship quality, but poor relationship quality did not predict future increases in texting (Halpern & Katz, 2017). This provides good evidence that it is not the case that people who are struggling in their relationships text more over time. Rather, those who text more tend to be more troubled in the future.

These negative consequences appear at any given moment in the day or on reflecting how the day went. During FtF social interactions, people feel more distracted when their smartphone is out compared with when it is not (Dwyer et al., 2018). More use of the phone during FtF interactions is associated with less social connection, more boredom, and less positive affect. Reflecting on the events of each day for two weeks, romantic couples reported that co-present device use (what the authors call techno-interference on the cellphone) happened on 21.5% of days (McDaniel & Drouin, 2019). However, this problem varied considerably between couples: 28% said it *never* happened over the course of fourteen days. McDaniel and Drouin (2019) also compared couples with each other and compared the same couple across days of the study. On any day when co-present device use was more frequent, there was lower relationship quality, more negative mood, less positive FtF interactions, and more conflict about technology. However, people who in general reported more co-present device use over the entire fourteen-day period reported higher conflict, poorer mood, and worse FtF interactions. Importantly, these effects were stronger than the day-by-day effects.

In the context of relationships, co-present device use is most harmful when it is chronic. McDaniel and Drouin (2019) not only confirm evidence of the long-term risks of the behavior (Halpern & Katz, 2017), but also suggest that part of what is happening is that people who perceive their partners to be overly attentive to the smartphone may have fewer positive interactions and are in a more negative mood, suggesting that it is not just conflict about the device that is a drag on the relationship.

There is an important caveat to this evidence: not all co-present device use is equally objectionable. For example, when two people are in a waiting room together, using a mobile phone may be a welcome distraction. If it is normative in that time and/or place, it does not have the same negative effects. In an observational field study of students waiting with friends for class to start, researchers found that looking at one's phone was remarkably common: for 62% of observed pairs, at least one person looked at their phone for around a minute (van den Abeele, Hendrickson, Pollman, & Ling, 2019). After observing these pairs of students for ten minutes, researchers approached the pair and asked them some questions. The observed participants more often than not inaccurately recalled their own and their partner's use of a smartphone during the ten-minute period of sitting together that had just occurred. It seems that people do not have a particularly accurate or keen awareness of smartphone use while sitting and waiting.

As an important clue about the direction of the problem, people did not report feeling distracted, no matter how much they used their phone. During get-to-know-you conversations, when partners used their phones for longer periods of time, they perceived their partners to be distracted, which was associated with less intimacy, supporting research on the effects of phone use. However, van den Abeele and colleagues (2019) were unconvinced that co-present device use was really a problem: they did not find that mobile phone use while waiting produced an attentional conflict in either party, nor did it seem to be harmful for processes that build relational intimacy. Most of the effects were small and unnoticeable to the observed participants themselves. Instead, the social norms of the location mattered quite a bit.

Another growing area of research is on device use among parents and children. Caplan (2018) notes that, unfortunately, there is a very limited amount of empirical research on the topic. The research tends to suggest that parents struggle with staying present and attending to their children. In my own work on social media displacement (e.g., Hall et al., 2019a), we found that time spent taking care of others was displaced by social media. When participants stopping using social media, they tended to spend more time taking care of family members. Some parents commented on this change in the open-ended responses, noting that having nothing to look at on their phone (because the social media apps had been removed) helped them to be more present. Co-present device use with children likely manifests in a lack of nonverbal cues, including diminished visual cues and infrequent gaze, both of which convey a lack of interest and concern (Caplan, 2018). Much more research is needed to know how children of different ages (e.g., infants, adolescents, teens) are affected by parent co-present device use.

2.4 What If You Have Good Phone Etiquette?

In the case of the mobile device, we have been in a time of technological transition for at least twenty years. Throughout history, times of transition are often vexed because society has yet to establish norms of conduct. Ling and McEwen (2010) suggest that when a person fails to follow the norms, they are violating standards of conduct and are subject to moral condemnation. Yet the degree to which a behavior is objectionable changes. Familiarity alone influences perceptions of the presence of a mobile device and thus its effects (Crowley et al., 2018). During times of transition, patterns of use change as well, perhaps even in response to emergent norms. For example, there has been a shift from voice calls in public to text messaging in public. This means that the "behavior" in question shifts *while* the norms of mobile device use are being established. The two key questions ought to be, What exactly is questionable or inappropriate behavior, and when it is objectionable (i.e., with whom and where)?

There is widespread agreement that people ought to limit co-present device use (Hall et al., 2014a; Rainie & Zickhur, 2015). Adolescents and young adults recognize that mobile devices increase availability to those far away, but create a risk of people becoming less available to the person nearby (Mihailidis, 2014). People have normative standards of when (e.g., beginning of a relationship, formal settings) and for whom (e.g., first date, close partners) they should put their mobile device out of sight and mind (Miller-Ott & Kelly, 2016). Young adults recognize the consequences of not doing so – it is considered rude and disrespectful, as if the mobile device is more important than the co-present partner.

My own work with Nancy Baym and Kate Miltner (2014a) attempted to take into account both perceptions of norms and perceptions of different social contexts. We explored perceptions of private and public uses of the phone when in the company of a specific relationship partner, and both people in the couple were part of the study. Neither perceptions of what was appropriate nor one's own behavior were associated with partner liking or relationship satisfaction. Instead, individuals who perceived their partners to be more strictly adherent to their own internalized standards liked their partners more and perceived the mobile phone to interfere less in the relationship. When a partner followed the rules of etiquette, it mitigated the potential damage a mobile device could cause. Furthermore, when people followed their own norms, they were more satisfied and committed to the relationship and liked their partners more. We speculated that committed and satisfied people follow their own mobile norms more conscientiously as a sign of commitment and satisfaction. Indeed, people tend to give less attention to incoming mobile messages when in the company of close friends and family (Lee et al., 2019).

In private settings, such as at home with a friend or romantic partner, whether co-present device use was a problem depended on whether relationship partners felt they were on the same page (Hall et al., 2014a): when a person felt their relationship partner was more similar to themselves in mobile device use, it was associated with a more committed and satisfied relationship. The perception of similarity seemed to mitigate the perception that mobile phones are interfering with the relationship, which may be why it is associated with greater satisfaction.

2.5 What If You Provide an Account?

It is worth noting that people might or might not provide an explanation for why they need to use their phone or have it available: "I have to respond to this text from mom" or "Just to let you know, I am expecting an important call" (Miller-Ott & Kelly, 2016). Very little research has explored whether these accounts save face or mitigate the potentially negative influence of breaking of the norm. There is good reason to believe that they might help.

Interpersonal accounts are the verbal and nonverbal messages we use to provide an explanation for our behavior (Cody & Dunn, 2007). People can justify their mobile phone use or provide a concession (e.g., where they admit they used it and apologize). Because the research on the harms of co-present mobile device use suggests that it more problematic for the person who witnesses the behavior and more harmful when the behavior is noticed, the situation really calls for an account. When properly done, an account can be quite effective (Cody & Dunn, 2007). When accounts are made politely, they address the wrongdoing and show respect for another person (e.g., "sorry, that was rude"), and therefore can reduce the potential harms. These politeness strategies may lessen or even eliminate the negative effects of co-present device use, especially given how small these effects are to begin with (van der Abeele et al., 2019).

Although this is speculative, I would expect that the reasons for device use matter. Why they are looking at their smartphone? Who are they expecting a call from? Are they expecting an important call about something or someone (e.g., "I am waiting to hear back from the pediatrician's office")? People feel that an interruption matters less when receiving messages from close others (Lee et al., 2019), and that may translate to how their co-present partner feels as well. The modality they use (e.g., text, voice call) and the partner on the other end will likely affect perceptions of appropriateness and attentiveness. As this research progresses, the research tradition of account giving and politeness theory will bring further attention to issues of power, positive and negative face, and the type of account in the study of the effects of co-present device use (Caplan, 2018; Cody & Dunn, 2007).

2.6 What If People Are Actually Trying to Ignore You?

Because so much of the evidence on the effects of co-present device use are correlational in nature, it is also possible that lower quality interactions or lower quality relationships trigger co-present mobile use. Certainly, my own work (e.g., Hall et al., 2014a) can be interpreted in that fashion. Just like romantic partners fighting about how the load the dishwasher, the fight is not really about what it seems to be about. It makes sense to me that people retreat into their mobile devices when they are already fighting with their romantic partner or are bored or irritated by the people they are hanging out with. There are very few experimental studies that look at the effect of attention to a mobile device in the context of already existing relationships, but one study suggests that it did not cause a reduction in liking (van den Abeele et al., 2016). That said, the single longitudinal design in the context of romantic couples did demonstrate that texting was associated with lower relationship quality in the future (Halpern & Katz, 2017). McDaniel and Drouin's (2019) work suggests that although this pattern of use may not *cause* problems in the relationship, both within the day and over time, chronic co-present device use may be a sign the relationship is distressed.

On another level, it seems to me that looking at one's mobile device in a public place is understood to make one socially unavailable. This is not dissimilar to reading a book or a newspaper – it sends a strong nonverbal signal of unavailability. Whether a person uses their mobile device to send out that message *intentionally* is another matter – it may be a habit that has no particular public social intent attached to it.

Finally, I would speculate that timing of device use matters quite a bit. I have observed people turn to their mobile device once a conversation has come to a conclusion. Young adults actively engage with one another during a meal, keeping their phones tucked away, but as the meal winds down and people are getting ready to leave, everyone takes a few minutes to check their mobile devices. And the content of that check is not just kept to themselves; people share what they see on the phone with others at the table (Brown et al., 2018; van den Abeele et al., 2016). In that case, is it possible that co-present mobile phone use can actually be a means of connection rather than disconnection? Again, further study is needed to know the answer with any confidence.

2.7 What If Co-present Device Use Tells Us Something about User?

One conclusion from research on the social displacement hypothesis seems to be that people who are socially active and have higher well-being seem to be socially engaged in a variety of ways – both online and offline. Research from the MMT tradition reinforces the idea that people use a variety of modalities to reach close relationship partners, and as relationships become interdependent, they add more modes of communication. These findings point to a possible implication for co-present device use research: people who engage in co-present displacement excessively may have characteristics that engender worse relationship outcomes. Is it possible that co-present device use is associated with people who might struggle interpersonally?

One study of young adults and adolescents in India suggests such a conclusion. Davey et al. (2018) found that co-present device use is associated with a host of negative outcomes, including distress and depression. Emotional stability and conscientiousness are both negatively associated with texting while eating with a friend (Briskin, Bogg, & Haddad, 2018). The perception that this behavior was not appropriate curbed texting while eating together somewhat, but it did not reduce the predictive value of negative personality traits on co-present device use.

Perhaps this behavior is a result of a lack of self-control. Many media habits, including social media use, are the result of insufficient self-regulation rather than intentional uses of time (Caplan, 2018; Meier et al., 2016; Schnauber-Stockmann, Meier, & Reinecke, 2018). Once established, habits are activated automatically with little awareness or attention (Schnauber-Stockmann et al., 2018). Co-present device use has been associated with a lack of self-control (Davey et al., 2018), and may be another manifestation of problematic internet use (Caplan, 2018). When the mobile device is highly accessible and use is habitual (Briskin et al., 2018; Dwyer et al., 2018), it may be difficult for people to not check constantly – whether in the company of others or alone.

Thus, a person who engages in co-present device use to excess may be someone who is quite challenging to be in a relationship with, not because of how they use their smartphone but because of their underlying disposition. Past research linking co-present device use to emotionally instability, less conscientiousness, depression, and poor self-regulation suggests such a reverse causal relationship is possible. Although I know of no evidence to support this idea, it seems quite possible to me that it is not the device that causes the relationship struggles, but the characteristics of the user.

SECTION THREE: CONCLUSION

Is it the case that increased internet use or increased social media use displaces time spent interacting FtF? The preponderance of evidence would suggest the answer is *no*. Rather, it seems that people who are quick adopters of personal media are also socially active people with higher levels of well-being.

Does the presence or use of a mobile device while in the company of other people harm relationships and ruin conversations? The evidence suggests that perceiving one's partner using their mobile device does diminish impressions of one's partner and may decrease the quality of conversation via a perception of incivility, lack of attention, or increased distraction. These negative effects are most salient when people are in a location where it is not normative to use one's mobile device, and when people make no attempt to mitigate or manage their distraction through an account and/or apology. There is mixed evidence whether this effect is stronger in closer or more distant relationships; however, there is good evidence that co-present device use can be a drag on romantic relationships when it is chronic, but individual incidents of co-present device use do not influence partner liking overall.

Therefore, it is a good idea to follow appropriate norms and minimize distraction during social engagements where attention is expected and the conversation steers toward connection. If an incoming call or text is of the utmost importance, provide a polite account of the behavior.

3.1 Three Caveats

Those overarching conclusions aside, I believe the social displacement hypothesis has three kernels of truth. As the evidence mounts that those who are lonely, depressed, or socially isolated turn to personal media, particularly social media, I am concerned that social media use will not alleviate their struggles (see Chapters 3 and 10). Just as socially skilled people with strong relationships will enact their relationships through any and all modalities available, I suspect that turning to a platform that encourages browsing over interacting and weak ties over strong ones will leave those in dire need of social connection unsatisfied. Thus, social media use may not make things worse for the majority of users, but for the loneliest or least socially skilled, social media use probably will not alleviate those feelings or build stronger connections.

Second, social media, particularly because it is accessible endlessly through a smartphone, may be like a small hole in a balloon when it comes to social connection. The balloon represents the motivation to connect inflated by a fundamental need to belong. Its size represents the cumulative motivation to act. As Hinsch and Sheldon (2013) suggest, "the social Internet tempts its users to acquire quick 'hits' of connection without strings that are often attached to ftf encounters" (p. 497). As argued in Chapter 3, I believe it is possible that perpetual social media use may, like a tiny hole in a balloon, redirect people away from more energy-intensive connection. When individuals experience a sense of isolation or exclusion, they will typically take ameliorative actions. A simple reminder of Facebook (i.e., seeing the icon on a computer screen) appears to circumvent this process (Knausenberger et al., 2015). As CBB theory would predict, when the unresolved need state arises again, social media are ultimately unable to satisfy the distal need to form enduring, close relationships (Pollet et al., 2011; Utz, Tanis, Vermeulen, & 2012).

Because the need to belong functions within a homeostatic system, I am suggesting that habitual social media use could reduce motivation to use more energy-intensive modalities (i.e., voice calls, video chat) and/or FtF interactions. Unfortunately, this motivation-reduction effect is particularly strong for those who rely mostly on Facebook to maintain relationships (Knausenberger et al., 2015). There may be greater risks of heavy or exclusive social media use for those who already experience social deficiencies.

My own research (Hall et al., 2019b) found additional evidence of this insufficient need-satisfaction hypothesis. People who used social media earlier in the day were more likely to experience lower future affective well-being *only* if they were alone when using it. In those moments, people are likely experiencing unmet relatedness needs. Thus, social media use decreases well-being in the future, but only when social media users do not get their relatedness needs met through more direct forms of social interaction.

Third and finally, I do not think it is necessarily a bad thing or even misguided to treat media consumption with a bit of suspicion, in particular, excessive media consumption. I do not think that social media use is bad in itself, but I do not think it is a great use of one's time either. Furthermore, people recognize that they need to adhere to social conventions when using mobile devices in the presence of others, and following these norms appears to be a good thing for relationships. In both cases, I believe that the worry about the diminishment of our relationships from both types of displacement is a reasonable response to a culture that enthusiastically promotes technology. I neither believe that social and mobile media are a source of evil, sapping our relationships and stultifying our personal growth, nor that they are salvation from isolation and loneliness or a particularly valuable use of our precious time here on earth.

Connectivity and Connection

Two remarkable studies have given us a window into what it takes to live a life well. Initiated in 1921, the Terman study followed 1,500 children throughout their entire lives (Friedman & Martin, 2011). The Harvard Study of Adult Development began in 1938 and tracked 268 men, recruited in their sophomore year at Harvard, into old age (Vaillant, 2012). Both studies archived the personality, life events, employment, hobbies, experiences in marriage and with children, and social lives of participants. Both studies revealed that regular contact with close friends is associated with a long life and greater well-being. These social habits and routines, firmly established by middle age, predicted the difference between dying before sixty-five or living in good health beyond seventy (Friedman & Martin, 2011), and predicted feeling close and connected to one's partner and children in those extended years (Vaillant, 2012).

Although making friends in early adulthood is important (Carmichael et al., 2015), people can change their social lives and relationships throughout adulthood (Vaillant, 2012). It is never too late to cultivate new friendships and social activities. Friedman and Martin (2011) conclude that "social networks represent an important – perhaps the most important – way to change one's life pathway" (p. 168). The directive is clear: to live a longer and healthier life, people should strengthen their social networks through routine, high-quality social interactions.

The mediated communication options now available were unimaginable for most of the lives of the men and women of the Terman and Harvard studies, as most were approaching the end of their lives during the rise of the internet. Yet family and friends continue to be a crucial source of meaning in Americans' lives (van Kessel, Smith, & Schiller, 2018). Will the benefits of keeping in touch through the letters and telephone calls of yesteryear translate to the social media habits and mobile app chats of today? Will the vast network of connectivity help us build similar practices of connection that contributed to the health, happiness, and longevity of the Terman and Harvard study participants?

In this final chapter, I explore what I believe to be one of the most important questions of our time: Does connectivity beget connection? If it does, what are the practices of online connection that really matter? As a preview, I offer these final take-home messages:

- Americans are spending less time socially interacting FtF, and one-to-one personal media use is not filling that gap.
- To capitalize on technology's potential, we must choose to build routines of high-quality mediated social interaction.
- Social media are not the answer to social isolation.
- To strengthen social bonds, tighten the circle of connection and send stronger communication signals.

SECTION ONE: AMERICAN SOCIABILITY AND THE ALWAYS-ON WORLD

One of the hallmarks of our digital age is what Barry Wellman (2001) identified as "networked individualism" nearly two decades ago. Rather than relying on a single community of closely knit friends and family for social connection and information, in the digital age people must be self-reliant and goal-oriented to find the people and resources they need (Boase et al., 2006; Wellman, 2001). The vision of networked individualism has the "individual as the autonomous center, and involve[s] both multiple users and multi-threaded multi-tasking" (Quinn & Papacharissi, 2018, p. 354). That is, each individual is situated in their personal communication command center, surrounded by mediated tools of connection and hundreds and hundreds of potential contacts. Advocates of this approach (e.g., Hampton, 2016; Rainie & Wellman, 2012) believe that the persistence of contact offered by social and mobile media is a counterweight to economic and geographic mobility. In other words, mobile media means that now you can take your family and friends with you wherever you go. Creating the kind of emotional and relational interdependence needed to sustain a relationship in the digital age requires intentional planning and new skills (Hampton, 2016; Rainie & Wellman, 2012). From the point of view of relating through technology, networked individualism makes relationship building and social interaction highly autonomous, highly agentic, highly strategic – and deeply exhausting.

In their analysis of how modern connectivity structures everyday life, Abeele, DeWolf, and Ling (2018) suggest that mobile technology's boundless and pervasive nature has dramatically reorganized the sociality of citizens of the global north. To gain the benefits of carrying along friends and family throughout the day (and throughout the caravan of life), we must *personally shoulder the burden* of keeping in touch with one another. Mobile communication has accelerated the already-existing trend of people being responsible for "maintaining frequent interactions in the context of stable affectively caring 'pure' relationships," typically without the benefits of routine contact, geographic proximity, and ample free time (Abeele et al., 2018, p. 8).

Collectively, we are likely unaware of how smartphone integration has shaped and constrained our personal, social lives because these changes have been very gradual and the freedom (and amusement) wireless technology has afforded has been so culturally celebrated. Throughout this book, I have explored how mobility has removed nearly all place-situated boundaries. With this removal of boundaries comes a dialectical tension: mobility unites while it invades, it connects as it leashes, and comforts and disrupts (Arnold, 2003; Baron, 2008; Hall & Baym, 2012). This is reflected in individuals' smartphone practices: nearly half of American teens say they are online almost constantly (Anderson & Jiang, 2018).

Thus, it is up to each and every one of us to define and police our own boundaries of mediated access and accessibility, while managing the obligations of responsiveness to others and coping with the missed social information and opportunities when unavailable – all of which contributes to pervasive digital stress (see Chapter 8). Curiously, this increase in responsibility for sociability is a product of both sides of the freedom–entrapment dialectic: without geographic or temporal boundaries, the freedom to be unavailable produces isolation; as norms of access and responsiveness rise to allow for connectivity, all places and co-present social interactions become subject to disruption (see Chapter 9). Paradoxically, internalized social pressure to be available to others through a smartphone throughout the day interrupts our autonomy and challenges our ability to achieve goals, but does little to satisfy our need for connection (Halfmann & Rieger, 2019; Licoppe, 2012).

Networked individualism ultimately renders mediated social interactions elective and intentional. Communicating with our most intimate ties through media, from friends to parents to romantic partners, has to be planned and thought through or risk interruption or non-response. Young adults recognize that the *choice* to communicate online is a built-in feature of mediated social interaction (Eden & Veksler, 2016). It is up to the individual to decide how and when to communicate, using what modality. The individual defines and manages their own practices of social engagement and relationship building through media.

This is in sharp contrast to historical patterns of sociability. For most of human history, even the very recent past, communication choices were implicit or structured into daily life through geographically situated places: the workplace, the community, and the home (Abeele et al., 2018; Hampton, 2016; Wellman, 2001). Although those locales of social interaction still structure our days (Small, 2017), the access afforded by mobile devices reduces the pull of place-situated social routines both in the moment and over time.

The promise and potential of personal media are intrinsically tied to intentionality and to access to responsive others. We increasingly believe that mobile and social media render social life available whenever and wherever it is needed. This promise, so strongly built into networked individualism, is tied up with the ideal of what technology has the potential to make possible.

However, I feel that there is a missing component to this conversation: the *possibility* of constant contact neither is ideal nor is it easily or frequently enacted in people's actual practices of sociality.

1.1 Are American Adolescents Spending Less Time Socializing?

A recent large study of American adolescents (Twenge et al., 2019) offered strong evidence that the amount of time spent socializing in-person is on the decline. In 1987, incoming college students spent 13.5 hours a week socializing with friends, but by 2016 this had shrunk to 9.1 hours a week. This appears to be a very recent phenomenon – most of this decline occurred between 2010 and 2017. Many of the in-person activities captured in Twenge et al. (2019) were social activities that take place outside the home, including going to the mall, going out to parties, taking a car ride for fun, and going to the movies. Time spent engaged in all of these activities has declined since 1987, and most sharply in the last ten years. At the same span of time, media use, particularly mobile and social media, dramatically increased. As opportunities to go out and about to socialize with friends decline, adolescents appear to turn to social and mobile media to connect (Twenge et al., 2018b).

Intriguingly, dana boyd may have identified the same trend in American teens years ago in her book *It's Complicated: The Social Lives of Networked Teens* (2014). However, she sees the role of social and mobile media in a different light. Namely, she reported that teens were forced to create *networked publics* through media because their physical mobility was increasingly monitored and restricted: "teens told me time and again that they would far rather meet up in person, but the hectic and heavily scheduled nature of their day-to-day lives, their lack of physical mobility, and the fears of their parents have made such face-to-face interactions increasingly impossible" (boyd, 2014, pp. 21–22). Compared with their physical mobility, teens feel free and capable of creating and shaping their networked public spaces. These places to connect complement and supplement FtF encounters at school, allowing important relationships to grow, and networked publics can be accessed on the go or at home, and are thus adaptable to a busy lifestyle (boyd, 2014).

Thus, two trends have co-occurred over the last two decades for adolescents: time spent in FtF contact is declining and time spent using social and mobile media is growing. It is tempting to tie these trends together, but as reviewed in Chapter 9, I do not believe that the explanation that social media is displacing social interaction has sufficient empirical support. I do believe that we lack a clear understanding of *why* teens do not (or cannot) spend time in one another's company. Perhaps broader societal fears about teens hanging out or being alone without parental supervision have contributed to their lack of FtF time. Perhaps parents' increasing focus on college preparation and/or programmed sports or activities have curtailed teens' social opportunities. In the face of such constraints, social and mobile media offer reasonable and efficient replacements for missed socialization (boyd, 2014). Indeed, all of the key components of what makes a friend a friend can be seen in adolescents' practices of mobile and social media (Yau & Riech, 2018). I believe that mobile and social media are being used to attempt to satisfy a strong need to belong among American adolescents that is unmet by FtF contact.

Is this also true among American adults?

1.2 Are American Adults Spending Less Time Socializing?

A few years ago, there was a great deal of public concern and debate about the declining state of Americans' personal relationships. People were confronted with data that implied that we are more socially isolated than we were twenty years ago. Hampton and colleagues (2011) conducted an important study in 2008 that challenged those findings, and found no evidence supporting a decline in the size of people's core networks. The average discussion network size (around two) was the same across decades, and the core network size included one more significant person not in the discussion network, which was also consistent with past data. Providing evidence contrary to the social displacement hypothesis, those who had more social ties also used more personal and social media (see Chapter 9) (Hampton et al., 2011). It seems likely that Americans have a similar number of close relationships partners now as in the past.

Because the number of core ties is not the same thing as amount of time in social interaction, I wanted to know whether there was any evidence of less time spent in social interaction. Luckily, the American Time Use Survey (United States Department of Labor, 2019) has taken a probability sample of American adults every year since 2003 to measure how the average American uses their time each day. In total, more than 200,000 Americans were interviewed over the last fifteen years to answer this question.

In my analysis, I focused primarily on the two categories measuring time spent socializing (i.e., FtF social communication and hosting or attending parties or social functions). Because time spent in mediated communication is not part of this category, I drew data from the category of "telephone calls" that included texting and internet voice and video calling (i.e., three forms of mediated social interaction). Finally, I combined several subcategories that constituted social interaction, including talking to and reading stories to children in one's household, socializing for work-related purposes, and attending meetings for volunteer activities (i.e., labeled "Other social time" in Figure 10.1).

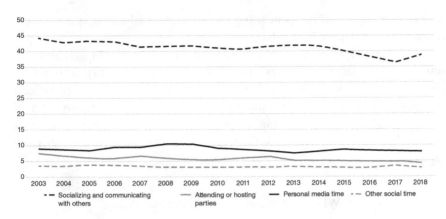

FIGURE 10.1 Time spent socializing, 2003–2018

I elected not to include social activities like religious or volunteer activities, as time spent there does not necessarily require or imply social interaction. As a final note, the American Time Use Survey does not measure secondary or simultaneous activities. Its manual states: "If respondents report doing more than one activity at the same time, they are asked to separate out the time spent on each activity or to specify which was their main activity" (United States Department of Labor, 2019). The minutes reported on the figure should be interpreted as time spent socializing for its own sake, not as a supplement to doing other things like eating, working, or driving.

The data were clear: among American adults, there has been a ten-minute decline in the number of minutes spent socializing per day over the last fifteen years. This amounts to a loss of over an hour a week of socializing. The majority of the decline is in two activities: socializing and attending or hosting parties. Using data drawn from LSAY collected during the same time period, we also (i.e., Hall et al., 2019b) reported a decline in the frequency of visiting friends among Generation Xers.

Mediated social interactions (i.e., telephone, video chat, texting, emails) also showed a tiny decline over fifteen years of approximately one minute. This means that time spent using personal media in ways most similar to social interaction *is not replacing* the lost time spent socializing FtF. In other words, it does not appear to be the case that Americans are spending more time in mediated social interaction to replace less time spent in FtF social interaction.

It is important to point out that Figure 10.1 does not capture the hour-plus per day that active users spend on social media (Hall et al., 2019a; *The Economist*, 2016). Social media use is likely captured in the American Time Use Survey's media use categories. Time spent using the computer is one of the top four activities in terms of increased uses of time over the last fifteen years (along with watching TV and playing games). Unfortunately for the sake of comparison, time spent using mobile and social media is not a well-differentiated category in the data.

It also appears that time spent socializing is one of the biggest shifts in time use in the last fifteen years. Since 2003, Americans have spent less time shopping, caring for children, and socializing, in that order. This likely reflects patterns of greater reliance on online shopping, but also is reminiscent of findings that teens are spending less time going to places like malls. This means that, compared with all of the ways people can use their time, socializing is on the decline.

1.3 What Is Associated with Time Socializing?

One question that might immediately come to mind is, What replaced that lost social time? Unfortunately, the data were collected in such a way that we cannot see individual trends in declining social time; we can only see year to year change. However, by exploring the correlates of time spent socializing across all fifteen years, we can answer the question in a slightly different way. Similar to Robinson's (2011) analysis on internet use patterns, we can determine what people who socialize a lot are doing *less* of and what people who are socializing a little are doing *more* of.

First, I do not believe that demographic changes in America provide many helpful clues. Women are more likely to spend time socializing than men, and older adults are spending less time socializing than younger adults. But these two correlations were very small, which suggests that they do not really tell us much about who socializes more. The three most strongly associated uses of time were at least four times larger in terms of size of correlation than demographic characteristics.

Working was the number one correlate of time spent socializing, and number three was commuting to work. If we include time spent at work-related events, working is by far the best and most clear negative correlate with socializing. People who work longer hours, commute longer, and have to stay at work for other events spend less time socializing.

The second largest correlate was time spent watching TV and streaming content. Although not as strong a correlate with socializing as work, Americans who watch more TV or stream more online content socialize less.

1.4 Conclusion

American adolescents and adults are spending less time interacting FtF at home and out in the community, and are not using personal media (i.e., video chat, voice calls) to compensate for this lost social time. People who work more, commute longer, and watch more TV spend less time socializing. And since 2003, time spent watching TV and using the computer is on the rise.

Taken together, these trends may mean that the portion of time in FtF contact may remain stable (as reported in Chapter 5) *and* that the most sociable people use several forms of media to keep in touch (as reported in Chapter 9), but the overall amount of social interaction is on the decline for both adults and for adolescents in America.

I fear we have built a society that does not prioritize the access to places, leisure, or free time, and allocation of time that enable people to engage in the amount of FtF connection they need to thrive.

One possible answer to this challenge is that we need to build routines of mediated connection that better integrate our online and offline social worlds.

SECTION TWO: ROUTINE SOCIAL INTERACTION

Only recently have researchers begun to appreciate the fundamentally inter-twined nature of online and offline communication in personal relationships. There has been push toward mixed-media (Parks, 2017), multimodal (Baym, 2009; Ramirez & Wang, 2008), and interdependent (Caughlin & Sharabi, 2013) relationships, but divisions between theories, methods, and research topics hamper high-quality research inquiry. Questions about how online media habits influence global well-being have been pursued, particularly for social media (see Chapter 8), but considerably less attention has been paid to how *offline* social habits and access to others FtF influence *online* social behavior. Granted, both personality (e.g., extroversion) and mental health (e.g., loneliness) influence online behaviors (Caplan, 2018). Yet the idea that users' offline social worlds – social routines, access to others, and relationship quality – play an important role in explaining media use is a topic given insufficient research attention. I suspect that the more routine access we have to important others offline, the less important and influential our online communication habits are in shaping our relational health and well-being.

These are the fundamental issues of social ecology in the digital age.

2.1 The Power of Convenience

But those space-independent [mediated] relationships, no matter how strong, long lasting or trusted – all of which they often are – cannot override people's responsiveness to everyday contact, the fact that, day in and day out, people encounter a stream of regular and new individuals with whom they must interact, to whom they must respond, and about whom they must make decisions. In spite of what is possible online, people are deeply responsive to the social interactions they encounter routinely.

—Mario Small (2017, p. 176)

Humans are creatures of habit and social habits are no exception. Routine conversations with other people in general, and emotional close others specifically, play a huge role in communication content, sometimes in unexpected ways. Small (2017) demonstrated this in his rich analysis of new graduate students' social lives. He found that people talk about important matters, not only with intimates or closest confidants but with the people they routinely interact with. When availability was taken into account, graduate students were far more likely (i.e., 59% of the time) to talk to those with whom they had weak ties than strong ties about important matters (Small et al., 2015). In other words, students talk about school to classmates, employees talk about work to coworkers, and parents talk about parenting to other parents because it helps to have an interaction partner who understands the issue at hand and is routinely available.

More so than any form of media, FtF conversation is habitual partly because it is obligatory and partly because it is convenient, especially in institutional settings like work and school, and, of course, at home. In my analysis of modality and interaction partners in Chapter 5, I found that people interacted FtF with a huge range of others on any given day – from close friends and family to strangers. Other modalities were much more linked to certain relationship partners. The frequency of these daily interactions with strong and weak ties alike are associated with a better quality of life (Hall & Merolla, 2020; Sandstrom & Dunn, 2014). Routine FtF interactions give us a wider group of people to talk to about important and mundane matters alike, which strengthens our bridging and bonding social capital.

Convenient social routines matter and the lack thereof has equally formative consequences.

2.2 Routine Contact Creates Relationships

Convenient contact is a boon to relationship maintenance. The greatest threat to losing touch with friends, and to a lesser degree family, is moving away from them (Mollenhorst et al., 2014; Small et al., 2015). In examining changes in Dutch citizens' personal network (i.e., the first fifteen) over the course of seven years, Mollenhorst et al. (2014) found that 53% of relationships were lost or displaced due to lack of meeting opportunities. In the largest meta-analysis of social network size and composition, Wrzus et al. (2013) concluded that relocation is the single greatest threat to friendship maintenance. Without contact, there is a day-by-day attrition of emotional closeness between friends (Roberts & Dunbar, 2011). When entering into a new environment, people maintain only their closest ties as time becomes scarce and opportunity to interact declines (Small et al., 2015). Other relationships, once routine and convenient, fade away.

Routine social interaction is crucial to having and keeping friends.

On the flip side, times of transition create new patterns of routine contact, which offer opportunities to make new friends (Hall, 2019; Mollenhorst et al.,

2014). Most students find new friends within the first few months of arriving at university (Saramaki et al., 2014; Small et al., 2015). New routines disrupt old patterns, and this frees up time and creates space for new friendships to form.

All of these studies point to an important fact: although people could use various mediated technologies to keep relationships close and connected, there is a great deal of research evidence that they often do not. The farther away people live, the less frequent the contact (Tillema et al., 2010). And this is not a new phenomenon. Fischer (1992) noted a similar attrition of faraway friends in the era of posted letters and phone calls. Only the closest relationships, especially those between parents and children and between romantic partners, manage to endure the loss of routine interaction opportunities.

In other words, people are not very good at keeping in touch. Why not?

2.3 Talk in a Homeostatic System

Overwhelmingly, routine social interactions are conducted with people whom we live with or are obliged to talk to. Only 2–6% of people are in daily contact with their closest friends and family who live outside their home (Tillema et al., 2010). Even when something serious comes up, we talk about important matters with the people who are around, not necessarily with the people who really matter to us (Small, 2017).

According to CBB theory (Hall & Davis, 2017), all of this talk exists within an individual's social system shaped by the need to belong and the homeostatic management of time spent in contact and time spent alone (see Chapter 3). When individuals get their fundamental need to belong met through one interaction, they are more likely to be alone later in the day (Hall, 2018a). When people lack opportunities to talk with close partners, they seem to get more out of interactions with weaker ties (Sandstrom & Dunn, 2014). Thus, CBB theory would suggest that once belongingness needs are sufficiently satisfied with the people who are around, people are more likely to seek isolation and avoid more social interactions (see also O'Connor & Rosenblood, 1996). This is also a matter of energy conservation.

Just as new contexts allow new relationships to form, when we lack people to talk to at home, CBB theory would suggest we have more social energy to talk to a wider group of others. When relationships are well established and routine, our social time is set and constrained. Freedom from routine contact (or a lack thereof) in one's home makes time available and motivates seeking contact elsewhere. In other words, having a partner at home decreases communication with others outside the home (van den Berg et al., 2012).

This can be observed in the difference between single and married people. Using seven nationally-representative data sets, Sarkisian and Gerstel (2016) found that compared with married people, single people were more likely to stay in touch with, provide help to, and receive help from a wide range of strong and weak ties. This aligns nicely with a classic study that found that starting a new romantic relationship leads to a 50% drop in interaction time with other friends, even close friends (Milardo, Johnson, & Huston, 1983). Forming a stable romantic partnership drops the interaction network size from thirty to twenty distinct individuals (Milardo et al., 1983). Taking a life-course perspective, both being single and moving away from one's home contribute to the dramatic rise in number of relationship partners starting at fifteen and continuing until around twenty-five years old (Wrzus et al., 2013). Around twenty-five, the formation of a family of one's own (i.e., marriage, children) reverses the acquisition of friends, and likely accelerates the decline in the number of social interactions outside the home. All of this suggests that a primary reason why people do not keep in touch is that they are getting their needs met and/or their social energy expended by social interactions with people who are physically near.

We are extremely selective in whom we keep in touch with through high-energy personal media (not social media) when we do not see them FtF (Small, 2017; Tillema et al., 2010; Wellman & Tindall, 1993). This trend goes back to the era of posted letters and the telephone (Fischer, 1992). Wellman and Tindall (1993) suggest that it is only the core people we feel obliged to keep in contact with when FtF contact is unavailable, not even the first fifteen, and we feel even less of an obligation to stay in touch with distant friends and family.

To me, these research findings imply several conclusions. People who are more alone on any given day – both emotionally or by lacking a co-present other on that day – are probably more likely to use personal media than on days when they have someone around to talk to. Other things being equal, single adults probably use more personal media to socially interact with others than do married people. People who feel more socially supported and connected to their offline relationships are less likely to seek new supportive relationship partners through media.

Without the benefit of routine FtF contact, keeping in touch with others is the exception not the rule.

Bringing this back to the challenges of networked individualism, I expect that the reason why people do not keep in touch is not because of a lack of technologically enabled access, but because of a lack of routine. The data suggest we are choosing *not* to build mediated routines of interaction because of insufficient need, energy, or time – with one major exception: social media.

SECTION THREE: SOCIAL ECOLOGY AND PRACTICES OF SOCIAL MEDIA

Nowhere is it easier or cheaper to keep in touch than it is on social media. Technologically enabled notifications and reminders to log on and attend to the pictures, posts, and stories of others create and reinforce this form of mediated sociality. If analysis of the American Time Use Survey data suggests that American adults are *not* turning to mediated social interactions (e.g., voice calls, video chat) to keep in touch, is it possible that social media is filling that gap? Is there evidence that social media use is a product of a lack of offline social contact?

3.1 Social Media Use Is Associated with Unmet Social Needs

The heaviest users of social media are those who do not have routine FtF interaction partners. Prior to the rise of social media, when people got lonelier or less satisfied with life, they turned to the internet to socialize (Stepanikova et al., 2010). Song and colleagues' (2014) meta-analysis of Facebook use showed that loneliness is a much better predictor of social media use than social media use is of loneliness. Similarly, adolescents who are depressed are more likely to browse on Instagram over time, but browsing Instagram was unassociated with future depression (Frison & Eggermont, 2017). A similar study found that when adolescents and young adults were more isolated, they were more likely to use social media in the future, but not the other way around (Heffer et al., 2019). Adolescents crave the time and connection with their friends, but lacking opportunities, time, and places to hang out with them, they turn to social and personal media to connect (boyd, 2014). When people lack strong offline connections, they turn to media to try to connect with others – through online forums, gaming, and IM, and, of course, through social media (Caplan, 2018; Wang et al., 2012).

Thus, people turn to social media to resolve unmet social needs. But do people use social media in a way that is likely to get their needs met?

As addressed in Chapter 6, social media were and continue to be a tool primarily used to people-watch. Through this type of passive consumption, users enjoy the feeling of being "in the loop" about others' life events. I would predict that by virtual people watching, people feel that the minimum standard of connection has been met, even in the absence of more direct forms of mediated contact (see Chapter 3). Without a doubt, this is an extremely efficient use of social time, so it has its own draw according to the principle of energy conversation (Hall & Davis, 2017). However, social media browsing is dramatically different from other forms of mediated social interaction (see Chapters 5 and 6). Importantly, social media do not seem to meet the needs of those who turn to them to alleviate a social deficiency or need (Caplan, 2018; Wang et al., 2012). Indeed, adolescents who have high social media use and low in-person interaction have the highest rates of loneliness (Twenge et al., 2019). Social media browsing does not promote the same degree of relationship connection, need satisfaction, and decreases in loneliness or gains in well-being that social interactions through FtF, voice call, and video chat do (Chapter 5).

Consider the results of a recent experimental study that found that social media users who typically spent time scrolling and browsing stand the most to gain by quitting, while users who typically use social media to share, comment, and privately message stand the most to lose by quitting (Hanley et al., 2019). In general, active social media use offers more gains to well-being than does passive use (Verduyn et al., 2015).

Even in the case that social media offer opportunities to reconnect with old friends, that reconnection tends to dwindle if routine contact off of social media does not transpire. Since its earliest incarnations, SNSs are widely used to reconnect with old friends (82% used it for that purpose) (Bryant et al., 2011). Once reconnected, sometimes there is a follow-up email, IM, voice call, or bout of texting, and occasionally a FtF meeting (Quinn, 2013; Ramirez et al., 2017). Yet it seems that people take those extra steps only when the value of keeping in touch with the lost partner is high (Ramirez et al., 2017). Once that extra mediated and FtF contact diminishes, relationships often return to being maintained only through SNS (Karakayali & Killic, 2013; Quinn, 2013), and only if both people continue to actively use it. Even though social media offer a great place to reconnect, their use does not seem to increase routine social interactions with renewed contacts.

It is important not to forget that the content of a social media feed is overwhelmingly composed of contributions from less close friendships and members of professional or organizational networks (Bryant et al., 2011; Quinn & Papacharissi, 2018). The question is, Does this contact reinforce further contact through other media or FtF? The *New York Times* (Badger & Bui, 2018) reported: "Nationwide, in the average county, 63 percent of friendship links are [within 100 miles], probably reflecting that many people on Facebook know one another through real-world sites like grade schools, colleges and offices." This means most of the people we see on social media are people we *could* meet up with in person. Yet I know of no research that explores whether the amount of social media contact increases the chance of FtF contact for geographically proximal weak ties. Does social media contact promote personal media connection in general, particularly for those less close relationship partners?

Considering what usually promotes social routines and habit, I am doubtful that it does. The communication interdependence perspective (Caughlin & Sharabi, 2013) strongly suggests that interdependence, not media use, comes first in tracking online communication prevalence and coordination. In other words, constant *access* does not produce interdependence. Madianou's (2014) study of migrant family communication concurs: the possibilities of smartphone-enabled communication will not "create relationships when there are none" (p. 677). Relationships must be fertile at first to grow habits of mediated communication that can sustain them.

In other words, a lack of closeness cannot be resolved by text or post.

Again, this means that it is up to us to take steps to fulfill the promise of media. Typical patterns of social media use are unlikely to build and sustain relationships.

SECTION FOUR: BUILDING HEALTHFUL SOCIAL MEDIA PRACTICES

4.1 When Interdependence Is Built Through Media

The internet has long been a place of personal connection (Baym, 2010) (see Chapter 4). As in offline relationships, mediated communication requires partner responsiveness to initiate relationships. In Chapter 7, I explored why media with high reach and/or low interactivity are more likely to dissuade audiences to attend to messages, much less to respond to them. If the trends of American time use are correct, we are not using personal and directed media (e.g., voice calls, video chat, email) to replace lost time in FtF contact, but we are increasingly using social media to observe the social news of a large network of close and distant relationships alike. Given this reliance on social media, what are relationship-supporting practices in that environment?

As discussed in Chapter 6, the pull of social media has long been to see and be seen by others (Donath, 2008). Humphreys's (2018) analysis of the everyday experience of social media suggests the receipt and reaction to presentations of the mediated self can "reinforce our social bonds" through "bearing witness" (p. 16). I personally believe that bearing witness to another's life as it is lived is a deeply intimate act, perhaps even existentially necessary. Humphreys's analysis reminds us that in its ideal form, attending to others' social media accounts can build togetherness, intimacy, and acknowledgment through knowledge of the "connective rhythms of the quotidian, shared expectations, or understandings of daily routines" (p. 7). It is possible for media to become a dwelling place (O'Hara et al., 2014), a place of intimacy through shared rhythms of interaction (Quan-Haase & Collins, 2008). But it is not enough to be a technologically adjacent yet silent witness.

To maintain interdependence among migrant families, smartphone conversations actively flow between platforms and modalities (Madianou, 2014). Texts, photos, emails, one-click acknowledgments, and comments buoy families' shared commitment to one another. Through those practices, life far away seems less distant; it becomes a background feature of the migrant's life abroad. Active, personalized use of technology can be a sign of ongoing commitment to one another (O'Hara et al., 2014). Between long-distance romantic couples, mediated communication, even the simple buzz of the mobile device, "can be understood as constitutive of the actual relationships" (Madianou, 2014, p. 676) (Chapter 2).

No doubt, media can be used to sustain intimate long-distance relationships. Is there any value to bearing witness to the lives of others with whom we are less interdependent?

4.2 Supporting One Another Through Media

As they unite geographically remote patients and caretakers who are coping with similar challenges, online support groups are a valuable component of modern health interventions (Rains & Young, 2009). People who use them show an improvement in quality of life and in ability to manage and cope with their medical condition. The interaction of support group members with one another appears to play a key role in promoting these outcomes. Importantly, when online support groups have chat-type options, it seems to boost positive outcomes for participants (Rains & Young, 2009). Focusing on the content of messages shared on online support groups, Rains, Peterson, and Wright's (2015) meta-analysis found that both emotional and informational support promotes positive outcomes. When coping with a serious illness, feeling validated and understood is a critical act of witness we can offer one another.

Drawing from the value of high-quality support in health contexts, it seems that receiving quality support through social media may hold a similar value. We often turn to social media to seek social support (Baker & Algorta, 2016; Lo, 2019). When users perceived that they were more supported through social media, they reported greater well-being (Kim & Lee, 2011) and less depression (Baker & Algorta, 2016). These results suggest that social media users have an important role to play for one another online. If the value of social media depends on the quality of interactions and support that people have there, then we all can contribute positively to one another's online experience. Supportive messages can be both informational and empathetic in nature (Rains et al., 2015), but, importantly, they should be *messages*, not merely passive viewing or one-click acknowledgments.

Echoing these findings, Facebook's own research team has found that directed messages from close others matter the most for promoting well-being (Burke & Kraut, 2016) and building relationship closeness (Burke & Kraut, 2014). Their analysis revealed that messages *to* and messages *from* are strongly correlated, which suggests that communicative reciprocity can be built in friendship-promoting ways on social media (Yau & Riech, 2018). By comparison, the frequency of broadcasting by itself was negatively associated with relationship closeness over time. Only composed communication explained the benefits of social media use, particularly in nonkin relationships (Burke & Kraut, 2014). This reinforces the importance of using social media in ways that promote social interaction – active, directed, composed, and personalized.

Considering this in combination with research that suggests people turn to social media in time of need suggests that those who are most in need of connection can benefit the most from having a supportive and responsive audience.

4.3 For Some, Mediated Contact Is Vital

It is important not to forget the vital importance of online communities and connection for those who are marginalized, particularly if marginalized in their geographically proximate community. Since its inception, online dating has been a critical route to intimacy for sexually marginalized groups (Finkel et al., 2012). Individuals who do not have suitable romantic partners in their local community benefit the most from the reach and discretion afforded by online dating sites and apps. This trend continues. In 2017, 65% of same-sex couples who got together met online, compared with 39% of straight couples (Rosenfeld, Thomas, & Falcon, 2016).

For some people, there is simply no substitute for the connection that online communities offer. Online support groups are particularly helpful for people who are geographically remote, whose mobility is impaired, or who have rare ailments (Rains & Young, 2009). Although they may start as a set of strangers brought together by a common experience, online support groups can transform into a vital community of mutual support and concern (Rains et al., 2015). This sort of connection would be nearly impossible without the capabilities of online media.

These benefits have been a part of the promise of technology from the inception. BBS communities united tech enthusiasts, and early online communities united fans of soap operas (Baym, 2000). The promise of technology can be fulfilled only when there is an attentive and receptive audience, with at least some portion of the membership devoted to doing the emotional (and sometimes technological) labor of sharing, responding, and cultivating a community. There is work to be done.

4.4 Tighten the Circle

Yet the time we devote to others is a finite resource and must be balanced with our time and attention to those who matter the most to us.

As the results of Burke and Kraut (2014; 2016) illustrate, direct mediated social interactions with our close partners seem to offer the strongest benefits to our own well-being. Such results mirror those found in offline relationships. Several studies have pointed out that there are diminishing returns to be gained in life satisfaction and well-being from an increasingly wider social circle (Binder, Roberts, & Sutcliffe, 2012; Helliwell & Wang, 2011; van der Horst & Coffe, 2012). It is not advantageous to spread ourselves too thin socially. Unfortunately, adding new contacts on SNS primarily increases superficial relationships (Manago et al., 2012; Quinn & Papacharissi, 2018).

Thus, one of my recommendations is to tighten the social circle when building and sustaining media routines. Keeping in touch with fewer people who are more personally important in both robust and routine ways is likely much more beneficial than broadcasting updates to a large group of those with whom one has a weaker relationship. Close friends and family are proportionally much more important than other friends and family for well-being (van der Horst & Coffee, 2012), particularly for stemming loneliness (Piquart & Sorensen, 2003). When people spend proportionally more of their social interaction time – both offline and online – with close relationship partners, they report lower levels of loneliness (Hall & Merolla, 2020).

One way to combine the above suggestions of social support and tightening the circle is to recognize that there are (at least) two important pathways to thriving through social interaction. Spend sustained and routine high-quality social time with close friends and family *and* frequently engage with less close others in warm and supportive ways. A few long conversations with close others online or offline can accompany brief, supportive, personalized exchanges with less close partners online and offline alike.

4.5 Increase the Signal Strength

Increasing the signal strength can be done in two ways: the message and the medium.

My own work (Hall, 2018a; 2019; Hall & Merolla, 2020) suggests that some conversations are more beneficial to our in-the-moment and long-term well-being than others, namely, joking around, catching up, affectionate communication, and meaningful conversation. But the good news is that we seem to need only a few of these types of conversations on any given day to experience their benefits (Hall & Merolla, 2020). That is, such types of conversation can be a small part of one's social practice – proportionally speaking – as long as they are a typical part of one's social life. Such conversations can be conducted FtF and through personal and social media and still carry weight (Vlahovic et al., 2012). Status updates and other social media messages that are more entertaining are also able to build connectedness (Utz, 2015). Fun and funny online and offline social interactions are an essential part of increasing signal strength. So, it does not all have to be deep talk or emotionally intense social support.

The medium can also be used to boost signal strength. As reported in Chapter 5, high social cue and low reach technologies such as the voice call and video chat are associated with a similar sense of connection as FtF communication, and are vital in keeping long-distance friends and family in touch. Indeed, the choice of media alone can convey a relationship-promoting message (see Chapter 5).

Carrying on an ancient tradition of keeping in touch – writing a letter – may also be a way to build a practice of closeness through media. Mourning its demise, Wayne (2015) compares a lengthy email to a candlelit dinner for two, especially in comparison to the low-calorie snack of social media (see Chapter 3). Email may be a complementary part of keeping in touch with long-distance friends (Ruppel & Burke, 2015).

Taking the time to compose and think through a long letter may, in itself, convey a message of concern and closeness. More effort in composition and creation signals commitment. In a clever article about how people imbue concern and care into their mediated communication, Kelly, Gooch, Patil, and Watts (2017) link the communication discipline's perspective on relationship maintenance with the functional design of technology. When a relational partner (e.g., friend, grandparent, lover) puts time and effort into correspondence, it is seen as a gift or something special and personal. Ironically, technologies tend to make things easier (i.e., less effort or energy), which may decrease the perception of signal strength. Taking the time and investing energy into keeping in touch and corresponding with friends is perceived as a sincere act of care, one that both the composition of the message and the choice of medium can convey.

SECTION FIVE: CONCLUSIONS

5.1 Social and Personal Media Are Not Built to Nourish Relationships

Never forget that you live in an ecosystem designed to disrupt you.
—Michael Harris (2014, p. 11)

It bears mentioning that while technology can be used to sustain meaningful, close relationships, it is not designed for that purpose. Most social media and smartphone apps are designed to capture our attention, to record our digital footprint, including our communication patterns, in order to generate advertising dollars for the host corporation. Apps essentially sell bits of our attention to advertisers. Consistent attention to media platforms and apps develops into habits, and habitual use increases the amount of information that can be harvested about you, with ever-greater precision. Moving forward, our patterns of social connection will be increasingly shaped by algorithms (Abeele et al., 2018), the logic of which is not visible and the use of which you cannot opt out of. In this environment, a greater degree of personalization helps corporations increase your attention to their product. Particularly when the platform or app is free, then you are the product – your data are aggregated, repackaged, and sold to generate advertising dollars.

We must remember that the aims of technology creators do not align with our social goals. Their motives are not in line with promoting interpersonal connection and well-being. Again, it is up to us to shape technology toward our social ends.

5.2 Cultural Dialectics of Connection

There is real, pervasive cultural anxiety about the disconnect we are experiencing. People feel distracted and trapped by their mobile connectedness. Chayko (2018) predicts that the social and instrumental costs of unplugging will continue to rise. Too much of our daily life has become integrated into our smartphone usage for us to simply unplug, and too much of our social connection is integrated into our personal and social media apps. Media have become interpersonalized (Parks, 2017).

If left to our own devices, we feel that our relationships with others will continue to decay, in part because of the lure and efficiency of mediated contact. Even in long-distance romantic relationships, where technology is a tremendous boon to staying in touch, it can also be a symbol of separation. One long-distance couple who relied on video chat for both sexual and emotional connection found that in using it, "they realized more fully that they couldn't actually touch each other and this caused them to miss each other more" (Pinsker, 2019). This lines up with analyses reported in Chapter 5 about piqued feelings of loneliness when using video chat. Young adults and adolescents already perceive a great deal of ambivalence with technology: using the smartphone causes anxiety and the lack of access to the smartphone causes anxiety (Mihailidis, 2014). Misplacing one's smartphone brings about fears of a loss of relationship connection (Hoffner, Lee, & Park, 2016) and actively using one's smartphone leads to a perception of a loss of in-person social connection (Mihailidis, 2014).

We may be entering into a time of two broader cultural shifts: toward freedom and independence and away from social and mobile media, and toward closer personal relationships and away from access to a multitude of relationship partners. Arnold (2003) suggested that technology is Janus-faced: looking forward as it looks back. Thus, dialectical theory would predict that at a societal level as connectivity increases, we may seek greater connection. Will this cultural shift steer us toward patterns of media use that promote more intimate connection? Will family, friends, and romantic couples seek greater independence and less connectivity in exchange for freedom and independence, especially if it refocuses time and attention on the in-person experience? Can meaningful mediated practices of connection show themselves to be a hallmark of a long, healthy, and well-lived life in the same way that quality FtF time was shown to be for the men and women of the Harvard and Terman studies?

Only time will tell as people continue to understand the consequences of relating through technology.

And so, I leave you with this advice. Connect mindfully to those who matter most, increase the signal strength when using media (i.e., more impactful conversations, more direct communication), and keep media habits in check, especially in places where they are the most disruptive. Many people are doing these things already, and when they do, they do so to show care and respect for their relationship partners both in-person and remote. Media can be used to nourish relationships, but to harness their capabilities, habits need to be established around practices of connection. These practices must be built by the users themselves, as media do not make us do anything and are not designed to promote connection over connectivity.

I offer my sincere thanks to you, the reader. I hope you enjoyed my DJ setlist on this curated tour of research on technology and relationships. I hope this book has contributed to your knowledge of how we can live mindfully in this digital age, and provided you with answers to questions that you had. I hope my playlist has opened your mind to relating to technology and will inspire repeat visits.

Until we meet again.

REFERENCES

Abeele, M. V., de Wolf, R., & Ling, R. (2018). Mobile media and social space: How anytime, anyplace connectivity structures everyday life. *Media and Communication, 6*(2), 5–14. doi:10.17645/mac.v6i2.1399

Ahn, D., & Shin, D.-H. (2013). Is the social use of media for seeking connectedness or for avoiding social isolation? Mechanisms underlying media use and subjective well-being. *Computers in Human Behavior, 29*(6), 2453–2462. doi:10.1016/j.chb.2012.12.022

Alberts, J. K., Yoshimura, C. G., Rabby, M., & Loschiavo, R. (2005). Mapping the topography of couples' daily conversation. *Journal of Social and Personal Relationships, 22*(3), 299–322. doi:10.1177/0265407505050941

Aledavood, T., López, E., Roberts, S. G., Reed-Tsochas, F., Moro, E., Dunbar, R. I., & Saramäki, J. (2015). Daily rhythms in mobile telephone communication. *PloS ONE, 10*(9), e0138098. doi:10.1371/journal.pone.0138098

Ambady, N., & Skowronski, J. J. (2008). *First impressions.* New York: Guilford Press.

Ancu, M. (2012) Older adults on Facebook: A survey examination of motives and use of social networking by people 50 and over. *Florida Communication Journal, 40*(2), 1–12.

Andalibi, N., Bentley, F., & Quehl, K. (2017). Multi-channel topic-based mobile messaging in romantic relationships. *Proceedings of the ACM on Human-Computer Interaction,* 1 (CSCW), 1–18.

Anderson, M., & Jiang, J. (2018). Teens, social media and technology 2018. *Pew Research Center.* Retrieved from www.pewinternet.org/wp-content/uploads/sites/9/2018/05/ PI_2018.05.31_TeensTech_FINAL.pdf.

Arminen, I. (2005). Social functions of location in mobile telephony. *Personal and Ubiquitous Computing, 10*(5), 319–323. doi:10.1007/s00779-005-0052-5

Arnold, M. (2003). On the phenomenology of technology: The "Janus" faces of mobile phones. *Information and Organization, 13*(4), 231–256. doi:10.1016/S1471-7727(03)00013-7

Axelsson, A. (2010). Perpetual and personal: Swedish young adults and their use of mobile phones. *New Media & Society, 12*(1), 35–54. doi:10.1177/1461444809355110

Badger, E., & Bui, Q. (2018). How connected is your community to everywhere else in America? Retrieved from: www.nytimes.com/interactive/2018/09/19/upshot/facebook-county-friendships.html.

Baker, D. A., & Algorta, G. P. (2016). The relationship between online social networking and depression: A systematic review of quantitative studies. *Cyberpsychology, Behavior, and Social Networking, 19*(11), 638–648. doi:10.1089/cyber.2016.0206

Barkhuus, L., & Polichar, V. E. (2011). Empowerment through seamfulness: Smart phones in everyday life. *Personal Ubiquitous Computing, 15*(6), 629–639. doi:10.1107/s00779-010-0342-4

Baron, N. (2008). *Always on: Language in an online and mobile world.* New York: Oxford University Press.

(2011). Concerns about mobile phones: A cross-national study. *First Monday, 6*(8). Retrieved from: http://firstmonday.org/ojs/index.php/fm/article/view/3335/3032.

Baron, N. S., & Campbell, E. M. (2012). Gender and mobile phones in cross-national context. *Language Sciences, 34*(1), 13–27. doi:10.1016/j.langsci.2011.06.018

Baron, N. S., & Hård af Segerstad, Y. (2010). Cross-cultural patterns in mobile-phone use: Public space and reachability in Sweden, the USA and Japan. *New Media & Society, 12*(1), 13–34. doi:10.1177/1461444809355111

Barry, C. T., Sidoti, C. L., Briggs, S. M., Reiter, S. R., & Lindsey, R. A. (2017). Adolescent social media use and mental health from adolescent and parent perspectives. *Journal of Adolescence, 61*, 1–11. doi:10.1016/j.adolescence.2017.08.005

Baumeister, R. F., & Leary, M. R. (1995). The need to belong: Desire for interpersonal attachments as a fundamental human motivation. *Psychological Bulletin, 117*(3), 497–529. doi:10.1037/0033-2909.117.3.497

Baxter, L. A., & Braithwaite, D. O. (2007). Social dialectics: The contradictions of relating. In B. B. Whaley & W. Samter (eds.), *Explaining communication* (pp. 275–292). Mahwah, NJ: Erlbaum.

Baxter, L. A., & Simon, E. P. (1993). Relationship maintenance strategies and dialectical contradictions in personal relationships. *Journal of Social and Personal Relationships, 10*(2), 225–242. doi:10.1177/026540759301000204

Bayer, J. B., Campbell, S. W., & Ling, R. (2015). Connection cues: Activating the norms and habits of social connectedness. *Communication Theory, 26*(2), 128–149. doi:10.1111/hcre.12067

Bayer, J. B., Ellison, N. B., Schoenebeck, S. Y., & Falk, E. B. (2016). Sharing the small moments: Ephemeral social interaction on Snapchat. *Information, Communication & Society, 19*(7), 956–977. doi:10.1080/136918X.1084349

Baym, N. K. (2000). *Tune in, log on: Soaps, fandom, and online community.* Thousand Oaks, CA: Sage.

(2009). A call for grounding in the face of blurred boundaries. *Journal of Computer Mediated Communication, 14*(3), 720–723. doi:10.1111/j/1083-6101.2009.01461.x

(2010). *Personal connections in the digital age.* Malden, MA: Polity Press.

(2015). *Personal connections in the digital age* (2nd ed.). Malden, MA: Polity Press.

(2018). *Playing to the crowd: Musicians, audiences, and the intimate work of connection.* New York: New York University Press.

Baym, N. K., & Ledbetter, A. M. (2009). Tunes that bind?: Predicting friendship strength in a music-based social network. *Information, Communication, & Society, 12*(3), 408–427. doi:10.1080/1369118082635430

Baym, N. K., Zhang, Y. B., & Lin, M-C. (2004). Social interactions across media. *New Media & Society, 6*(3), 299–318. doi:10.1177/1461444804041438

Bazarova, N. N. (2012). Public intimacy: Disclosure interpretation and social judgments on Facebook. *Journal of Communication, 62*(5), 815–832. doi:10.1111/j.1460-2466.2012.01664.x

BBC News (2010, July 9). Over 5 billion mobile phone connections worldwide. Retrieved from: www.bbc.co.uk/news/10569081.

Beck, J. (2019, February 4). Facebook: Where friendships go to never quite die. Retrieved from: www.theatlantic.com/family/archive/2019/02/15-years-facebook-friendships-wont-die/581824/.

Becker, J. A., Johnson, A. J., Craig, E. A., Gilchrist, E. S., Haigh, M. M., & Lane, L. T. (2009). Friendships are flexible, not fragile: Turning points in geographically-close and long-distance friendships. *Journal of Social and Personal Relationships, 26*(4), 347–369. doi:10.1177/0265407509344310

Bernstein, M. S., Bakshy, E., Burke, M., & Karrer, B. (2013, April 27–May 2). Quantifying the invisible audience in social networks. Presented at the ACM Conference on Human Factors in Computing Systems: CHI 2013 in Paris. doi:10.1145/2470654.2470658

Bevan, J. L., Galvan, J., Villasenor, J., & Henkin, J. (2016). "You've been on my mind ever since": A content analysis of expressions of interpersonal attraction in Craigslist.org's Missed Connections posts. *Computers in Human Behavior, 54,* 18–24. doi:10.106/j.chb.2015.07.050

Beyens, I., Frison, E., & Eggermont, S. (2016). "I don't want to miss a thing": Adolescents' fear of missing out and its relationship to adolescents' social needs, Facebook use, and Facebook related stress. *Computers in Human Behavior, 64,* 1–8. doi:10.1016/j.chb.2016.05.083

Bhattacharya, K., Ghosh, A., Monsivais, D., Dunbar, R. I., & Kaski, K. (2016). Sex differences in social focus across the life cycle in humans. *Royal Society Open Science, 3*(4), 160097. doi:10.1098/rsos.160097

Binder, J. F., Roberts, S. G. B., & Sutcliffe, A. G. (2012). Closeness, loneliness, support: Core ties and significant ties in personal communities. *Social Networks, 34*(2), 206–214. doi:10.1016/j.socnet.2011.12001

Blease, C. R. (2015). Too many "friends," too few "likes"? Evolutionary psychology and "Facebook depression." *Review of General Psychology, 19*(1), 1–13. doi:10.1037/gpr0000030

Boase, J., Horrigan, J. B., Wellman, B., & Rainie, L. (2006). The strength of internet ties. *Pew Internet & American Life Project.* www.pewinternet.org/.

boyd, d. (2014). *It's complicated: The social lives of networked teens.* New Haven, CT: Yale University Press.

Braithwaite, D. O., & Schrodt, P. (2015). *Engaging theories in interpersonal communication: Multiple perspectives* (2nd ed.). Los Angeles, CA: Sage.

Brandtzæg, P. B. (2012). Social networking sites: Their users and social implications – A longitudinal study. *Journal of Computer Mediated Communication, 17*(4), 467–488. doi:10.1111/j.1083-6101.2012.01580.x

Briskin, J. L., Bogg, T., & Haddad, J. (2018). Lower trait stability, stronger normative beliefs, habitual phone use, and unimpeded phone access predict distracted college student messaging in social, academic and driving contexts. *Frontiers in Psychology, 9*(2633). doi:10.3389/fpsyg.2018.02633

Brown, B., O'Hara, K., McGregor, M., & McMillan, D. (2018). Text in talk: Lightweight messages in co-present interaction. *ACM Transactions on Computer-Human Interaction (TOCHI), 24*(6), 42. doi: 10.1145/3152419

Brown, C. J., & Brown, R. M. (2006). Selective investment theory: Recasting the functional significance of close relationships. *Psychological Inquiry, 17*(1), 1–29. doi:10.1207/s15327965pli1701_01

Bryant, E. M., & Marmo, J. (2012) The rules of Facebook friendship: A two-stage examination of interaction rules in close, casual, and acquaintance friendships. *Journal of Social & Personal Relationships, 29*(8), 1013–1035. doi:10.1177/0265407512443616

Bryant, E. M., Marmo, J., & Ramirez, A., Jr. (2011). A functional approach to social networking sites. In K. B. Wright & L. M. Webb (eds.), *Computer-mediated communication in personal relationships* (pp. 3–20). New York: Peter Lang.

Bryant, J., & Fondren, W. (2009). Displacement effects. In R. L. Nabi & M. B. Oliver (eds.), *The SAGE handbook of media processes and effects* (pp. 505–516). Los Angeles, CA: Sage.

Bucher, T., & Helmond, A. (2018). The affordances of social media platforms. In J. Burgess, A. Marwick, & T. Poell (eds.), *The SAGE handbook of social media* (pp. 233–253). Los Angeles, CA: Sage Publications.

Buntain, C., & Golbeck, J. (2014, April). Identifying social roles in Reddit using network structure. In *Proceedings of the 23rd international conference on World Wide Web* (pp. 615–620). Seoul: ACM. doi:10.1145/2567948.2579231

Bureau of Labor Statistics (2016). 69.7% of 2016 high school graduates enrolled in college. Retrieved from: www.bls.gov/opub/ted/2017/69-point-7-percent-of-2016-high-school-graduates-enrolled-in-college-in-october-2016.htm.

Burke, M., & Kraut, R. E. (2014, April). Growing closer on Facebook: Changes in tie strength through social network site use. In *Proceedings of the SIGCHI conference on human factors in computing systems* (pp. 4187–4196). Toronto: ACM. doi:10.1145/2556288.2557094

(2016). The relationship between Facebook use and well-being depends on communication type and tie strength. *Journal of Computer-Mediated Communication, 21*(4), 265–281. doi:10.1111/jcc4.12162

Burke, M., Kraut, R., & Marlow, C. (2011). Social capital on Facebook: Differentiating uses and users. In *Proceedings of the SIGCHI conference on human factors in computing systems* (pp. 571–580). Vancouver, CA doi:10.1145/1978942.1979023

Cacioppo, J. T., Cacioppo, S., Gonzaga, G. C., Ogburn, E. L., & VanderWeele, T. J. (2013). Marital satisfaction and break-ups differ across on-line and off-line meeting venues. *Proceedings of the National Academy of Sciences, 110*(25), 10135–10140. doi:10.1073/pnas.1222447110

Caplan, S. E. (2018). *The changing face of problematic internet use: An interpersonal approach.* New York: Peter Lang.

Carmichael, C. L., Reis, H. T., & Duberstein, P. R. (2015). In your 20s it's quantity, in your 30s it's quality: The prognostic value of social activity across 30 years of adulthood. *Psychology and Aging, 30*(1), 95–105. doi:10.1037/pag0000014

Carlson, J. R., & Zmud, R.W. (1999). Channel expansion theory and the experiential nature of media richness perceptions. *Academy of Management Journal, 42*(2), 153–170. doi:10.2307/257090

Cather, W. (1918). *My Antonia.* New York: Library of America.

Caughlin, J. P., & Sharabi, L. L. (2013). A communication interdependence perspective of close relationships: The connections between mediated and unmediated interactions matter. *Journal of Communication, 63*(5), 873–893. doi:10.1111/jcom/12046

Caughlin, J. P., & Wang, N. (2020). Relationship maintenance in the age of technology. In B. G. Ogolsky & J. K. Monk (eds.), *Relationship maintenance: Theory, process, and context.* New York: Cambridge University Press.

Center for Humane Technology (2019, June). Learn about the Center for Humane Technology & meet our team. Retrieved from https://humanetech.com/about-us/.

Chan, D. K. S., & Cheng, G. H. L. (2004). A comparison of offline and online friendship qualities at different stages of relationship development. *Journal of Social and Personal Relationships, 21*(3), 305–320. doi:1177/0265407504042834

Chan, M. (2015). Multimodal connectedness and quality of life: Examining the influences of technology adoption and interpersonal communication on well-being across the life span. *Journal of Computer-Mediated Communication, 20*(1), 3–18. doi:10.1111/jcc4.12089

Chayko, M. (2014). Techno-social life: The internet, digital technology, and social connectedness. *Sociology Compass, 8*(7), 976–991. doi:10.1111/soc4.12190

(2018). *Superconnected: The internet, digital media, and techno-social life* (2nd ed.). Los Angeles, CA: Sage.

Chotpitayasunondh, V., & Douglas, K. M. (2018). The effects of phubbing on social interaction. *Journal of Applied Social Psychology, 48*(6), 304–316. doi:10.1111/jasp.12506

Clark, M. S., Mills, J., & Powell, M. C. (1986). Keeping track of needs in communal and exchange relationships. *Journal of Personality and Social Psychology, 51*(2), 333–338. doi:10.1037/0022-3514.51.2.333

Cody, M. J., & Dunn, D. (2007). Accounts. In B. B. Whaley & W. Samter (eds.), *Explaining communication: Contemporary theories and exemplars* (pp. 237–256). Mahwah, NJ: Erlbaum.

Crowley, J. P., Allred, R. J., Follon, J., & Volkmer, C. (2018). Replication of the mere presence hypothesis: The effects of cell phones on face-to-face conversations. *Communication Studies, 69*(3), 283–293. doi:10.1080/10510974.2018.1467941

Crystal, D. (2008). *Txtng: The gr8 db8.* Oxford: Oxford University Press.

Cummings, J. N., Butler, B., & Kraut, R. (2002). The quality of online social relationships. *Communications of the ACM, 45*(7), 103–108. doi:10.1145/514236.514242

Daft, R. L. & Lengel, R. H. (1984). Information richness: A new approach to managerial behavior and organizational design. In L. L. Cummings & B. M. Staw (eds.), *Research in organizational behavior* (pp. 191–233). Homewood, IL: JAI Press.

Davey, S., Davey, A., Raghav, S. K., Singh, J. V., Singh, N., Blachnio, A., & Przepiórkaa, A. (2018). Predictors and consequences of "Phubbing" among adolescents and youth in India: An impact evaluation study. *Journal of Family & Community Medicine, 25*(1), 35–42. doi:10.4103/jfcm.JFCM_71_17

Davis, D. A. C. (1997). Development and initial tests of a human energy management theory of communication. Doctoral dissertation. Available from ProQuest Dissertations and Theses database (UMI No. 9835087).

DeAndrea, D. C., & Walther, J. B. (2011). Attributions for inconsistencies between online and offline self-presentations. *Communication Research, 38*(6), 805–825. doi:10.1177/0093650210385340

Delwiche, A. (2018). Early social computing: The rise and fall of the BBS scene (1977–1995). In J. Burgess, A. Marwick, & T. Poell (eds.), *The SAGE handbook of social media* (pp. 35–52). Los Angeles, CA: Sage Publications.

Dienlin, T., Masur, P. K., & Trepte, S. (2017). Reinforcement or displacement? The reciprocity of FtF, IM, and SNS communication and their effects on loneliness and life satisfaction. *Journal of Computer-Mediated Communication, 22*(2), 71–87. doi:10.1111/jcc4.12183

Dimmick, J., Feaster, J. C., & Ramirez, A., Jr. (2011). The niches of interpersonal media: Relationships in time and space. *New Media & Society, 13*(8), 1265–1282. doi:10.1177/1461444811403445

Dimmick, J., Kline, S., & Stafford, L. (2000). The gratification niches of personal e-mail and the telephone. *Communication Research, 27*(2), 227–248. doi:10.1177/009365000027002005

Domahidi, E. (2018). The associations between online media use and users' perceived social resources: A meta-analysis. *Journal of Computer-Mediated Communication, 23*(4), 181–200. doi:10.1093/jcmc/zmy007

Donath, J. (2008). Signals in social supernets. *Journal of Computer-Mediated Communication, 13*(1), 231–251. doi:10.1111/j.1083-6101.2007.00394.x

Donner, J., Rangaswamy, N., Steenson, M. W., & Wei, C. (2008). "Express yourself" and "stay together": The middle-class Indian family. In J. E. Katz (ed.), *Handbook of mobile communication studies* (pp. 325–338). Cambridge, MA: MIT Press.

Duck, S. (1994a). *Meaningful relationships: Talking, sense, and relating.* Thousand Oaks, CA: Sage.

(1994b). Relationship maintenance as a shared meaning system. In D. J. Canary & L. Stafford (eds.), *Communication and relational maintenance.* (pp. 45–60). San Diego, CA: Academic Press.

Duck, S., & Pittman, G. (1994). Social and personal relationships. In M. L. Knapp & G. R. Miller (eds.), *The SAGE handbook of interpersonal communication* (2nd ed., pp. 676–695). Thousand Oaks, CA: Sage.

Duggan, M., Ellison, N. B., Lampe, C., & Lenhart, A. (2015). *Social media update 2014.* Retrieved from: www.pewinternet.org/2015/01/09/social-media-update-2014/.

Dunbar, R. I. M. (1996). *Grooming, gossip, and the evolution of language.* Cambridge, MA: Harvard University Press.

(2010). *How many friends does one person need? Dunbar's number and other evolutionary quirks.* Cambridge, MA: Harvard University Press.

(2012). Social cognition on the internet: Testing constrains on social network size. *Philosophical Transactions of the Royal Society of London B Biological Sciences, 367*(1599), 2192–2201. doi:10.1098/rstb.2012.0121.

(2016). Do online social media cut through the constraints that limit the size of offline social networks? *Royal Society Open Science, 3*(1), e150292. doi:10.1098/rsos.150292

Duran, R. L., & Kelly, L. (2017). Knapp's model of relational development in the digital age. *Iowa Journal of Communication, 49*, 22–45.

Duran, R. L., Kelly, L. & Rotaru, T. (2011). Mobile phones in romantic relationships and the dialectic of autonomy versus connection. *Communication Quarterly, 59*(1), 19–36. doi:10.1080/01463373.2011.541336

Dutta-Bergman, M. J. (2004). Community participation and Internet use after September 11: Complementarity in channel consumption. *Journal of Computer-Mediated Communication, 11*(2), 469–484. doi:10.1111/j.1083-61-1.2006.00022.x

Dwyer, R. J., Kushlev, K., & Dunn, E. W. (2018). Smartphone use undermines enjoyment of face-to-face social interactions. *Journal of Experimental Social Psychology, 78*, 233–239. doi:10.1016/j.jesp.2017.10.007

The Economist (2016, May 21). Censors and sensibility (pp. 23–24).

Eden, J. & Veksler, A. E. (2016). Relational maintenance in the digital age: Implicit rules and multiple modalities. *Communication Quarterly, 64*(2), 119–144. doi:10.1080/01463373.2015.1103279

Ellison, N. B., Hancock, J. T., & Toma, C. L. (2012). Profile as promise: A framework for conceptualizing veracity in online dating self-presentations. *New Media & Society, 14*(1), 45–62. doi:10.1177/1461444811410395

Ellison, N. B., & Vitak, J. (2015). Social network site affordances and their relationship to social capital processes. In S. S. Sundar (ed.), *The handbook of the psychology of communication technology* (pp. 205–227). Chichester: John Wiley & Sons.

Ellison, N. B., Vitak, J., Gray, R., & Lampe, C. (2014). Cultivating social resources on social network sites: Facebook relationship maintenance behaviors and their role in social capital processes. *Journal of Computer-Mediated Communication, 19*(4), 855–870. doi:10.1111/jcc4.12078

Evans, S. K., Pearce, K. E., Vitak, J., & Treem, J. W. (2017). Explicating affordances: A conceptual framework for understanding affordance in communication research. *Journal of Computer-Mediated Communication, 22*(1), 35–52. doi:10.1111/jcc4.12180

Farman, J. (2018). *Delayed: The art of waiting from the ancient to the instant world.* New Haven, CT: Yale University Press.

Finkel, E. J., Eastwick, P. W., Karney, B. R., Reis, H. T., & Sprecher, S. (2012). Online dating: A critical analysis from the perspective of psychological science. *Psychological Science in the Public Interest, 13*(1), 3–66. doi:10.1177/1529100612436522

Fischer, C. S. (1992). *America calling: A social history of the telephone to 1940.* Berkeley: University of California Press.

Flaherty, L. M., Pearce. K. J., & Rubin, R. B. (1998). Internet and face-to-face communication: Not functional alternatives. *Communication Quarterly, 46*(3), 250–268. doi:10.1080/01463379809370100

Flanagin, A. J., & Metzger, M. J. (2001). Internet use in the contemporary media environment. *Human Communication Research, 27*(1), 153–181. doi:10.1111/j.1468-2958.2001.tb00779.x

Foote, J., Shaw, A., & Hill, B. M. (2018). A computational analysis of social media scholarship. In J. Burgess, A. Marwick, & T. Poell (eds.), *The SAGE handbook of social media* (pp. 111–134). Los Angeles, CA: Sage Publications.

Fox, J., & Frampton, J. (2017). Social media stressors in romantic relationships. In N. M. Punyanunt-Carter & J. S. Wrench (eds.), *The impact of social media in modern romantic relationships* (pp. 181–196). Lanham, MD: Lexington Books.

Fox, J. & Moreland, J. J. (2015). The dark side of social networking sites: An exploration of the relational and psychological stressors associated with Facebook use and affordances. *Computers in Human Behavior, 45*(11), 168–176. doi:10.1016/j.chb.2014.11.083

French, M., & Bazarova, N. N. (2017). Is anybody out there?: Understanding masspersonal communication through expectations for response across social media platforms. *Journal of Computer-Mediated Communication, 22*(6), 303–319. doi:10.1111/jcc4.12197

Frenkel, S., Confessore, N., Kang, C., Rosenberg, M., & Nicas, J. (2018, November 14). Delay, deny and deflect: How Facebook's leaders fought through crisis. Retrieved from: www.nytimes.com/2018/11/14/technology/facebook-data-russia-election-racism.html.

Friedman, H. S., & Martin, L. R. (2011). *The longevity project: Surprising discoveries for health and long life from the landmark eight-decade study.* New York: Hudson Stress Press.

Frison, E., & Eggermont, S. (2017). Browsing, posting, and liking on Instagram: The reciprocal relationships between different types of Instagram use and adolescents' depressed mood. *Cyberpsychology, Behavior, and Social Networking, 20*(10), 603–609. doi:10.1089/cyber.2017.0156

Fu, J. S., & Lai, C-H. (2020). Mapping the intellectual structure and roots of online social networks 1997–2017: Challenges and opportunities for computer-mediated communication research. *Journal of Computer-Mediated Communication. 25*(1), 111–128, doi:10.1093/jcmc/zmz020

Fulk, J. (1993). Social construction of communication technology. *Academy of Management Journal, 36*(5), 921–950. doi:10.5465/256641

Gardner, W. L., Pickett, C. L., & Knowles, M. (2005). Social snacking and shielding: Using social symbols, selves, and surrogates in the service of belonging needs. In K. D. Williams, J. P. Forgas, & W. von Hippel (eds.), *The social outcast: Ostracism, social exclusion, rejection, and bullying* (pp. 227–241). New York: Psychology Press.

Goffman, E. (1959). *The presentation of self in everyday life.* Garden City, NY: Doubleday Anchor Books.

(1963). *Behavior in public places: Notes on the social organization of gatherings.* New York: Free Press.

Goldsmith, D. J., & Baxter, L. A. (1996). Constituting relationships in talk: A taxonomy of speech events in social and personal relationships. *Human Communication Research, 23*(1), 87–114. doi:10.1111/j.1468-2958.1996.tb00388.x

Gramlich, J. (2019). 10 facts about Americans and Facebook. *Pew Research Center.* Retrieved from: www.pewresearch.org/fact-tank/2019/02/01/facts-about-americans-and-facebook/.

Grebe, J. P., & Hall, J. A. (2013). Affinity in instant messaging. *Northwest Journal of Communication, 41*, 81–108. Open source: http://hdl.handle.net/1808/9964.

Greitemeyer, T., Mugge, D. O., & Bollerman, I. (2014). Having responsive Facebook friends affects the satisfaction of psychological needs more than having many Facebook friends. *Basic and Applied Social Psychology, 36*(3), 252–258. doi:10.1080/01973533.2014.900619

Halfmann, A., & Rieger, D. (2019). Permanently on call: The effects of social pressure on smartphone users' self-control, need satisfaction, and well-being. *Journal of Computer-Mediated Communication, 24*(4), 165–181. doi:10.1093/jcmc/zmz008

Hall, J. A. (2011). Sex differences in friendship expectations: A meta-analysis. *Journal of Social and Personal Relationships, 28*(6), 723–747. doi:10.1177/0265407510386192

(2012). Friendship standards: The dimensions of ideal expectations. *Journal of Social and Personal Relationships, 29*(7), 884–907. doi:10.1177/0265407512448274

(2017a). The experience of mobile entrapment in daily life. *Journal of Media Psychology, 29* (Special Issue), 148–158. doi:10.1027/1864-1105/a000228

(2017b). The regulation of social interaction in everyday life. *Journal of Social and Personal Relationships, 34*(5), 699–716. doi:10.1177/0265407516654580

(2018a). Energy, episode, and relationship: A test of communicate bond belong theory. *Communication Quarterly, 66*(4), 380–402. doi:10.1080/01463373.2017.1411377

(2018b). When is social media use social interaction? Defining mediated social interaction. *New Media & Society, 20*(1), 162–179. doi:10.1177/1461444816660782

(2019). How many hours does it take to make a friend? *Journal of Social and Personal Relationships, 36*(4), 1278–1296. doi:10.1177/0265407518761225

Hall, J. A., & Baym, N. K. (2012). Calling and texting (too much): Mobile maintenance expectations, (over)dependence, entrapment, and friendship satisfaction. *New Media & Society, 14*(2), 316–331. doi:10.1177/1461444811415047

Hall, J. A., Baym, N. K., & Miltner, K. M. (2014a). Put down that phone and talk to me: Understanding the roles of mobile phone norm adherence and similarity in relationships. *Mobile Media & Communication, 2*(2), 134–153. doi:10.1177/2050157913517684

Hall, J. A., & Davis, D. A. C. (2017). Proposing the communicate bond belong theory: Evolutionary intersections with episodic interpersonal communication. *Communication Theory, 27*(1), 21–47. doi:10.111/comt/12106

Hall, J. A., Johnson, R. M., & Ross, E. M. (2019a). Where does the time go? An experimental test of what social media displaces and displaced activities' associations with affective well-being and quality of day. *New Media & Society, 21*(3), 674–692. doi:10.1177/1461444818804775

Hall, J. A., Kearney, M., & Xing, C. (2019b). Two tests of social displacement through social media use. *Information, Communication and Society, 22*(10), 1396–1413. doi:10.1080/1369118X.2018.1430162

Hall, J. A., Larson, K. A., & Watts, A. (2011). Satisfying friendship maintenance expectations: The role of friendship standards and biological sex. *Human Communication Research, 37*(4), 529–552. doi:10.1111/j.1468-2958.2011.01411.x

Hall, J. A., & Merolla, A. (2020). Connecting everyday talk and time alone to global well-being. *Human Communication Research*, *46*(1), 594–619. doi:10.1093/hcr/hqz014

Hall, J. A., Pennington, N., & Lueders, A. (2014b). Impression management and formation on Facebook: A lens model approach. *New Media & Society*, *16*(6), 958–982. doi:10.1177/1461444813495166

Hall, J. A., Xing, C., Ross, E. M., & Johnson, R. M. (in press). Experimentally manipulating social media abstinence: Results of a four-week diary study. *Media Psychology*. doi:10.1080/15213269.2019.1688171

Halpern, D., & Katz, J. E. (2017). Texting's consequences for romantic relationships: A cross-lagged analysis highlights its risks. *Computers in Human Behavior*, *71*, 386–394. doi:10.1016/j.chb2017.01.051

Hampton, K. N. (2016). Persistent and pervasive community: New communication technologies and the future of community. *American Behavioral Scientist*, *60*(1), 101–124. doi:10.1177/0002764215601714

Hampton, K. N., Lu, W., & Shin, I. (2016). Digital media and stress: The cost of caring 2.0. *Information, Communication & Society*, *19*(9), 1267–1286. doi:10.1080/1369118X.2016.1186714

Hampton, K. N., Sessions, L. F., & Her, E. J. (2011). Core networks, social isolation, and new media. *Information, Communication & Society*, *14*(1), 130–155. doi:10.1080/139118x.2010.513417

Hanley, S. M., Watt, S. E., & Coventry, W. (2019). Taking a break: The effect of taking a vacation from Facebook and Instagram on subjective well-being. *PloS ONE*, *14*(6), e0217743. doi:10.1371/journal/pone.0217743

Harris, M. (2014). *The end of absence: Reclaiming what we've lost in a world of constant connection*. New York: Penguin.

Haselton, M. G., & Funder, D. (2006). The evolution of accuracy and bias in social judgment. In M. Schaller, J. A. Simpson, & D. T. Kendrick (eds.), *Evolution and social psychology* (pp. 15–37). New York: Psychology Press.

Haythornthwaite, C. (2005). Social networks and internet connectivity effects. *Information, Communication, & Society*, *8*(2), 125–147. doi:10.1080/13691180500146185

Heffer, T., Good, M., Daly, O., MacDonell, E., & Willoughby, T. (2019). The longitudinal association between social media use and depressive symptoms among adolescents and young adults: An empirical reply to Twenge et al. (2018). *Clinical Psychological Science*, *7*(3), 462–470. doi:10.1177/2167702618812727

Hefner, D., & Vorderer, P. (2016). Digital stress: Permanent connectedness and multitasking. In L. Reinecke, & M.-B. Oliver (eds.), *Handbook of media use and well-being* (pp. 237–249). New York: Routledge.

Helliwell, J. F., & Huang, H. (2013). Comparing happiness effects of real and on-line friends. *PLoS ONE*, *8*(9), e72754. doi:10.1371/journal.pone.0072754

Helliwell, J. F., & Putnam, R. D. (2004). The social context of well-being. *Philosophical Transactions of the Royal Society of London B Biological Sciences*, *359*(1449), 1435–1446. doi:10.1098/rstb.2004.1522

Helliwell, J. F., & Wang, S. (2011). Trust and wellbeing. *International Journal of Wellbeing*, *1*(1), 42–78. doi:10.5502/ijw.v1i1.9

Hinsch, C., & Sheldon, K. M. (2013). The impact of frequent social internet consumption: Increased procrastination and lower life satisfaction. *Journal of Consumer Behaviour, 12*(6), 496–505. doi:10.1002/cb.1453

Hoffner, C. A., Lee, S., & Park, S. J. (2016). "I miss my mobile phone!": Self-expansion via mobile phone and responses to phone loss. *New Media & Society, 18*(11), 2452–2468. doi:10.1177/1461444815592665

Hruschka, D. J. (2010). *Friendship: Development, ecology, and evolution of a relationship.* Berkeley: University of California Press.

Huang, C. (2010). Internet use and psychological well-being: A meta-analysis. *Cyberpsychology, Behavior, and Social Networking, 13*(3), 241–249. doi:10.1089/cyber.2009.0217

(2017). Time spent on social network sites and psychological well-being: A meta-analysis. *Cyberpsychology, Behavior and Social Networking, 20*(6), 346–354. doi:10.1089/cyber.2016.0758

Hull, C. L. (1943/1970). Characteristics of innate behavior under conditions of need. In W. A. Russell (ed.), *Milestone in motivation: Contribution to the psychology of drive and purpose* (pp. 520–530). New York: Meredith Corporation. (Reprinted from *Principles of Behavior* [D. Appleton-Century, 1943], pp. 57–67.)

Humphreys, L. (2005). Cellphones in public: Social interactions in a wireless era. *New Media & Society, 7*(6), 810–833. doi:10.1177/1461444805058164

(2018). *The qualified self: Social media and the accounting of everyday life.* Cambridge, MA: MIT Press.

Humphreys, L., Gill, P., Krishnamurthy, B., & Newbury, E. (2013). Historicizing new media: A content analysis of Twitter. *Journal of Communication, 63*(3), 413–431. doi:10.1111/jcom.12030

Humphreys, L., von Pape, T., & Karnowski, V. (2013). Evolving mobile media: Uses and conceptualizations of the mobile internet. *Journal of Computer-Mediated Communication, 18*(4), 491–507. doi:10.111/jcc4.12019

Hunt, M. G., Marx, R., Lipson, C., & Young, J. (2018). No more FOMO: Limiting social media decreases loneliness and depression. *Journal of Social and Clinical Psychology, 37*(10), 751–768. doi:10.1521/jscp.2018.37.10.751

International Telecommunications Union (2010). Global ICT development, 2000–2010. Retrieved from: www.itu.int/ITU-D/ict/statistics/material/graphs/2010/Global_ICT_Dev_00-10.jpg.

Johnson, A. J., & Becker, J. A. H. (2011). CMC and the conceptualization of "friendship": How friendships have changed with the advent of new methods of interpersonal communication. In K. B. Wright & L. M. Webb (eds.), *Computer-mediated communication in personal relationships* (pp. 225–243). New York: Peter Lang.

Johnson, A. J., Bostwick, E., & Bassick, M. (2017). Long-distance versus geographically close romantic relationships: The effects of social media on the development and maintenance of these relationships. In N. M. Punyanunt-Carter & J. S. Wrench (eds.), *The impact of social media in modern romantic relationships* (pp. 113–130). Lanham, MD: Lexington Books.

Joinson, A. N. (2008) Looking at, looking up, or keeping up with people?: Motives and use of Facebook. In *Proceedings of the Twenty-sixth Annual SIGCHI Conference* on *Human Factors in Computing Systems* (1027–1036). Florence, IT: ACM Press. doi:10.1145/1357054.1357213

Karakayali, N., & Kilic, A. (2013). More network conscious than ever? Challenges, strategies, and analytic labor of users in the Facebook environment. *Journal of Computer-Mediated Communication, 18*(2), 61–79. doi:10.1111/jcc4/12005

Kim, H., Kim, G. J., Park, H. W., & Rice, R. E. (2007). Configurations of relationships in different media: FtF, email, instant messenger, mobile phone, and SMS. *Journal of Computer-Mediated Communication, 12*(4), 1183–1207. doi:10.1111/j.1083-6101.2007.00369

Kim, J., & Lee, J-E. R. (2011). The Facebook paths to happiness: Effects of the number of Facebook friends and self-presentation on subjective well-being. *Cyberpsychology, Behavior, and Social Networking, 14*(6), 359–364. doi:10.1089/cyber.2010.0374

Kelley, H. H., & Thibaut, J. W. (1978). *Interpersonal relations: A theory of interdependence.* New York: Wiley.

Kelly, R., Gooch, D., Patil, B., & Watts, L. (2017, February). Demanding by design: Supporting effortful communication practices in close personal relationships. In *Proceedings of the 2017 ACM Conference on Computer Supported Cooperative Work and Social Computing* (pp. 70–83). ACM.

Kelly, R., & Watts, L. (2015). Characterising the inventive appropriation of emoji as relationally meaningful in mediated close personal relationships. In *Experiences of technology appropriation: Unanticipated users, usage, circumstances, and design.* Retrieved from: https://researchportal.bath.ac.uk/en/publications/characterising-the-inventive-appropriation-of-emoji-as-relational.

Knapp, M. L., & Daly, J. A. (2011). Background and current trends in the study of interpersonal communication. In M. L. Knapp & J. A. Daly (eds.), *The SAGE handbook of interpersonal communication* (4th ed., pp. 3–24). Los Angeles, CA: Sage.

Knausenberger, J., Hellmann, J. H., & Echterhoff, G. (2015). When virtual contact is all you need: Subtle reminders of Facebook preempt social-contact restoration after exclusion. *European Journal of Social Psychology, 45*(3), 279–284. doi:10.1002/ejsp.2035

Knowles, M. L., Haycock, N., & Shaikh, I. (2015). Does Facebook magnify or mitigate threats to belonging? *Social Psychology, 46*(6), 313–324. doi:10.1027/1864-9335/a000246

Krasnova, H., Spiekermann, S., Koroleva, K., & Hildebrand, T. (2010). Online social networks: Why we disclose. *Journal of Information Technology, 25*(2), 109–125. doi:10.1057/jit.2010.6

Kraut, R., Kiesler, S., Boneva, B., Cummings, J. N., Helgeson, V., & Crawford, A. M. (2002). Internet paradox revisited. *Journal of Social Issues, 58*(1), 49–74. doi:10.1111/1540-4560/00248

Kraut, R., Patterson, M., Lundmark, V., Kiesler, S., Mukopadhyay, T., & Scherlis, W. (1998). Internet paradox: A social technology that reduces social involvement and psychological well-being? *American Psychologist, 53*(9), 1017–1031. doi:10/1037/0003-066x.53.9.1017

Kross, E., Verduyn, P., Demiralp, E., Park, J., Lee, D. S., Lin, N., . . . Ybarra, O. (2013). Facebook use predicts declines in subjective well-being in young adults. *PLoS ONE, 8*(8), e69841. doi:10.1371/journal.pone.0069841

Lane, B. L., & Piercy, C. W. (2017). Making sense of becoming Facebook official: Implications for identity and time. In N. M. Punyanunt-Carter & J. S. Wrench (eds.), *The impact of social media in modern romantic relationships* (pp. 31–46). Lanham, MD: Lexington Books.

LaRose, R., Connolly, R., Lee, H., Li, K., & Hales, K. D. (2014). Connection overload? A cross-cultural study of the consequences of social media connection. *Information Systems Management, 31*(1), 59–73. doi:10.1080/10580530.2014.854097

Larsson, A. O. (2015). Comparing to prepare: Suggesting ways to study social media today – And tomorrow. *Social Media + Society, 1*(1), 1–2. doi:10.1177/2056305115578680

Lasén, A., & Casado, E. (2012). Mobile telephony and the remediation of couple intimacy. *Feminist Media Studies, 12*(4), 550–559. doi:10.1080.14680777.2012.741871

Latané, B. (1981). The psychology of social impact. *American Psychologist, 36*(4), 343–356.

Leary, M. R. (2001). The self we know and the self we show: Self-esteem, self-presentation, and the maintenance of interpersonal relationships. In G. J. O. Fletcher & M. S. Clark (eds.), *Interpersonal processes* (pp. 457–477). Malden, MA: Blackwell.

Leary, M. R., & Kelly, K. M. (2008). Belonging motivation. In M. R. Leary & R. H. Hoyle (eds.), *Handbook of individual differences in social behavior* (pp. 400–409). New York: Guilford Press.

Leatham, G., & Duck, S. (1990). Conversations with friends and the dynamics of social support. In S. Duck & R. C. Silver (eds.), *Personal relationships and social support* (pp. 1–29). London: Sage.

Ledbetter, A. M. (2010). Content- and medium-specific decomposition of friendship relational maintenance: Integrating equity and media multiplexity approaches. *Journal of Social and Personal Relationships, 27*(7), 938–955. doi:10.1177/0265407510376254

    (2015). Media multiplexity theory: Technology use and interpersonal tie strength. In D. O. Braithwaite & P. Schrodt (eds.), *Engaging theories in interpersonal communication: Multiple perspectives* (2nd ed., pp. 363–376). Los Angeles, CA: Sage.

Ledbetter, A. M., Taylor, S. H., & Mazer, J. P. (2016). Enjoyment fosters media use frequency and determines its relational outcomes: Toward a synthesis of uses and gratifications theory and media multiplexity theory. *Computers in Human Behavior, 54*, 149–157. doi:10.1016/j.chb.2015.07.053

Lee, H. P., Chen, K. Y., Lin, C. H., Chen, C. Y., Chung, Y. L., Chang, Y. J., & Sun, C. R. (2019). Does who matter?: Studying the impact of relationship characteristics on receptivity to mobile IM messages. In *Proceedings of the 2019 CHI Conference on Human Factors in Computing Systems* (p. 526). Glasgow UK: ACM.

Lenhart, A. (2012). Teens, smartphones & texting. Pew Internet & American Life Project, 1–34. Retrieved from: www.pewresearch.org/internet/2012/03/19/teens-smartphones-texting/.

Lenhart, A., & Duggan, M. (2014). Couples, the internet, and social media. Retrieved from: www.pewinternet.org/2014/02/11/couples-the-internet-and-social-media/.

Levordashka, A., & Utz, S. (2016). Ambient awareness: From random noise to digital closeness in online social networks. *Computers in Human Behavior, 60,* 147–154. doi:10.1016/j.chb.2016.02.037

Licoppe, C. (2004). "Connected" presence: The emergence of a new repertoire for managing social relationships in a changing communication technoscape. *Environment and Planning D: Society and Space, 22*(1), 135–156. doi:10.1068/d323t

(2012). Understanding mediated appearances and their proliferation: The case of phone rings and the "crisis of the summons." *New Media & Society, 14*(7), 1073–1091. doi:10.1177/1461444812452410

Licoppe, C., & Heurtin, J. P. (2001). Managing one's availability to telephone communication through mobile phones: A French case study of the development dynamics of mobile phone use. *Personal and Ubiquitous Computing, 5*(2), 99–108. doi:10.1007/s007790170013

Lieberman, M. D. (2013). *Social: Why our brains are wired to connect.* New York: Crown Publishers/Random House.

Ling, R. (2004). *The mobile connection: The cell phone's impact on society.* San Francisco, CA: Elsevier.

(2008). Mobile telephones and the disturbance of the public sphere. *Europe, 115,* 1–17. Retrieved from: http://richardling.com/papers/2004_disturbance_of_social_sphere.pdf

(2010). Texting as a life phase medium. *Journal of Computer-Mediated Communication, 15*(2), 277–292. doi:10.1111/j.1083-6101.2010.01520.x

Ling, R., Bertel, T., & Sundsøy, P. (2012). The socio-demographics of texting: An analysis of traffic data. *New Media & Society, 14*(2), 280–297. doi:10.1177/1461444811412711

Ling, R., & Lai, C.-H. (2016). Microcoordination 2.0: Social coordination in the age of smartphones and messaging apps. *Journal of Communication, 66*(5), 834–856. doi:10.111/jcom.12251

Ling, R. & McEwen, R. (2010). Mobile communication and ethics: Implications of everyday actions on social order. *Etikk i Praksis, 4*(2), 11–25. doi:10.5324/eip.v4i2.1760

Ling, R., & Ytrri, B. (2002). Hyper-coordination via mobile phones in Norway. In J. E. Katz, & M. Aakhus (eds.), *Perpetual contact: Mobile communication, private talk, public performance* (pp. 139–169). Cambridge: Cambridge University Press.

Litt, E. (2012). Knock, knock. Who's there? The imagined audience. *Journal of Broadcasting & Electronic Media, 56*(3), 330–345. doi:10.1080/08838151.2012.705195

Liu, D., Ainsworth, S. E., & Baumeister, R. F. (2016). A meta-analysis of social networking online and social capital. *Review of General Psychology, 20*(4), 369–391. doi:10.1037/gpr0000091

Liu, D., & Yang, C-C. (2016). Media niche of electronic communication channels in friendship: A meta-analysis. *Journal of Computer-Mediated Communication, 21*(6), 451–466. doi:10.1111/jcc4.12175

Lo, J. (2019). Exploring the buffer effect of receiving social support on lonely and emotionally unstable social networking users. *Computers in Human Behavior, 90,* 103–116. doi:10.1016/j.chb.2018.08.052

Lomas, N. (2017, August 22). Teens favoring Snapchat and Instagram over Facebook, says eMarketer. Retrieved from: https://techcrunch.com/2017/08/22/teens-favoring-snapchat-and-instagram-over-facebook-says-emarketer/.

Lucas, R. E., & Dyrenforth, P. S. (2006). Does the existence of social relationships matter for subjective well-being? In K. D. Vohs & E. J. Finkel (eds.), *Self and relationships: Connecting intrapersonal and interpersonal processes* (pp. 254–273). New York: Guilford Press.

Madianou, M. (2014). Smartphones as polymedia. *Journal of Computer-Mediated Communication, 19*(3), 667–680. doi:10.1111/jcc4.12069

Madianou, M., & Miller, D. (2012). Polymedia: Towards a new theory of digital media in interpersonal communication. *International Journal of Cultural Studies, 16*(2), 169–187. doi:10.1177/1367877912452486

Mai, L. M., Freudenthaler, R., Schneider, F. M., & Vorderer, P. (2015). "I know you've seen it!" Individual and social factors for users' chatting behavior on Facebook. *Computers in Human Behavior, 49*, 296–302. doi:10.1016/j.chb.2015.01.074

Manago, A. M., Taylor, T., & Greenfield, P. M. (2012). Me and my 400 friends: The anatomy of college students' Facebook networks, their communication patterns, and well-being. *Developmental Psychology, 48*(2), 369–380. doi:10.1037/a0026338

Manago, A. M., & Vaughn, L. (2015). Social media, friendship, and happiness in the millennial generation. In M. Demir (ed.), *Friendship and happiness* (pp. 187–206). New York: Springer.

Manley, T. (2017). Millennials' use of online applications for romantic development. In N. M. Punyanunt-Carter & J. S. Wrench (eds.), *The impact of social media in modern romantic relationships* (pp. 47–64). Lanham, MD: Lexington Books.

Marcus, B., Machilek, F., & Schütz, A. (2006). Personality in cyberspace: Personal websites as media for personality expressions and impressions. *Journal of Personality and Social Psychology, 90*(6), 1014–1031. doi:10.1037/0022-3514.90.6.1014

Marwick, A. E. (2012). The public domain: Social surveillance in everyday life. *Surveillance & Society, 9*(4), 378–393. doi:10.24908/ss.v9i4.4342

Masur, P. K., Reinecke, L., Ziegele, M., & Quiring, O. (2014). The interplay of intrinsic need satisfaction and Facebook specific motives in explaining addictive behavior on Facebook. *Computers in Human Behavior, 39*, 376–386. doi:10.1016/j.chb.2014.05.047

McAndrew, F. T., & Jeong, H. S. (2012). Who does what on Facebook? Age, sex, and relationship status as predictors of Facebook use. *Computers in Human Behavior, 28*(6), 2359–2365. doi:10.1016/j.chb.2012.07.007

McDaniel, B. T., & Drouin, M. (2019). Daily technology interruptions and emotional and relational well-being. *Computers in Human Behavior, 99*, 1–8. doi:10.1016/j.chb.2019.04.027

McEwan, B. (2013) Caring, sharing, and surveilling: An actor-partner interdependence model examination of Facebook relational maintenance strategies. *Cyberpsychology, Behavior, and Social Networking, 16*(12), 863–869. doi:10.1089/cyber.2012.0717

McLaughlin, C., & Vitak, J. (2012). Norm evolution and violation on Facebook. *New Media & Society, 14*(2), 299–315. doi:10.1177/1461444811412712

Meier, A., Reinecke, L., & Meltzer, C. E. (2016). "Facebocrastination"? Predictors of using Facebook for procrastination and its effects on students' well-being. *Computers in Human Behavior, 64*, 65–76. doi:10.1016/j.chb.2016.06.011

Merolla, A. M., Hall, & J. A. (2018). Unpublished dataset. Open Science Framework: https://osf.io/9pwb4?view_only=a71c471a456d445fbca10892187d9558.

Merolla, A. M., Hall, J. A., & Bernhold, Q. (2019). Perseverative cognition, distracted communication, and well-being in everyday social interaction. *Personal Relationships*, 26(3), 507–528. doi:10.1111/pere.12286

Mesch, G. S., & Talmud, I. (2006). The quality of online and offline relationships: The role of multiplexity and duration of social relationships. *The Information Society*, 22, 137–148. doi:10.1080/01972240600677805

Mesch, G. S., Talmud, I., & Quan-Haase, A. (2012). Instant messaging social networks: Individual, relational, and cultural characteristics. *Journal of Social and Personal Relationships*, 29(6), 736–759. doi:10.1177/0265407512448263

Middleton, C. A., & Cukier, W. (2006). Is mobile email functional or dysfunctional?: Two perspectives on mobile email usage. *European Journal of Information Systems*, 15(3), 252–260. doi:10.1057/palgrave.ejis.3000614

Mihailidis, P. (2014). A tethered generation: Exploring the role of mobile phones in the daily life of young people. *Mobile Media & Communication*, 2(1), 58–72. doi:10.1177/2050157913505558

Milardo, R. M., Johnson, M. P., & Huston, T. L. (1983). Developing close relationships: Changing patterns of interaction between pair members and social networks. *Journal of Personality and Social Psychology*, 44(5), 964–976.

Milardo, R. M., Helms, H. M., Widmer, E. D., & Marks, S. R. (2014). Social capitalization in personal relationships. In C. R. Agnew (ed.), *Social influences on romantic relationships: Beyond the dyad* (pp. 33–57). Cambridge: Cambridge University Press.

Miller, G. R., & Steinberg, M. (1975). *Between people: A new analysis of interpersonal communication*. Chicago, IL: Science Research Association.

Miller, J. D. (2014). *Longitudinal study of American youth, 1987–1994, 2007–11. User guide*. Inter-University Consortium for Political and Social Research. Retrieved from: www.lsay.org/about.html.

Miller-Ott, A. E., & Kelly, L. (2016). Competing discourses and meaning-making in talk about romantic partners' cell-phone contact with non-present others. *Communication Studies*, 67(1), 58–67. doi:10.1080/10510974.2015.1088876

Miritello, G., Moro, E., Lara, R., Martinez-Lopez, R., Belchamber, J., Roberts, S. B. G., & Dunbar, R. I. M. (2013). Time as a limited resource: Communication strategy in mobile phone networks. *Social Networks*, 35, 89–95. doi:10.1016/j.socnet.2013.01.003

Misra, S., Cheng, L., Genevie, J., & Yuan, M. (2016). The iPhone effect: the quality of in-person social interactions in the presence of mobile devices. *Environment and Behavior*, 48(2), 275–298. doi:10.1177/0013916514539755

Misra, S., & Stokols, D. (2012). Psychological and health outcomes of perceived information overload. *Environment and Behavior*, 44(6), 737–759. doi:10.1177/0013916511404408

Mollenhorst, G., Volker, B., & Flap, H. (2014). Changes in personal relationships: How social contexts affect the emergence and discontinuation of relationships. *Social Networks*, 37, 65–80. doi:10.1016/j.socnet.2013.12.003

Morgan, D. (2009) *Acquaintances: The space between intimates and strangers*. Berkshire: Open University Press.

Morgan, D. L., Neal, M. B., & Carder, P. (1996). The stability of core and peripheral networks over time. *Social Networks, 19*(1), 9–25. doi:10.1016/SO378-8733 (96)00288-2

Nagi, Ariel. (2012). 9 ways technology can ruin your relationship. *Cosmopolitan for Latinas*. Retrieved from: www.cosmopolitan.com/cosmo-latina/how-technology-ruins-relationships.

Nesi, J., Choukas-Bradley, S., & Prinstein, M. J. (2018). Transformation of adolescent peer relations in the social media context: Part 1 – A theoretical framework and application to dyadic peer relationships. *Clinical Child and Family Psychology Review, 21*(3), 267–294. doi:10.1007/s10567-018-0261

Neustaedter, C., & Greenberg, S. (2012). Intimacy in long-distance relationships over video chat. In *Proceedings of the SIGCHI Conference on Human Factors in Computing Systems (CHI '12)* (pp. 753–762). New York: ACM. doi:10.1145/2207676.2207785

New York Times (2016). Facebook bends the rules of audience engagements to its advantage. Retrieved from: www.nytimes.com/2016/05/06/business/facebook-bends-the-rules-of-audience-engagement-to-its-advantage.html?_r=0.

Nie, N. H. (2001). Sociability, interpersonal relations, and the internet: Reconciling conflicting findings. *American Behavior Scientist, 45*(3), 420–435. doi:10.1177/00027640121957277

Nie, N. H., & Hillygus, D. S. (2002). The impact of internet use on sociability: Time-diary findings. *IT & Society, 1*(1), 1–20. doi:10.1002/9780470774298.ch7

Nielsenwire (2008, September 22). In US, SMS text messaging tops mobile phone calling. Retrieved from: http://blog.nielsen.com/nielsenwire/online_mobile/in-us-text-messaging-tops-mobile-phone-calling/.

(2010). U.S. teen mobile report: Calling yesterday, texting today, using apps tomorrow. Retrieved from: http://blog.nielsen.com/nielsenwire/online_mobile/u-s-teen-mobile-report-calling-yesterday-texting-today-using-apps-tomorrow/.

(2013). The mobile consumer: A global snapshot. Retrieved from: www.nielsen.com/wp-content/uploads/sites/3/2019/04/Mobile-Consumer-Report-2013-1.pdf.

Nonnecke, B., & Preece, J. (2001). Why lurkers lurk. *Proceedings from Americas Conference on Information Systems*. Boston.

O'Connor, S. C., & Rosenblood, L. K. (1996). Affiliation motivation in everyday experience: A theoretical comparison. *Journal of Personality and Social Psychology, 70*(3), 513–522. doi:10.1037/0022-3514.70.3.513

Oh, H. J., Ozkaya, E., & LaRose, R. (2014). How does online social networking enhance life satisfaction? The relationships among online supportive interaction, affect, perceived social support, sense of community, and life satisfaction. *Computers in Human Behavior, 30*, 69–78. doi:10.1016/j.chb.2013.07.053

O'Hara, K., Massimi, M., Harper, R., Rubens, S., & Morris, J. (2014). Everyday dwelling with WhatsApp. In *Proceedings of the 17th ACM Conference on Computer Supported Cooperative Work* (pp. 1131–1143). Baltimore, MD.

Okun, M. A., Stock, W. A., Haring, M. J., & Witter, R. A. (1984). The social activity/subjective well-being relation: A quantitative synthesis. *Research on Aging, 6*(1), 45–65. doi:10.1177/0164027584006001003

Olmstead, K., Lampe, C. & Ellison, N. B. (2016). Social media and the workplace. *Pew Research Center*. Retrieved from: www.pewresearch.org.

Orben, A., Dienlin, T., & Przybylski, A. K. (2019). Social media's enduring effect on adolescent life satisfaction. *Proceedings of the National Academy of Sciences of the United States of America*, 116(21), 10226–10228. doi:10.1073/pnas.1902058116

Orchard, L. J., Fullwood, C., Morris, N., & Galbraith, N. (2015). Investigating the Facebook experience through Q methodology: Collective investment and a "Borg" mentality. *New Media & Society*, 17(9), 1547–1565. doi:10.1177/1461444814530099

Osnos, E. (2018). Can Mark Zuckerberg fix Facebook before it breaks democracy? *The New Yorker Magazine*. Retrieved from: www.newyorker.com/magazine/2018/09/17/can-mark-zuckerberg-fix-facebook-before-it-breaks-democracy.

O'Sullivan, P. B. (2005). Masspersonal communication: Rethinking the mass interpersonal divide. Paper presented at the annual meeting of the International Communication Association, New York, NY.

O'Sullivan, P. B., & Carr, C. T. (2018). Masspersonal communication: A model bridging the mass-interpersonal divide. *New Media & Society*, 20(3), 1161–1180. doi:10.1177/1461444816686104

Park, N., Chung, J. E., & Lee, S. (2012). Explaining the use of text-based communication media: An examination of three theories of media use. *Cyberpsychology, Behavior, and Social Networking*, 15(7), 357–363. doi:10.1089/cyber.2012.0121.

Parks, M. R. (2007). *Personal relationships and personal networks*. Mahwah, NJ: Erlbaum.

(2011). Boundary conditions for the application of three theories of computer-mediated communication to MySpace. *Journal of Communication*, 61(4), 557–574. doi:10.1111/j.1460-2466.2011.01569.x

(2017). Embracing the challenges and opportunities of mixed-media relationships. *Human Communication Research*, 43(4), 505–517. doi:10.1111/hcre.12125

Pennington, N. (2015). Building and maintaining relationships in the digital age: Using social penetration theory to explore communication through social networking sites. PhD dissertation, University of Kansas.

Pennington, N., & Hall, J. A. (2014). An analysis of humor orientation on Facebook: A lens model approach. *Humor*, 27(1), 1–21. doi:10.1515/humor-2013-0053

Pew Research Center (2018). Mobile fact sheet. Retrieved from: www.pewinternet.org/fact-sheet/mobile/.

Pinsker, J. (2019). The new long-distance relationship. Retrieved from: www.theatlantic.com/family/archive/2019/05/long-distance-relationships/589144/.

Piquart, M. & Sorensen, S. (2003). Risk factor for loneliness in adulthood and old age: A meta-analysis. In S. P. Shohov (ed.), *Advances in psychology research* (vol. 19, pp. 111–143). Hauppauge, NY: Nova Science.

Platt, C. A., Bourdeaux, R., & DiTunnariello, N. (2014). Should I text or should I call?: How college students navigate mediated connections with family. In L. Robinson, S. R. Cotton, & J. Schulz (eds.), *Communication and Information Technologies Annual* (pp. 75–101). Bingley: Emerald Group Publishing.

Pollet, T. V., Roberts, S. G. B., & Dunbar, R. I. M. (2011). Use of social network sites and instant messaging does not lead to increased offline social network size, or to emotionally closer relationships with offline network members. *Cyberpsychology, Behavior, and Social Networking, 14*(4), 253–258. doi:10.1089/cyber.2010.0161

Poushter, J. (2016). Smartphone ownership and internet usage continues to climb in emerging economies. *Pew Research Center*. Retrieved from: www.pewglobal.org/2016/02/22/smartphone-ownership-and-internet-usage-continues-to-climb-in-emerging-economies/

Prentice, M., Halusic, M., Sheldon, K. M. (2014). Integrating theories of psychological needs-as-requirements and psychological needs-as-motives: A two process model. *Social and Personality Psychology Compass, 8*, 73–85. doi:10.1111/spc3.12088

Primack, B. A., Shensa, A., Escobar-Viera, C. G., Barrett, E. L., Sidani, J. E., Colditz, J. B., & James, A. E. (2017). Use of multiple social media platforms and symptoms of depression and anxiety: A nationally-representative study among U.S. young adults. *Computers in Human Behavior, 69*, 1–9. doi:10.1016/j.chb.2016.11.013

Przybylski, A. K., Murayama, K., DeHaan, C. R., & Gladwell, V. (2013). Motivational, emotional, and behavioral correlates of fear of missing out. *Computers in Human Behavior, 29*(4), 1841–1848. doi:10.1016/j.chb.2013.02.014

Przybylski, A. K., & Weinstein, N. (2013). Can you connect with me now? How the presence of mobile communication technology influences face-to-face conversation quality. *Journal of Social and Personal Relationships, 30*(3), 237–246. doi:10.1177/0265407512453827

Quan-Haase, A. (2007). University students' local and distant social ties: Using and integrating modes of communication on campus. *Information, Communication & Society, 10*(5), 671–693. doi:10.1080/13691180701658020

Quan-Haase, A., & Collins, J. L. (2008). I'm there, but I might not want to talk to you. *Information, Communication & Society, 11*, 526–543. doi:10.1080/13691180801999043

Quinn, K. (2013). We haven't talked in 30 years! Relationship reconnection and internet use at midlife. *Information, Communication, and Society, 16*(3), 397–420. doi:10.1080/1369118x.2012.756047

Quinn, K., & Papacharissi, Z. (2018). Our networked selves: Personal connection and relational maintenance in social media use. In J. Burgess, A. Marwick, & T. Poell (eds.), *The SAGE handbook of social media* (pp. 353–371). Los Angeles, CA: Sage Publications.

Rae, J. R., & Lonborg, S. D. (2015). Do motivations for using Facebook moderate the association between Facebook use and psychological well-being? *Frontiers in Psychology, 6*(771), 271–280. doi:103389/fpsyg.2015.00771

Rainie, L., & Wellman, B. (2012). *Networked: The new social operating system.* Cambridge, MA: MIT Press.

Rainie, L., & Zickhur, K. (2015, August 26). Americans' views on mobile etiquette. Retrieved from: www.pewinternet.org/2015/08/26/americans-views-on-mobile-etiquette/.

Rains, S. A., Brunner, S. R., & Oman, K. (2016). Self-disclosure and new communication technologies: The implications of receiving superficial self-disclosures from friends. *Journal of Social and Personal Relationships, 33*(1), 42–61. doi:10.117/0265407514562561

Rains, S. A., Peterson E. B., & Wright, K. B. (2015). Communicating social support in computer-mediated contexts: A meta-analytic review of content analyses examining support messages shared online among individuals coping with illness. *Communication Monographs, 82*(4), 403–430. doi:10.1080/03637751.2015.1019530

Rains, S. A., & Young, V. (2009). A meta-analysis of research on formal computer-mediated support groups: Examining group characteristics and health outcomes. *Human Communication Research, 35*(3), 309–336. doi:10.1111/j.1468-2958.2009.01353.x

Ramirez, A., Jr., & Broneck, K. (2009). "IM me": Instant messaging as relational maintenance and everyday communication. *Journal of Social and Personal Relationships, 26*(2–3), 291–314. doi:10.1177/025407509106719

Ramirez, A., Jr., Dimmick, J., Feaster, J., & Lin, S.-F. (2008). Revisiting interpersonal media competition: The gratification niches of instant messaging, e-mail, and the telephone. *Communication Research, 35*(4), 529–547. doi:10.1177/0093650208315979

Ramirez, A., Jr., Sumner, E. M., Fleuriet, C., & Cole, M. (2015). When online dating partners meet offline: The effect of modality switching on relationship communication between online daters. *Journal of Computer-Mediated Communication, 20*(1), 99–115. doi:10.1111/jcc4.12101

Ramirez, A., Jr., Sumner, E. M., & Spinda, J. (2017). The relational reconnection function of social network sites. *New Media & Society, 19*(6), 807–825. doi:10.1177/1461444815614199

Ramirez, A., Jr., & Wang, Z. (2008). When online meets offline: An expectancy violation theory perspective on modality switching. *Journal of Communication, 58*, 20–39. doi:10.1111/j.1460-2466.2007.00372.x

Rawlins, W. K. (1992). *Friendship matters: Communication, dialectics, and the life course.* Berlin: De Gruyter.

(2009). *The compass of friendship.* Thousand Oaks, CA: Sage.

Reinecke, L. (2017). POPC and well-being: A risk-benefit analysis. In. P. Vorderer, D. Hefner, L. Reinecke, & C. Klimmt (eds.), *Permanently online, permanently connected: Living and communicating in a POPC world* (pp. 233–243). New York: Routledge.

Reinecke, L., Aufenanger, S., Beutel, M. E., Dreier, M., Quiring, O., Stark, B., . . . Müller, K. W. (2017). Digital stress over the life span: The effects of communication load and Internet multitasking on perceived stress and psychological health impairments in a German probability sample. *Media Psychology, 20*(1), 90–115. doi:10.1080/15213269.2015.1121832

Reinecke, L., Vorderer, P., & Knop, K. (2014). Entertainment 2.0? The role of intrinsic and extrinsic need satisfaction for the enjoyment of Facebook use. *Journal of Communication, 64*(3), 417–438. doi:10.1111/jcom.12099

Reis, H. T. (2001) Relationship experiences and emotional well-being. In C. D. Ryff & B. H. Singer (eds.), *Emotion, social relationships, and health* (pp. 57–85). New York: Oxford University Press.

Requena, F., & Ayuso, L. (2018). Individualism or complementarity? The effect of digital personal networks on face-to-face personal networks. *Information, Communication & Society, 22*(14), 2097–2111. doi:10.1080/1369118X.2018.1477968

Rettberg, J. W. (2018). Self-representation in social media. In J. Burgess, A. Marwick, & T. Poell (eds.), *The SAGE handbook of social media* (pp. 429–443). Los Angeles, CA: Sage Publications.

Rettie, R. (2007). Texters not talkers: Phone aversion among mobile phone users. *Psychology Journal, 5*(1), 33–57.

Roberts, J. A., & David, M. E. (2016). My life has become a major distraction from my cell phone: Partner phubbing and relationship satisfaction among romantic partners. *Computers in Human Behavior, 54*, 134–141. doi:10.1016/j.chb.2015.07.058

Roberts, S. B. G., & Dunbar, R. I. M. (2011). The costs of family and friends: An 18-month longitudinal study of relationship maintenance and decay. *Evolution and Human Behavior, 32*(3), 186–197. doi:10.1016/j.evolhumbehav.2010.08.005

Robinson, J. P. (2011). IT use and leisure time displacement: Convergent evidence over the last 15 years. *Information, Communication & Society, 14*(4), 495–509. doi:10.1080/1369118x.2011.562223

Rook, K. S. (1984). Promoting social bonding: Strategies for helping the lonely and socially isolated. *American Psychologist, 39*(12), 1389–1407. doi:10.1037/0003-066X.39.12.1389

Rosenfeld, M. J., Thomas, R. J., & Falcon, M. (2016). *How couples meet and stay together (HCMST), Wave 1 2009, Wave 2 2010, Wave 3 2011, Wave 4 2013, Wave 5 2015, United States.* Ann Arbor, MI: Inter-university Consortium for Political and Social Research [distributor]. doi:10.3886/ICPSR30103.v8

Rowling, J. K. (2000). *Harry Potter and the chamber of secrets.* New York: Scholastic Press.

Rudd, D. C. (1989, October). AT&T plans cuts in long-distance rates. *Chicago Tribune.* Retrieved from: www.chicagotribune.com/news/ct-xpm-1989-12-20-8903190444-story.html.

Ruppel, E. K., & Burke, T. J. (2015). Complementary channel use and the role of social competence. *Journal of Computer-Mediated Communication, 20*(1), 37–51.

Ruppel, E. K., Burke, T. J., & Cherney, M. R. (2018). Channel complementarity and multiplexity in long-distance friends' patterns of communication technology use. *New Media & Society, 20*(4), 1564–1579. doi:10.1177/1461444817699995

Ruppel, E. K., Gross, C., Stoll, A., Peck, B., Allen, M. R., & Kim, S. (2017). Reflecting on connecting: Meta-analysis of differences between mediated and face-to-face self-disclosure. *Journal of Computer-Mediated Communication, 22*(1), 18–34. doi:10.1111/jcc4.12179

Sacco, D. F., & Ismail, M. M. (2014). Social belongingness satisfaction as a function of interaction medium: Face-to-face interactions facilitate greater social belonging and interaction enjoyment compared to instant messaging. *Computers in Human Behavior, 36*, 359–364. doi:10.1016/j.chb.2014.04.004

Sagioglou, C., & Greitemeyer, T. (2014). Facebook's emotional consequences: Why Facebook causes a decrease in mood and why people still use it. *Computers in Human Behavior, 35*, 359–363. doi:10.1016/j.chb.2014.03.003

Sandstrom, G. M., & Dunn, E. W. (2014). Social interactions and well-being: The surprising power of weak ties. *Personality and Social Psychology Bulletin, 40*(7), 910–922. doi:10.1177/0146167214529799

Saramaki, J., Leicht, E. A., Lopez, E., Roberts, S. G. B., Reed-Tsochas, F., & Dunbar, R. I. M. (2014). Persistence of social signatures in human communication. *Proceedings of the National Academy of Sciences*, *111*(3), 942–947. doi:10.1073/pnas.1308540110

Sarkisian, N., & Gerstel, N. (2016). Does singlehood isolate or integrate? Examining the link between marital status and ties to kin, friends, and neighbors. *Journal of Social and Personal Relationships*, *33*(3), 361–384. doi:10.1177/0265407515597564

Schlenker, B. R. (1980). *Impression management: The self-concept, social identity, and interpersonal relations*. Monterey, CA: Brooks/Cole Publishing.

Schnauber-Stockmann, A., Meier, A., & Reinecke, L. (2018). Procrastination out of habit? The role of impulsive versus reflective media selection in procrastinatory media use. *Media Psychology*, *21*(4), 640–668. doi:10.1080/152132269.2018.1476156

Scissors, L. E., & Gergle, D. (2013). Back and forth, back and forth: Channel switching in romantic couple conflict. In *Proceedings of the 2013 Conference on Computer Supported Cooperative Work*, 237–248. San Antonio, TX.

Scott, C. R. (2009). A whole-hearted effort to get it half right: Predicting the future of communication technology scholarship. *Journal of Computer-Mediated Communication*, *14*(3), 753–757. doi:10.111/j.1083-6101.2009.01467.x

Scott, V. M., Mottarella, K. E., & Lavooy, M. J. (2006). Does virtual intimacy exist? A brief exploration into reported levels of intimacy in online relationships. *Cyberpsychology & Behavior*, *9*(6), 759–761.

Seltzer, L. J., Ziegler, T. E., & Pollak, S. D. (2010). Social vocalizations can release oxytocin in humans. *Proceedings of the Royal Society B: Biological Sciences*, *277*(1694), 2661–2666. doi:10.1098/rspb.2010.0567

Seyfarth, R. M., & Cheney, D. L. (2012). The evolutionary origins of friendship. *Annual Review of Psychology*, *63*, 153–177. doi:10.1146/annurev-psych-120810-100337

Shakya, H. B., & Christakis, N. A. (2017). Association of Facebook use with compromised well-being: A longitudinal study. *American Journal of Epidemiology*, *185*(3), 203–211. doi:10.1093/aje/kww189

Sharabi, L. & Caughlin, J. P. (2017a). Usage patterns of social media across stages of romantic relationships. In N. M. Punyanunt-Carter & J. S. Wrench (eds.), *The impact of social media in modern romantic relationships* (pp. 15–30). Lanham, MD: Lexington Books.

Sharabi, L. L., & Caughlin, J. P. (2017b). What predicts first date success? A longitudinal study of modality switching in online dating. *Personal Relationships*, *24*(2), 370–391. doi:10.1111/pere.12188

Sharabi, L. L., & Dykstra-DeVette, T. A. (2019). From first email to first date: Strategies for initiating relationships in online dating. *Journal of Social and Personal Relationships*, *36*(11–12), 3389–3407. doi:10.1177/0265407518822780

Sheer, V. C. (2011). Teenagers' use of MSN features, discussion topics, and online friendship development: The impact of media richness and communication control. *Communication Quarterly*, *59*, 82–103. doi:10.1080/01463373.2010.525702

Sheldon, K. M., Abad, N., & Hinsch, C. (2011). A two-process view of Facebook use and relatedness need-satisfaction: Disconnection drives use, and connection rewards it. *Journal of Personality and Social Psychology*, 100(4), 766–775. doi:10.1037/a0022407

Sheldon, K. M., & Gunz, A. (2009). Psychological needs as basic motives, not just experiential requirements. *Journal of Personality*, 77(5), 1467–1492. doi:10.1111/j.1467-6494.2009.00589.x

Short, J., Williams, E., & Christie, B. (1976). *The social psychology of telecommunications*. London: John Wiley & Sons.

Small, M. L. (2017). *Someone to talk to*. New York: Oxford University Press.

Small, M. L., Pamphile, V. D., & McMahan, P. (2015). How stable is the core discussion network? *Social Networks*, 40, 90–102. doi:10.1016/j/socnet/2014.09.001

Smock, A. D., Ellison, N. B., Lampe, C., & Wohn, D. Y. (2011) Facebook as a toolkit: A uses and gratification approach to unbundling feature use. *Computers in Human Behavior*, 27(6), 2322–2329. doi:10.1016/j.chb.2011.07.011

Song, H., Zmyslinski-Seelig, A., Kim, J., Drent, A., Victor, A., Omori, K., & Allen, M. (2014). Does Facebook make you lonely?: A meta-analysis. *Computers in Human Behavior*, 36, 446–452. doi:10.1016/j.chb.2014.04.011

Sprecher, S. (2014). Initial interactions online-text, online-audio, online-video, or face-to-face: Effects of modality on liking, closeness, and other interpersonal outcomes. *Computers in Human Behavior*, 31, 190–197. doi:10.1016/j.chb.2013.10.029

Sprecher, S., Hampton, A. J., Heinzel, H. J., & Felmlee, D. (2016). Can I connect with both you and my social network? Access to network-salient communication technology and get-acquainted interactions. *Computers in Human Behavior*, 62, 423–432. doi:10.1016/j.chb.2016.03.090

St. Clair, B. (2016, June 30). The real reason so many millennials are living at home. *Washington Post*. Retrieved from: www.washingtonpost.com/news/wonk/wp/2016/06/30/the-real-reason-so-many-millennials-are-living-at-home/.

Stafford, L. (2015). Long-distance relationships. In C. R. Berger, M. E. Roloff, S. R. Wilson, J. P. Dillard, J. P. Caughlin, & D. Solomon (eds.), *The international encyclopedia of interpersonal communication* (pp. 1–3). New York: Wiley Blackwell. doi:10.1002/9781118540190.wbeic075

Standlee, A. (2019). Friendship and online filtering: The use of social media to construct offline social networks. *New Media & Society*, 21(3), 770–785. doi:10.1177/1461444188806844

Steele, R. G., Hall, J. A. & Christofferson, J. L. (2019). Conceptualizing digital stress in adolescents and young adults: Toward the development of an empirically based model. *Clinical Child and Family Psychology Review*, 23(1), 15–26, doi:10.1007/s10567-019-00300-5

Steers, M.-L. N., Wickham, R. E., & Acitelli, L. K. (2014). Seeing everyone else's highlight reels: How Facebook usage is linked to depressive symptoms. *Journal of Social and Clinical Psychology*, 33(8), 701–731.

Stepanikova, I., Nie, N. H., & He, X. (2010). Time on the Internet at home, loneliness, and life satisfaction: Evidence from panel time-diary data. *Computers in Human Behavior*, 26(3), 329–338. doi:10.1016/j.chb.2009.11.002

Stevenson, M. (2018). From hypertext to hype and back again: Exploring the roots of social media in early web culture. In J. Burgess, A. Marwick, & T. Poell (eds.), *The SAGE handbook of social media* (pp. 69–88). Los Angeles, CA: Sage Publications.

Stieger, S., & Lewetz, D. (2018). A week without using social media: Results from an ecological momentary intervention study using smartphones. *Cyberpsycholgy, Behavior, and Social Networking, 21*(10), 618–624. doi:10.1089/cyber.2018.0070

Stone, A. R. (1995). *The war of desire and technology at the close of the mechanical age.* Cambridge, MA: MIT Press.

Stoycheff, E., Liu, J., Wibowo, K. A., & Nanni, D. P. (2017). What have we learned about social media by studying Facebook? A decade in review. *New Media & Society, 19*(6), 968–980. doi:10.1177/1461444817695745

Sutcliffe, A., Dunbar, R., Binder, J., & Arrow, H. (2012). Relationships and the social brain: Integrating psychological and evolutionary perspectives. *British Journal of Psychology, 103*(2), 149–168. doi:10.1111/j.2044-8295.2011.02061.x

Taylor, S. H., & Bazarova, N. N. (2018). Revisiting media multiplexity: A longitudinal analysis of media use in romantic relationships. *Journal of Communication, 68*(6), 1104–1126. doi:10.1093/joc/jqy055

Terrell, J. E. (2015). *A talent for friendship: Rediscovery of a remarkable trait.* New York: Oxford University Press.

Thomée, S., Härenstam, A., & Hagberg, M. (2011). Mobile phone use and stress, sleep disturbances, and symptoms of depression among young adults – A prospective cohort study. *BMC Public Health, 11*(66), 1–9. doi:10.1186/1471-2458-11-66

Thompson, A. K. (2018). *Creative quest.* New York: HarperCollins.

Thulin, E., & Vilhelmson, B. (2005). Virtual mobility of urban youth: ICT-based communication in Sweden. *Tijdschrift voor Economische en Sociale Geografie, 96*(5), 477–487. doi:10.1111/j.1467-9663.2005.00480.x

Tillema, T., Dijst, M., & Schwanen, T. (2010). Face-to-face and electronic communications in maintaining social networks: The influence of geographical and relational distance and of information content. *New Media & Society, 12*(6), 965–983. doi:10.1177/1461444809353011

Tinbergen, N. (1951/1970). An attempt at a synthesis. In W. A. Russell (ed.), *Milestones in motivation: Contribution to the psychology of drive and purpose* (pp. 53–79). New York: Meredith Corporation. (Reprinted from *The study of instinct* (Oxford: Clarendon Press, 1951).)

Tokunaga, R. S. (2016a). An examination of functional difficulties from Internet use: Media habit and displacement theory explanations. *Human Communication Research, 42*(3), 339–370. doi:10.1111/hcre/12081

(2016b). Interpersonal surveillance over social network sites: Applying a theory of negative relational maintenance and the investment model. *Journal of Social and Personal Relationships, 33*(2), 171–190. doi:10.1177/02654075168749

Tokunaga, R. S., & Rains, S. A. (2016). A review and meta-analysis examining conceptual and operational definitions of problematic Internet use. *Human Communication Research, 42*(2), 165–199. doi:10.111/hcre.12075

Toma, C. L., & D'Angelo, J. D. (2017). Connecting profile-to-profile: How people self-present and form impressions of others through online dating profiles. In N. M. Punyanunt-Carter & J. S. Wrench (eds.), *The impact of social media in modern romantic relationships* (pp. 147–162). Lanham, MD: Lexington Books.

Tong, S. T., van der Heide, B., Langwell, L., & Walther, J. B. (2008). Too much of a good thing? The relationship between number of friends and interpersonal impressions on Facebook. *Journal of Computer-Mediated Communication, 13*(3), 531–549. doi:10.111/j.1083-6101.2008.00409.x

Tong, S. T., & Walther, J. B. (2011). Relational maintenance and computer-mediated communication. In K. Wright & L. Webb (eds.), *Computer-mediated communication in personal relationships* (pp. 98–118). New York: Peter Lang.

(2015). The confirmation and disconfirmation of expectancies in computer-mediated communication. *Communication Research, 42*(2), 186–212. doi:10.1177/0093650212466257

Tooby, J., & Cosmides, L. (2008). The evolutionary psychology of emotions and their relationship to internal regulatory variables. In M. Lewis, J. M. Haviland-Jones, & L. F. Barrett (eds.), *Handbook of emotions* (3rd ed., pp. 114–137). New York: Guilford Press.

Tosun, L. P. (2012). Motives for Facebook use and expressing "true self" on the internet. *Computers in Human Behavior, 28*(4), 1510–1517. doi:10.1016/j.chb.2012.03.018

Tromholt, M. (2016). The Facebook experiment: Quitting Facebook leads to higher levels of well-being. *Cyberpsychology, Behavior, and Social Networking, 19*(11), 661–666. doi:10.1089/cyber.2016.0259

Trottier, D. (2012). Interpersonal surveillance on social media. *Canadian Journal of Communication, 37*(2), 319–332. doi:10.22230/cjc.2012v37n2a2536

Tskhay, K. O. & Rule, N. O. (2014). Perceptions of personality in text-based media and OSN: A meta-analysis. *Journal of Research in Personality, 49*, 25–30. doi:10.1016/j.jrp.2013.12.004

Tufecki, Z. (2008). Grooming, gossip, Facebook, and MySpace: What can we learn about these sites from those who won't assimilate? *Information, Communication, & Society, 11*(4), 544–564. doi:10.1080/13691180801999050

(2010, May). Who acquires friends through social media and why? "Rich get richer" versus "seek and ye shall find." In *Fourth International AAAI Conference on Weblogs and Social Media*. Washington, DC.

Turel, O., Cavagnaro, D. R., Meshi, D. (2018). Short abstinence from online social networking sites reduces perceived stress, especially in excessive users. *Psychiatry Research, 270*, 947–953. doi:10.1016/j.psychres.2018.11.017

Turkle, S. (2011). *Alone together*. New York: Basic Books.

Twenge, J. M., Joiner, T. E., Rogers, M. L., & Martin, G. N. (2018a). Increases in depressive symptoms, suicide-related outcomes, and suicide rates among U.S. adolescents after 2010 and links to increased new media screen time. *Clinical Psychological Science, 6*(1), 3–17. doi:10.1177/2167702617723376

Twenge, J. M., Martin, G. N., & Spitzberg, B. H. (2018b). Trends in U.S. adolescents' media use, 1976–2016: The rise of digital media, the decline of TV, and the (near) demise of print. *Psychology of Popular Media Culture, 8*(4), 329–345. doi:10.1037/ppm0000203

Twenge, J. M., Spitzberg, B. H., & Campbell, W. K. (2019). Less in-person social interaction with peers among US adolescents in the 21st century and links to loneliness. *Journal of Social and Personal Relationships, 36*(6), 1892–1913. doi:10.1177/0265407519836170

US Department of Labor (2015). American time use survey 2014. Retrieved from: www .bls.gov/tus/.

(2019). American time use survey 2003–2018. Retrieved from: www.bls.gov/tus/ atususersguide.pdf.

Utz, S. (2010). Show me your friends and I will tell you what type of a person you are: How one's profile, number of friends, and type of friends influence impression formation on social network sites. *Journal of Computer-Mediated Communication*, 15(2), 314–335. doi:10.1111/j.1083-6101.2010.01522.x

(2015). The function of self-disclosure on social networking sites: Not only intimate, but also positive and entertaining self-disclosures increase the feeling of connection. *Computers in Human Behavior*, 45, 1–10. doi:10.1016/j.chb.2014.11.076

Utz, S., Tanis, M., & Vermeulen, I. (2012). It is all about being popular: The effects of need for popularity on social network site use. *Cyberpsychology, Behavior, and Social Networking*, 15(1), 37–42. doi:10.1089/cyber.2010.0651

Vaillant, G. E. (2012). *Triumphs of experience: The men of the Harvard Grant study*. Cambridge, MA: Belknap Press.

Valente, T. W. (1995). *Network models of the diffusion of innovations*. Cresskill, NJ: Hampton Press.

Valkenburg, P. M., & Peter, J. (2009). Social consequences of the internet for adolescents: A decade of research. *Current Directions in Psychological Science*, 18(1), 1–5. doi:10.1111/j.1467-8721.2009.01595.x

(2013). The differential susceptibility to media effects model. *Journal of Communication*, 63(2), 221–243. doi:10.1111/jcom.12024

van den Abeele, M. M., Antheunis, M. L., & Schouten, A. P. (2016). The effect of mobile messaging during a conversation on impression formation and interaction quality. *Computers in Human Behavior*, 62, 562–569. doi:10.1016/j/ chb.2016.04.005

van den Abeele, M. M., Hendrickson, A., Pollman, M. H., & Ling, R. (2019). Phubbing behavior in conversations and its relation to perceived conversation intimacy and distraction: An exploratory observation study. *Computers in Human Behavior*, 100, 35–47. doi:10.1016/j.chb.2019.06.004

van den Berg, P. E. W., Arentze, T. A., & Timmermans, H. J. P. (2012). New ICTs and social interaction: Modeling communication frequency and communication mode choice. *New Media & Society*, 14(6), 987–1003. doi:10.1177.146144812437518

van der Horst, M., & Coffe, H. (2012). How friendship network characteristics influence subjective well-being. *Social Indicators Research*, 107(3), 509–529. doi:10.1007/s11205-011-9861-2

van Kessel, P., Smith, G. A., & Schiller, A. (2018). Where Americans find meaning in life. *Pew Research Center*. Retrieved from: www.pewforum.org/2018/11/20/where-americans-find-meaning-in-life/.

van Kruistum, C., Leseman, P. P., & de Haan, M. (2014). Youth media lifestyles. *Human Communication Research*, 40(4), 508–529. doi:10.1111/hcre.12033

Vanman, E. J., Baker, R., & Tobin, S. J. (2018). The burden of online friends: The effects of giving up Facebook on stress and well-being. *The Journal of Social Psychology*, 158(4), 496–508. doi:10/1080/00224545.2018.1453467

Vazire, S., & Gosling, S. D. (2004). e-Perceptions: Personality impressions based on personal websites. *Journal of Personality and Social Psychology, 87*(1), 123–132. doi:10.1037//0022-3514.87.1.123

Vejnoska, J. (2016, December 21). 1.6 billion reasons Christmas cards aren't going away anytime soon. Retrieved from: www.ajc.com/lifestyles/billion-reasons-christmas-cards-aren-going-away-anytime-soon/0B43hRjOxd5j6TS1q3IYZN/.

Velasquez, A. (2018). Parents' mobile relational maintenance in resource-constrained contexts: Barriers and facilitating access conditions. *New Media & Society, 20*(12), 4415–4435. doi:10.1177/1461444818774256

Verduyn, P., Lee, D. S., Park, J., Shablack, H., Orvell, A., Bayer, J., . . . Kross, E. (2015). Passive Facebook usage undermines affective well-being: Experimental and longitudinal evidence. *Journal of Experimental Psychology: General, 144*(2), 480–488. doi:10.1037/xge0000057

Vilhelmson, B., Thulin, E., & Elldér, E. (2017). Where does times spent on the internet come from? Tracing the influence of information and communications technology use on daily activities. *Information, Communication & Society, 20*(2), 250–263. doi:10.1080/1369118x.2016.1164741

Vlahovic, T. A., Roberts, S., Dunbar, R. (2012). Effects of duration and laughter on subjective happiness within different modes of communication. *Journal of Computer-Mediated Communication, 17*(4), 436–450. doi:10.1111/j.1083-6101.2012.01584.x

Walther, J. B. (1992). Interpersonal effects in computer-mediated interaction: A relational perspective. *Communication Research, 19*(1), 52–90. doi:10.1177/009365092019001003

   (1995). Relational aspects of computer-mediated communication: Experimental observations over time. *Organization Science, 6*(2), 186–203. doi:10.1287/orsc.6.2.186

   (1996). Computer-mediated communication: Impersonal, interpersonal, and hyperpersonal interaction. *Communication Research, 23*(1), 3–43. doi:10.1177/009365096023001001

   (2010). Computer-mediated communication. In C. R. Berger, M. E. Roloff, & D. R. Roskos-Ewoldsen (eds.), *Handbook of communication science* (2nd ed., pp. 489–505). Los Angeles, CA: Sage.

   (2011). Theories of computer-mediated communication and interpersonal relations. In M. L. Knapp & J. A. Daly (eds.), *The SAGE handbook of interpersonal communication* (4th ed., pp. 443–480). Los Angeles, CA: Sage.

   (2015). Social information processing theory. In D. O. Braithwaite & P. Schrodt (eds.), *Engaging theories in interpersonal communication: Multiple perspectives* (2nd ed., pp. 417–428). Los Angeles, CA: Sage.

   (2017). The merger of mass and interpersonal communication via new media: Integrating metaconstructs. *Human Communication Research, 43*(4), 559–572. doi:10.1111/hcre.12122

Walther, J. B., Anderson, J. F., & Park, D. W. (1994). Interpersonal effects in computer-mediated interaction: A meta-analysis of social and antisocial communication. *Communication Research, 21*(4), 460–487. doi:10.1177/009365094021004002

Walther, J. B., Carr, C. T., Choi, S. S. W., DeAndrea, D. C., Kim, J., Tong, S. T., & van der Heide, B. (2010). Interaction of interpersonal, peer, and media influence sources online. In Z. Papacharissi (ed.), *A networked self: Identity, community, and culture on social network sites* (pp. 17–38). New York: Routledge.

Walther, J. B., van der Heide, B., Hamel L. M., & Shulman, H. C. (2009). Self-generated versus other-generated statements and impressions in computer-mediated communication: A test of warranting theory using Facebook. *Communication Research*, 36(2), 229–253. doi:10.1177/0093650208330251

Wang, X., Xie, X., Wang, Y., Wang, P., & Lei, L. (2017). Partner phubbing and depression among married Chinese adults: The roles of relationship satisfaction and relationship length. *Personality and Individual Differences*, 110, 12–17. doi:10.1016/j.paid.2017.01.014

Wang, Z., Tchernev, J. M., Solloway, T. (2012). A dynamic longitudinal examination of social media use, needs, and gratifications among college students. *Computers in Human Behavior*, 28(5), 1829–1839. doi:10.1016/j.chb2012.05.001

Watzlawick, P., Beavin, J. H., & Jackson, D. D. (1967). *Pragmatics of human communication*. New York: W. W. Norton.

Wayne, T. (2015). A eulogy for the long, intimate email. Retrieved from: www.nytimes.com/2015/07/12/style/a-eulogy-for-the-long-intimate-email.html.

Weidman, A. C., Fernandez, K. C., Levinson, C. A., Augustine, A. A., Larsen, R. J., & Rodebaugh, T. L. (2012). Compensatory internet use among individuals higher in social anxiety and its implications for well-being. *Personality and Individual Differences*, 53(3), 191–195. doi:10.1016/j.paid.2012.03.003

Weinstein, E. C., & Selman, R. L. (2014). Digital stress: Adolescents' personal accounts. *New Media & Society*, 22(3), 191–195. doi:10.1177/1461444814543989

Wellman, B. (2001). Physical place and cyberspace. *International Urban and Regional Research*, 25(2), 227–252. doi:10.1111/1468-2427.00309

Wellman, B., Carrington, P. J., & Hall, A. (1988). Networks as personal communities. In B. Wellman & S. D. Berkowitz (eds.), *Social structures: A network approach* (pp. 130–184). Cambridge: Cambridge University Press.

Wellman, B., & Tindall, D. (1993). Reach out and touch some bodies: How social networks connect telephone networks. *Progress in Communication Sciences*, 12, 63–93.

Werner, C. M., & Baxter, L. A. (1994). Temporal qualities of relationships: Organismic, transactional, and dialectical views. In M. L. Knapp & G. R. Miller (eds.), *The SAGE handbook of interpersonal communication* (2nd ed., pp. 323–379). Thousand Oaks, CA: Sage.

Wiessner, P. W. (2014). Embers of society: Firelight among the Ju/'hoansi Bushmen. *PNAS*, 111(39), 14027–14035. doi:10.1073/pnas.1404212111

Wilson, R. E., Gosling, S. D., & Graham, L. T. (2012). A review of Facebook research in the social sciences. *Perspectives on Psychological Science*, 7(3), 203–220. doi:1177/1745691612442904

Wrzus, C., Hänel, M., Wagner, J., & Neyer, F. J. (2013). Social network changes and life events across the life span: A meta-analysis. *Psychological Bulletin*, 139(1), 53–80. doi:10.1037/a0028601

Yang, C. C., Brown, B. B., & Braun, M. T. (2014). From Facebook to cell calls: Layers of electronic intimacy in college students' interpersonal relationships. *New Media & Society*, *16*(1), 5–23. doi:10.1177/1461444812472486

Yau, J. C., & Reich, S. M. (2018). Are the qualities of adolescents' offline friendships present in digital interactions? *Adolescent Research Review*, *3*(3), 339–355. doi:10.1007/240894-017-0059-y

INDEX

accounts, 31, 74, 175, 183, 186, 201
acquaintances, 123, 126, 128, 130–131, 149, 168
affordances, 7–8, 29, 77, 86, 136
ambient awareness, 121, 134, 146–147
American Time Use Survey, 71, 178, 192–194, 199
apology. *See* accounts
appropriation of technology (AT), 35–36
approval anxiety, 165–166
audience, 135–136, 140–149, 151–152, 156, 201–204
availability stress, 163–165

Baym, Nancy, 3, 6–7, 27, 32–34, 38, 40, 49–50, 53,
  56, 59–60, 63, 77–78, 83–84, 86, 88, 90, 92–96,
  98, 101, 104, 106, 108, 110, 113, 120, 138–143,
  147–149, 163–166, 177, 182, 190, 195, 201, 203
belongingness, 9, 30, 62–66, 68–69, 71, 74, 92–93,
  99, 105, 161–162, 179, 186, 192, 197
blogs/blogging, 77, 82, 108, 131, 135, 145
bonding social capital, 130–133, 196
bridging social capital, 10, 15, 112, 130–134
broadcasting, 114, 120, 131, 168–169, 202
browsing, 105, 114–115, 120, 122–123, 131, 142, 148,
  159, 161–162, 166–167, 176, 186, 198–200
bulletin board system (BBS), 4, 130, 140–141, 143,
  203

channel comparison, 95–105
channel expansion theory (CET), 51–52, 69
channel switching, 61, 94–95
chat programs/apps, 23, 67, 76, 85, 89, 91, 103, 106,
  108, 110, 112–114, 133, 139, 142, 164
chat room, 10, 27, 38, 77–79, 116, 140
comments, 23, 115, 120–121, 144–145, 150, 152, 174, 201
communicate bond belong (CBB) theory, 9, 35,
  62–69, 71, 91, 93, 104–105, 122, 149, 161–162,
  187, 197–198
communication episode, 63, 66–67, 104–105

communication interdependence perspective,
  60–62, 136, 200
computer-mediated communication (CMC)
  theory, 9, 49–59, 61
connection, 1, 9–12, 28–30, 34, 49, 51, 62, 66,
  77–79, 92, 95, 98–101, 104–105, 115, 117, 119,
  121–123, 128, 135, 140, 142–143, 145, 147,
  151–153, 155–156, 160–163, 167, 171, 175, 178,
  180, 185–186, 188–190, 195, 199–207
  overload, 166–168
connectivity, 6–7, 11–12, 59, 67–69, 79, 137–138,
  153, 161, 171, 188–190, 206–207
context collapse, 126–127
co-presence. *See* social presence
co-present device use, 38, 160, 171, 178–186
core network, 9, 18–19, 36, 39–40, 81, 107–108, 192
cost, of caring, 147, 168–169

dialectical theory, 43, 135–137, 140, 143, 206
digital stress, 25–27, 157–158, 161–164, 166–170, 190
domestication, 34–47, 72, 179
Duck, Steve, 43–47, 60, 136, 141–142
Dunbar, Robin, 17–20, 24, 28, 65, 108, 119, 171, 173,
  175, 196

email, 5, 10, 39–40, 50, 54, 58, 60, 62, 73–74, 76,
  78–79, 81, 83–84, 86, 88, 95, 97–98, 100,
  108–111, 113–114, 130–133, 140, 142, 144,
  150–151, 169, 173–175, 177, 200–201, 205, 219,
  223
emoji, 51, 115, 140, 142, 152
energy conservation, 9, 35, 63, 65–69, 71, 87–88,
  93, 122, 162, 197–198
entrapment, 25, 97, 138–139, 163, 190
etiquette, 38, 183
everyday talk, 3, 43–44, 46, 58, 136
evolution, 13–17, 48, 68

CPSIA information can be obtained
at www.ICGtesting.com
Printed in the USA
LVHW051228010723
751335LV00005B/111

9 781108 483308